Hugo Chávez and the Bolivarian Revolution

Also by Richard Gott

The Appeasers (with Martin Gilbert), 1963

Guerrilla Movements in Latin America, 1971

Land Without Evil, Utopian Journeys across the Latin American Watershed, 1991

Cuba, A New History, 2004

Hugo Chávez and the Bolivarian Revolution

RICHARD GOTT

With photographs by
GEORGES BARTOLI

VERSO
London • New York

First published by Verso in 2000 under the title
*In the Shadow of the Liberator, Hugo Chávez and the
Transformation of Venezuela*
This edition first published by Verso 2005
© Richard Gott 2005
Photographs © Georges Bartoli
All rights reserved

The moral rights of the author have been asserted

1 3 5 7 9 10 8 6 4 2

Verso
UK: 6 Meard Street, London W1F 0EG
USA: 180 Varick Street, New York, NY 10014–4606
www.versobooks.com

Verso is the imprint of New Left Books

ISBN 1–84467–533–5

British Library Cataloguing in Publication Data
A catalogue record for this book is available from the British Library

Library of Congress Cataloging-in-Publication Data
A catalog record for this book is available from the Library of Congress

Typeset in Bembo
Printed and bound in Great Britain by William Clowes Ltd, Beccles, Suffolk

Once upon a time a traveller arrived in Caracas as night was falling, and, not pausing even to shake off the dust of the road, asked – no, not where he could eat or sleep, but how he could get to the statue of Bolívar. They say that, alone beside the tall, fragrant trees of the square, the traveller stood in front of the statue as tears ran down his cheeks; the statue seemed to move, like a father when his son draws close to him. The traveller was right to do this, because all of us in the Americas should love Bolívar like a father – Bolívar and all the others who fought as he did, so that the Americas would belong to their own people.

José Martí, *La Edad de Oro*, New York, 1889

CONTENTS

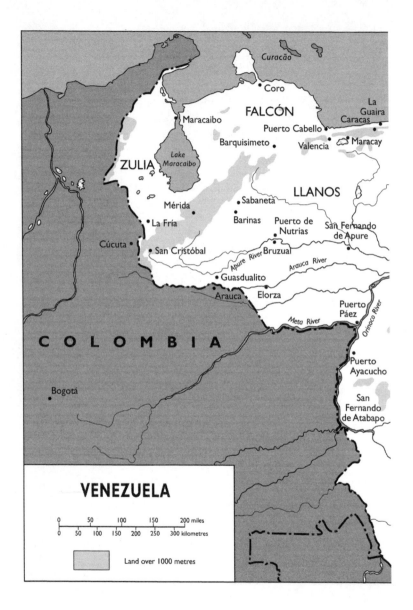

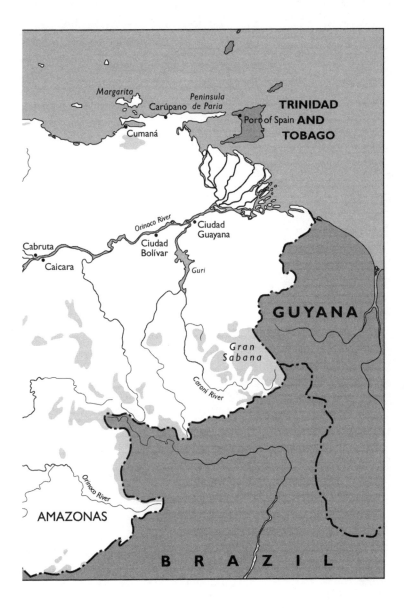

INTRODUCTION

Colonel Hugo Chávez, President of Venezuela, first came to serious world attention when he was overthrown in a *coup d'état* in April 2002 – and then miraculously returned to power two days later by popular demand. Suddenly what had been seen by many outsiders as a bizarre populist experiment in an obscure Latin American country became the subject of international interest and concern. The fierce internal conflict in Venezuela, an important supplier of oil to the United States market, began to be examined with interest outside the country and analysed in detail – by both left and right.

The overtly fascistic nature of that April coup, with a figurehead leader from *Fedecámeras*, the country's employers' federation, who abandoned his co-plotter in the trade union movement and moved swiftly to suppress parliament, the supreme court, local government institutions and the new Chávez constitution, recalled the overthrow of Salvador Allende and the establishment of the Pinochet regime in Chile in September 1973. Such an obviously right-wing coup led many people to consider that perhaps the Chávez government might have been more innovative and radical than they had previously supposed.

The subsequent airing of a wonderful Irish television programme, 'The Revolution Will Not Be Televised', which gave a fly-on-the-wall treatment of events in the Miraflores presidential palace in Caracas before, during, and after the coup and its providential reversal, gave many foreign viewers a timely and unforgettable insight into the nature of the crisis affecting Venezuela's politics, society and culture. The programme also revealed the exceptional role of the local private media in promoting and orchestrating the coup – and then in refusing to film or broadcast the popular mobilisation supported by loyal troops that led to the return of the president.

An earlier version of this book – *In the Shadow of the Liberator* – was written in the course of 1999, during Chávez's first year in power, and published in 2000. The book's original purpose was to introduce Chávez and his 'Bolivarian Revolution' to an external, largely Anglo-Saxon audience, at a time when outside interest in Latin American developments was at a low ebb. It seemed then to this writer that the election of Chávez on December 6, 1998, with 56 per cent of the vote, might well mark the start of a significant new era, not just in Venezuela but in inter-American affairs generally. Here was an impressive young leader, enjoying popular support, with a radical programme that sought to change the politics of the continent.

Not least among his ambitions was a desire to restore the image of the armed forces of the continent, fallen into low repute after the dictatorships of the period from the 1960s to the 1980s. The right-wing officers who seized power in Argentina, Bolivia, Brazil, Chile and Uruguay had so discredited the military institutions of Latin America that people had begun to question whether they could ever again recover the respect of their peoples.

Chávez himself had organised a *coup d'état* in 1992, with the partic-ipation of a group of radical young officers – and he paid the price of failure. Yet it was clear at the time that this was an attempted act of radical liberation, not that of a fascist or vainglorious colonel. His plan was to cut through the logjam of the Venezuelan political system that had long failed to address the problems facing the country. His essen-tially democratic vocation was made clear later in that decade when he decided to stand for election as president in 1998, when there was no guarantee that the country would warm to him. Subsequently he was to submit himself and his government to a succession of elections and referenda that bore witness both to his continuing commitment to democracy and to his extraordinary popularity.

What I had not envisaged when I wrote the earlier version of this book was that Chávez would become such a controversial figure, both in Venezuela and abroad. How could this attractive, intelligent, well-educated officer, with a reputation as a popular teacher in the country's war academy and possessed of unique communications skills, be transformed by the old Caracas political elite into an ogre comparable to the great dictators of the twentieth century? In this new version, expanded and brought up to date, I also address the problem of the reception and interpretation of his government by his friends and enemies.

A slow-burning revolution is now under way in Venezuela, to the surprise of both the supporters and the opponents of President Chávez. The revolution is not the work of the charismatic colonel himself – he is just the visible and vocal tip of the iceberg – but the result both of the unusual combativity of the Venezuelan underclass and of the political ineptitude of the opposition to his government. This drama may yet end in tragedy, and the sight of the president's bodyguards – half a dozen seven-feet-high black security officers equipped with the latest technology who stand alertly behind him at all public appearances – is a chilling reminder that politics in Latin America is often still conducted in the shadow of the gun. Political assassination is an ever-present possibility. Yet disasters aside, Venezuela's revolutionary course is now well established, and Latin America is witnessing the most extraordinary and unusual political process since the Cuban revolution nearly half a century ago.

Forget Chile and Nicaragua. Salvador Allende in the 1970s was at heart a skilful bourgeois politician, not a revolutionary. He used to say, before he became president, that if he were to start a guerrilla movement in the Chilean Andes the authorities would have to send out an ambulance to rescue him from frostbite. The Sandinistas in the 1980s made a good initial stab at organising a revolution, but coming from a small country with a withered political culture, they had little chance of resisting the inevitable United States counter-attack. The Cold War still cast its baleful shadow over the continent.

The Venezuelan experience is both different and unexpected. An oil-rich country with an economic weight far beyond the present capacity of its impoverished population of 24 million to generate by other means, Venezuela has always seemed an improbable candidate for revolution, although it spawned an active Castroite guerrilla movement in the 1960s. With the most Americanised middle class in Latin America, and an underclass (two-thirds of the population) seemingly crushed in perpetuity by hunger and poverty, Venezuela had virtually disappeared from the map during the last three decades of the twentieth century. It aroused no external interest, it was never a popular diplomatic posting, and foreign academics specialising in Latin America had long disregarded its history and politics. Few serious studies of the country have been published in recent years.

Yet at a time when few outsiders were taking much notice of events in Latin America – during the decade after the end of the Cold War – Venezuela suddenly emerged at the front of the field. It was the first country in Latin America to suffer from serious and debilitating government corruption, the first to react violently against externally imposed policies of neo-liberalism and the so-called Washington Consensus, and the first to experiment with an entirely fresh and original programme of anti-globalisation.

Contemporary politics in Venezuela begin with the so-called *Caracazo* of February 1989, an explosion of political rage by the underclass in Caracas and a handful of other cities against a neo-liberal programme imposed by a once-popular president, Carlos Andrés Pérez, who had just been elected to do something entirely different. For two days Caracas degenerated into violence of a kind not seen in Venezuela since the nineteenth century, sparked off by an increase in bus fares but reflecting a much wider political discontent. A thousand people, perhaps more, were killed in the subsequent repression by the armed forces.

This event was as important for Latin America as the fall of the Berlin Wall – which took place later that year – was for Europe. It marked the first occasion when the neo-liberal agenda imposed on the continent was dramatically rejected by a popular uprising. Comparable rebellions occurred subsequently in several other countries of the continent, but Venezuela was in at the start.

Ten years later, the crisis of neo-liberalism had exploded all over Latin America, with scenes of mounting hostility to these economic strategies in almost every country. In Brazil in 2003 a new leftist president took office, Luiz Inacio da Silva (Lula), the candidate of the Workers' Party that had a long track record of hostility to globalisation. In Bolivia that same year the businessman president had to be rescued from his palace in La Paz by an ambulance, as the city was given over to rioters protesting against privatisation and the imposition of fresh taxes. The police force, itself on strike, confronted armed soldiers, while the people poured down from the hills to trash the US fast-food outlets and the supermarkets. In Ecuador, in 2000, a similar story unfolded. An alliance of indigenous peoples and radical young officers brought down the neo-liberal government that had dollarised the currency.

In Argentina, almost unprecedented scenes of revolt occurred in the early years of the twenty-first century, in which even the middle class was mobilised. The normally sober citizens of Buenos Aires were to be seen banging on the doors of defaulting banks, and the underclass became increasingly active all over the country. Elections, with a dour cast of political has-beens competing for the presidency with no popular support, led to the emergence of President Nestor Kirchner, perceived as a different and new broom.

In neighbouring Uruguay, the heirs to the Tupamaros, the urban guerrilla movement of the 1970s, were elected into office in 2004.

In Colombia, the civil war waged since the 1950s is still very much alive, its impact exacerbated by the continuing US military intervention. Substantial areas of the country are out of the control of the central government, as they have been for much of the past five hundred years.

Venezuela, throughout these recent years, has been at the epicentre of this continental storm. When Hugo Chávez was first elected as president, in December 1998, the country had already suffered a prolonged crisis over many years. Mired in corruption, with the oil wealth dwindling, successive governments had imposed neo-liberal programmes with scant success. Riots in 1989, attempted coups in 1992, the successful impeachment of the president in 1993, the collapse of the banks in 1994, and the implosion of the once-powerful political parties, were all signs of impending breakdown.

Chávez appeared as the popular choice in 1998, and many prominent figures, despairing of the old politics, jumped onto his bandwagon. Millionaire businessmen and media owners hoped that he would not be too radical, and maybe they believed that he might fall under their influence. Most of them failed to appreciate his innate radicalism, and were destined to be disappointed.

Chávez is a genuinely original figure in Latin America. He is not a Marxist like Allende, or a populist like Perón. He is a radical left-wing nationalist, closer in his internationalist vision to that of Fidel Castro than to that of any other Latin American figure. He comes from the provinces of Venezuela, the son of two schoolteachers, and he has inherited their skills. Once a brilliant and popular lecturer at the war college in Caracas, he is a spell-binding orator and still has the didactic manner of a born teacher. He has the physical characteristics of a typical Venezuelan mestizo, with African and Indian features. He is a friendly and approachable man, always with a welcoming smile, and blessed with a great capacity to put people at their ease.

Chávez is a master communicator, and he speaks every Sunday morning on his own radio programme (later transferred to television) called '*Alo Presidente*. The entire country is familiar with his pedagogic formulations. He talks like a teacher and listens like a teacher, picking up an implicit question and throwing it back at the questioner. On the radio, he is at his didactic best, illustrating, explaining, and arguing, with all the sophistry at his command. This is a world with which he has always been familiar, and it is no accident that one of his great nineteenth century heroes is Simón Rodríguez, sometimes called Samuel Robinson, who worked as the organiser of a radical programme of education – in Venezuela, Bolivia, Chile and Ecuador – for the poor, the Indians, and the blacks.

It is difficult to overestimate the impact that Chávez's broadcasts make on the largest and poorest section of the Venezuelan population. On television, he often appears to be speaking to an invited audience immediately in front of him. Then he suddenly turns, as though to another camera, to address the real audience out there in the rural areas and the shanty towns. It is always an electrifying performance, for he speaks as though he is in instant communion with his own people, the people who understand what he is trying to say and do.

The privileged middle class in Caracas, and a plethora of hostile newspaper columnists, complain about his rough and simple language – he is accused of sounding dull and provincial. They fail to grasp that he is talking to people with whom he has a close rapport, who appreciate what he is doing, and who are buoyed up by a feeling of expectancy that something is going to happen, something is going to be done, and things are going to change. He conveys this sense of excitement in a way that the middle classes are unable to capture, for they are tuned to a different wavelength. Throughout his first years in office, much of the old Venezuelan political and cultural elite, grossly overblown by oil rent and petro-dollars, and rotten with corruption, stood back aghast and horrified, hypnotised by the activities of this messianic officer whose interests and preoccupations were not theirs. They could not quite believe what was happening to their country.

Chávez's support has come from the impoverished and politically inarticulate section of society, in the shanty towns of Caracas and in the great forgotten regions of the interior of the country. He speaks to them every day, in words that they understand, in the vivid, often biblical, language of the evangelical preacher. God and Satan, good and evil, pain and love, are the combinations that he often uses. As a result, the mass of the *pueblo* are with Chávez, just as, in other countries of Latin America and at other times, they have been with Perón, with Velasco Alvarado, with Torríjos, with Allende, and with Fidel.

PART ONE:
PORTRAIT OF A PRESIDENT

1

A BASEBALL GAME IN HAVANA, NOVEMBER 1999

On a hot evening in November 1999, Comandante Hugo Chávez, then aged forty-three, came jogging out onto the ground of the main baseball stadium in Havana, followed by his Venezuelan team. Beside him was Comandante Fidel Castro, aged seventy-three, the 'manager' of the Cuban squad. Chávez, the principal pitcher for the Venezuelans, was wearing his country's colours of orange, blue and crimson. Beside him stood his wife Marisabel, a handsome blonde woman with a dazzling smile. Castro wore a blue jacket and sported a red cap; he was accompanied by his vice-president, Carlos Lage, and his foreign minister, Felipe Pérez Roque, both dressed in Cuban colours.

The event that evening was a friendly match, designed to cement the close links developing between the two *comandantes* of Venezuela and Cuba. It had been agreed beforehand that all the players would be veterans over forty, although Castro had warned of a little 'surprise'. For the thousands of spectators in the Havana stadium – and for the millions watching on television all over Latin America – this was an historic sporting encounter between two political giants. Fidel Castro was the oldest and most famous revolutionary in Latin America in the twentieth century, while Hugo Chávez was perceived as the 'new kid on the block' with everything to play for, a radical former army officer whose anti-imperialist rhetoric echoed that of Castro. His dramatic plans for Venezuela and for Latin America were as wide-ranging as those of the Cuban leader had once been.

By an accident of history, the game of baseball, the favourite sport of these two presidents and the national sport of both their countries, is also the preferred game of the United States, the chief imperial power in the region and the champion of the neo-liberal philosophy against which both these radical leaders have directed their rhetoric. Che Guevara, an Argentinian-turned-Cuban, once argued that the Cuban revolution would never make much headway in Latin America unless the Cubans learnt to play soccer, while Henry Kissinger, a US secretary of state of German origin, believed that the future of US hegemony in the continent would depend on the capacity of the United States to adapt to the same game. In practice, the Cubans and the Venezuelans (and the Nicaraguans) have remained content to engage in the demonstrably imperialist sport of baseball – and are very good at it.

Despite the disparity in age between Castro and Chávez, both men share a number of similarities. Just as Fidel Castro became a national hero in Cuba after his failed attempt to seize the Moncada barracks in Santiago de Cuba in July 1953, so Colonel Chávez was projected onto the national stage after leading an unsuccessful military coup in February 1992. Moncada, it should be recalled, to illuminate the generational difference between the two men, took place just a year before Chávez was born.

Castro came to power in Cuba in 1959 after a period of prison, exile, and a two-year guerrilla war; Fulgencio Batista, his defeated predecessor, fled from the country. Chávez also spent time in prison, two years encarcerated at San Francisco de Yare, but he took a less spectacular, though no less intriguing, route to the top. He formed his own political movement when released from prison, and his presidential bid in 1998 was supported by radical nationalist officers and a number of well-known left-wing journalists and intellectuals, many of whom had been supporters of Venezuela's *fidelista* guerrilla movement in the 1960s. So corrupt and detested had the country's existing 'democratic' regime become that Chávez stormed his way through to electoral victory in December 1998 over the ashes of a dismayed and dispirited *ancien régime*. His principal civilian opponent in the 1990s, former president Carlos Andrés Pérez, though not in exile, was forced to spend time under house arrest facing charges of corruption.

The close friendship of Chávez with Castro, forged over the years, and celebrated with an official state visit to Havana in 1999 and a game of baseball, provided Chávez with incomparable revolutionary credentials, of the kind that are recognised in the shanty towns of Venezuela, where the majority of the population lives. They have not been so warmly approved by Venezuela's rich and tiny elite, whose Cuban friends live in Miami not Havana, and whose lives are spent in a constant state of alarm about the future of their property and their bank accounts.

Chávez sought to stir up the nationalist passions of his country's population with a dose of revolutionary rhetoric that had long been out of fashion, both in Latin America and the rest of the world. He has tried to combat the unquestioning acceptance of neo-liberalism and globalisation by means of a revival of radical nationalism, drawing on the words and actions of Venezuela's pantheon of nineteenth-century heroes. He has exalted the figure of Simón Bolívar in much the same way as Castro used the example of the Cuban patriot José Martí. Bolívar and Martí both fought against the Spanish empire, and Castro and Chávez have revived the memory of those nineteenth-century struggles in their campaign against the US attempt to rule the world.

Chávez took up this theme during his visit to Havana for the baseball game. 'Venezuela is travelling towards the same sea as the Cuban people,' he told an astonished audience at the University of Havana, 'a sea of happiness and of real social justice and peace.' Then turning to Castro, and calling him 'brother', he enlarged on one of his central themes, the indivisibility of the Latin American revolution:

> Here we are, as alert as ever, Fidel and Hugo, fighting with dignity and courage to defend the interests of our people, and to bring alive the ideas of Bolívar and Martí. In the name of Cuba and of Venezuela, I appeal for the unity of our two peoples, and of the revolutions that we both lead. Bolívar and Martí, one country united!

Castro, who had spent forty years searching for allies on the Latin American mainland, was more than satisfied with the rhetoric, but he had no intention of allowing this newfound friendship to stand in the way of winning the baseball game. In the stadium, at the start of the sixth game, his promised 'surprise' materialised. Two members of the Cuban reserve were brought on: two of Cuba's most famous young professionals, Oresty Kinderlan and Luís Ulasia. They were disguised with wigs and beards to make them look like veterans, but no one was fooled – although Chávez claimed to have been. With such guerrilla tactics, Cuba won the game without much difficulty, 5-4.

Chávez's visit to Cuba was not just about baseball. Other, more serious matters were under consideration. Cuba's long-established sugar-for-oil swap with Russia was scheduled to end in 1999, and the Cubans were hoping that they might now be able to secure Venezuelan oil at preferential rates. There was a precedent for this, in that under the terms of an agreement signed in 1980 in San José, Costa Rica, Venezuela and Mexico had agree to provide oil at a low price to eleven countries of the Caribbean and Central America. Cuba now joined this select group.

Meanwhile, in another part of Cuba, Héctor Ciávaldini, then the head of *Petróleos de Venezuela*, the Venezuelan state oil company, was examining what could be done with Cuba's Cienfuegos oil refinery, built by the Russians in the 1960s and now in a dilapidated condition. The Cubans had expressed hopes that Venezuela might invest US$200 million in the refinery, but the eventual agreement was more modest. *Petróleos de Venezuela* and Cupet, the Cuban state oil company, would set up a joint company to run the Cienfuegos operation, and Venezuela would supply it with 50,000 barrels a day.

Ciávaldini was asked by journalists what effect this agreement might have on the United States. 'We don't ask questions when the US buys things from China. Thirty per cent of the mass consumption articles that the US imports come from China. If they have these kinds of relationships, I don't think we should feel inhibited from having relations with whoever we want – with China, with Malaysia, or with Cuba.' A week later, Ali Rodríguez, then Venezuela's minister of energy and mines, visited Saddam Hussein in Baghdad to seek support for the revival of OPEC, the Organisation of Petroleum Exporting Countries.

Venezuela and Cuba have had a long and troubled interaction over the past half century, and it is appropriate to begin a book about Hugo Chávez with an account of the reconciliation of these two countries and their governments. For the radical programme embraced by Chávez has its roots in the conflictive events in Latin America of the past fifty years. During that time, revolutionary movements in Venezuela, inspired and directly assisted by Castro and Che Guevara, sought to spread the revolutionary message of the Cuban revolution from the island to the continent. Castro visited Caracas in 1959, just after his victory over Batista, to thank the Venezuelans for their moral and practical support. At that moment, he was the most popular man in the country, spontaneously welcomed by thousands of people demonstrating in the great space of El Silencio in the city centre.

A popular uprising had broken out in Caracas in January 1958, a year before Castro's guerrilla victory. A revolt at the military base at Maracay west of Caracas (later to be the base from which Chávez launched his own coup in 1992) had been followed by rioting in the capital. A left-wing Patriotic Junta appealed successfully for a general strike which led to the resignation of the Venezuelan dictator, Marcos Pérez Jiménez. Venezuela and Cuba appeared to be moving forward on parallel tracks.

The eventual beneficiary of the Venezuelan revolt was not a revolutionary but a reformist politician of great skill and ruthlessness. Rómulo Betancourt was a founder of *Acción Democrática*, a party that enjoyed the active support of the United States. The Americans saw Betancourt's Venezuela as a model for Latin America, and held it up as a favoured alternative to Castro's Cuba. Yet this was not the general view of the population of Caracas. Castro was cheered to the echo when he came to thank the Venezuelans for their support, while for Betancourt, standing at his side, there was only a storm of booing. Betancourt's Venezuela soon became a bastion of the anti-Cuban cause in the Americas, and his government's secret service was put in the charge of anti-Castro exiles from Miami.

Many left-wing Venezuelans, following the example of the Cuban revolution, took to the hills and organised a guerrilla insurrection in the 1960s that lasted until the end of the decade. Some of them came from the Communist Party, others from splinter groups that broke away from *Acción Democrática*. Still others worked hand in glove with radical groups within the armed forces – a significant development in the light of subsequent history.

Civilian activists from the Communist and other parties took part in two military revolts against the *Acción Democrática* government in 1962, at Carúpano and Puerto Cabello. The revolts were unsuccessful but left a powerful trace in popular imagination. In a statement after Carúpano, one of the Communist leaders, Guillermo García Ponce, described the political programme of the rebel officers as 'far-reaching, nationalistic, and patriotic', and praised it for calling on Venezuelans 'to work for democratic reconstruction'. García Ponce thought the rebels had 'done Venezuela a great service'. Nearly four decades later, in 1999, he was a Chávez supporter in the Assembly elected to draft a new constitution.

Chávez did not emerge from a vacuum. He was the heir to the revolutionary traditions of the Venezuelan left. Many survivors of the guerrilla insurrection of the 1960s were still participating in politics in the first decade of the twenty-first century – some on the side of Chávez, others in the opposition. Chávez had spent time cultivating the civilian left when planning his coup of 1992, and when in government he was able to draw on the talents of many of those who came from this radical tradition.

Half a dozen former guerrillas were to be found among the Chávez supporters in the National Assembly elected in 2000. Ali Rodríguez Araque, the minister of energy and mines who was to spearhead the revival of OPEC (and later became foreign minister), was a guerrilla fighter in Falcón state in the 1960s, and was subsequently active in a significant left-wing party, *La Causa Radical*. Lino Martínez, the minister of labour, was also once a guerrilla.

Chávez relied initially for political advice on two veteran civilian politicians – Luís Miquilena and José Vicente Rangel, both historic stars in the firmament of the Venezuelan left. Both had been in the public arena for close on half a century, some of that time spent in prison or in exile. Rangel, in his seventies and one of the great charmers of Latin

American politics, had been the presidential candidate of the left on three occasions, and became an active and vocal defender of the Chávez government – as foreign minister and later as vice-president. Miquilena, in his eighties, became president of the National Assembly and was Chávez's first minister of the interior. He had been a leader of the bus drivers' union in Caracas in the 1940s, and the co-founder of an anti-Stalinist communist party in 1946. He retained a tough Leninist streak, which proved useful when helping to construct the political movement of soldiers and civilians – the Fifth Republic Movement – that supported Chávez's election campaign in 1998, though eventually he abandoned Chávez in December 2001, and joined forces with the opposition.

Several other ministers came from the Venezuelan left. Ignácio Arcaya was Miquilena's godson and the son of a former foreign minister who was sacked in 1960 for failing to sign a US-inspired anti-Cuban motion at a meeting of the Organisation of American States. Jorge Giordani, the planning minister, was formerly the economic adviser to the Movement for Socialism, another left-wing party that had emerged after the end of the guerrilla rebellion in the 1970s.

Not all the surviving revolutionaries of the 1960s supported Chávez. Opposing him from the right was a group of former guerrillas led by Teodoro Petkoff, once a Communist leader and a prominent minister in the reformist government that preceded the first Chávez electoral victory. Petkoff had also on occasion been the presidential candidate of the left, and throughout Chávez's first year in power he was the influential editor of an evening paper, *El Mundo*, that was fiercely opposed to the president. Sacked by his paper's proprietor in December that year, Petkoff reappeared in subsequent years as editor of *Tal Cual*, a formidable pamphleteering paper. Among his columnists were several former guerrillas who had made the journey from Cuban-style socialism to social democracy – and beyond.

Opposing Chávez from the left, almost from the start, was Douglas Bravo, the guerrilla leader in Falcón in the 1960s and perhaps the most well-known of the uncompromising leftists of earlier years. Bravo had collaborated with Chávez on his revolutionary military project in the 1980s, on the assumption that this was going to be a genuinely civilian–military operation. He withdrew after 1992 when he felt that civilians were being by-passed, and that Chávez's programme was insufficiently radical.

Years ago, in 1968, I spent a couple of weeks in Caracas awaiting a call to interview Bravo in the hills. As so often used to happen, the contacts were never established, but some three decades later, in November 1999, I finally caught up with him, and he came to see me in the apartment of a friend. Then in his late sixties, Bravo had remained a cheerful and resilient revolutionary, though not in Chávez's camp. He explained how he had got to know Chávez quite well, at a time when the future president was a junior officer conspiring against the government. 'Chávez is an intelligent man,' said Bravo, 'bold, charismatic, and an excellent speaker; he has a natural ability to command.'

The old guerrilla leader was not without a few criticisms. 'Chávez is quite capable of making sudden changes in direction. These can be positive or negative. He can easily make agreements with one group, and then abandon them when he makes a deal with another. This was a very serious characteristic when Chávez was a conspirator, and it is quite dangerous now that he is the president.'

When I talked to Rangel, who is of the same generation as Bravo, he took a less critical view: 'It's a mistake to demonise Chávez, just as it is an error to sanctify him. If he had not emerged, there would certainly have been somebody else. Fortunately, this has proved the best way to secure change, peacefully and with civilians. After all, we might easily have had a Pinochet.'

The debate within the Venezuelan left about revolutionary tactics, and about the alliance between soldiers and civilians, continued into the Chávez era, unremitting and unresolved. Yet Chávez's capacity to survive in power, and to reinforce his Bolivarian Revolution, left his former leftist opponents high and dry, without arguments or supporters.

2

THE DISINTEGRATION
OF THE *ANCIEN RÉGIME*

Caracas was once a small town circled by relatively friendly *ranchos*, or makeshift shanties, on the surrounding hills. At night, the lights of the poor twinkled like candles. Yet the wealth and luxury of the city centre, and the visible poverty and misery of the *ranchos*, were dramatic reminders of Latin America's most famous characteristic – inequality of income and opportunity based on deep-seated attitudes of unacknowledged racism.

The middle class is not as large and as privileged as it once was, yet those not squeezed by the economic crisis remain informally convivial, with an international standard of living. Enjoy Saturday lunch in one of the *cervecerías*, or beer restaurants, of El Rosal or Sabana Grande, and you could easily be in Barcelona, Turin or Frankfurt. Visit the multi-storey shopping mall at the Centro Sambíl and you could be in any city of the US Midwest. Even at the height of a prolonged economic and political crisis, this is a social group that continues to live extraordinarily well, importing their food and consumer goods from all over the world, though chiefly from the United States, and preferring the cosmopolitan to the national. A country that once exported chocolate now imports Hershey bars.

In recent years the scale of inequality has changed, and the danger inherent in the urban situation has become increasingly obvious. Caracas is now a North American-style metropolis that always looks spectacular. The visitor is greeted by an urban jungle of freeways and concrete intersections, of pedestrianised precincts and shopping malls. A forest of gigantic skyscrapers, in every architectural style, reflects half a century of unbridled urban development.

Some of the shanty towns have been absorbed and upgraded; some, from a distance, now have the apparent charm of an Italian hill town. Yet above and beyond, on the sprawling cliffs to the south and east of the city, the shacks of wood and concrete are still growing in number, stretching over new ground, ring after ring of impoverished suburb and dormitory town. They remain as a permanent and seemingly ineradicable threat to the good life on the valley floor.

There was a time when the hilltop *ranchos* were able to use their height to remind the Venezuelan rich of their existence, but nowadays the construction of skyscrapers has symbolically turned the tables. The great tall blocks in the middle of the city are able to flaunt the wealth of the consumer society over the small hills of misery, while the poor have been driven ever further from the centre.

Like many of the other megacities of Latin America, Caracas is characterised by the virtual absence of law and order. It is a city under siege, with each shopping centre barricaded by fences of steel, each residential street marked off with a guardhouse and a lifting road barrier, and each block of flats protected by armed wardens. The rich live behind high walls with their own private security guards; the youthful poor survive by organising their own armed gangs. The middle class, sandwiched miserably in between, live in constant fear for their property and their lives.

On one dramatic day in February 1989, their worst nightmares were realised. The poor from the surrounding hills descended for a week of indiscriminate looting throughout the city. Hundreds of people were killed during the subsequent period of fierce military repression, a reminder to the country of just how thin the veneer of tolerance between the classes had become. The event, soon called the *Caracazo*, had a simple cause: the price of petrol went up; the bus fares went up; and simmering anger turned to active rebellion. The police, on strike at the time for a pay increase, were ill-prepared for an urban riot. When television screens began to show people looting in Caracas, and the police standing around and letting it happen, citizens in other cities saw this as an invitation to join in. Even today, years after those extraordinary and frightening days, many middle-class inhabitants of Caracas no longer feel really 'safe'.

The country's *ancien régime*, like that of the Soviet Union at the time, had been groping blindly towards new models, and the urban revolt of February 1989 occurred partly because of the movement towards reform. Since the late 1950s, Venezuela had had all the attributes of a one-party state, not unlike those that once existed in Communist Eastern Europe. Venezuela's peculiarity, shared with neighbouring Colombia, was that two parties rather than one were given the chance to control the state, turn and turn about. The largest and most significant party, *Acción Democrática*, had the predominant and hegemonic role, but to keep up the pretence that Venezuela was a 'democracy', an alternative Christian Democrat party, Copei, was allowed on occasion to win elections. The two political movements carved out this cynical agreement in the so-called Pact of Punto Fijo, signed in 1958, which effectively ensured that other parties, of left or right, would be prevented from ever taking power.

Acción Democrática and Copei both had large memberships. You joined a party to get a job, and to keep it. The party leaders, and the bosses of their tame trade unions, grew accustomed to the perks of power, and particularly to the pickings from the blossoming state industries created from the revenues from oil. Corruption on an almost unimaginable scale became endemic, particularly within the ranks of *Acción Democrática* but also in the wider banking and commercial community, and it snowballed with the years. The corruption and conspicuous consumption of the Venezuelan political elite became famous throughout the continent. They also created a deep anger within the poorer strata of society, and an unquenchable desire for revenge.

During the boom years of the 1970s, everything had seemingly gone well. President Carlos Andrés Pérez of *Acción Democrática*, an archetypal Third World leader with a penchant for stealing from the state, ruled from 1974 to 1979, and took the strong statist line that was popular at that time. Shell and Exxon and other foreign oil companies were nationalised, and state money was poured into the development of industry, to the applause of left-wing nationalists everywhere. Such was the flow of oil money in those years that even today there is still much visible to show for it, mostly in the southern region of Guayana: iron ore extraction, smelting operations, steel and aluminium plants, industrial complexes, and the gigantic hydro-electric dam at Guri on the Caroní river, capable of supplying Venezuela's electricity needs – and those of much of northern Brazil as well.

Yet over the years the state sector began to ossify. It was revealed to be inefficient and uncompetitive, overmanned and corrupt. Short of fresh investment, the great industrial enterprises began to rust away. Projects begun were quickly abandoned. As elsewhere in Latin America, encouraged by greedy international bankers, the country accumulated an immense foreign debt, saddling future generations with the costs of the riotous living of today. In the course of the 1980s, both economically and politically, the country was spiralling towards disaster.

Finally, in 1989, plans were produced to restructure the economy on neo-liberal lines. Returned to power that year with a mandate to revive the atmosphere of the 'good old days' of his earlier presidency, President Pérez unexpectedly changed tack. With no advance warning, his government steered the economy out into the difficult and turbulent waters of the free market, the liberalised economy, and international competition.

The new economic programme soon undermined the established political system, meeting with sustained opposition in the streets and within the ruling parties. The peoples of Latin America, in spite of the surface opulence of the middle-class sectors of the cities, are much closer to the breadline than their counterparts in Eastern Europe. The old party bosses, understandably, were bitterly opposed to *perestroika*, Venezuelan-style. Quite apart from the inherent difficulty of making the country more competitive, a huge structure of vested interests would have to be dismantled.

In February 1992, three years after the *Caracazo*, Colonel Chávez made his dramatic appearance – a 38-year-old military leader who promised to overthrow the corrupt politicians, to improve the conditions of the poor, and to move the country onto a fresh course. Then the commanding officer of a parachute regiment in Maracay, an hour's drive from Caracas, he was well positioned to challenge the *ancien régime* by staging a coup.

Although the rebellion was successful in other parts of the country, the attempt to seize the presidential palace in Caracas was a failure. Chávez surrendered and appeared on television to urge his fellow conspirators elsewhere to put down their arms. 'Comrades,' he said, 'unfortunately, for the moment, the objectives that we had set ourselves have not been achieved in the capital.' Maybe, he implied, we'll have better luck next time.

The phrase 'for the moment', *por ahora*, caught the popular imagination. The aims of the rebellion had not been secured, but most people read his message optimistically, as a sign that Chávez would return to the struggle at a later date. *Por ahora* became his trademark slogan, and the red beret of the parachute regiment became his signature logo. José Vicente Rangel cited the television appearance to me when explaining his conviction that Chávez would always be a strong supporter of press freedom. 'He knows that the word is much more powerful than the gun. He failed when he used the gun, and triumphed when he had access to the media. He spent ten years preparing a *coup d'état* that failed militarily; the single minute they allowed him to appear on television was enough to conquer the country.'

Chávez's intervention, at a time of national disintegration, was to turn him into a national hero overnight, celebrated all over the country in poetry and song. In a continent where evangelical sects have been increasing exponentially over the past twenty years, to rival the power and influence of the Catholic Church, the arrival of Colonel Chávez was greeted as though it were the Second Coming.

Chávez spent two years in prison, but news of the revolutionary project on which he had been working with fellow officers soon leaked out. Resurrecting three South American heroes from the nineteenth century – Bolívar himself, Bolívar's revolutionary teacher Simón Rodríguez, and Ezequiel Zamora, leader of the peasants against the landed oligarchy in the Federal wars of the 1840s and 1850s – Chávez began to sketch the outline of a politics of revolutionary nationalism, destined to have considerable popular appeal. From the country in Latin America that has been most deeply immersed in North American culture and politics, he launched a fierce counter-attack on the programme of globalisation imposed on the world by the United States in the aftermath of the Cold War. Soon he was topping the polls of public opinion. In December 1998, he was elected president.

3

PROVINCIAL ORIGINS IN BARINAS

The small, hot town of Barinas stands beneath the final range of the Andes, the gateway to the great plains of the Orinoco basin. I came here on the bus from Caracas, an eight-hour journey on a good road along the foot of the hills, through Maracay and Carabobo and Acarígua. Here begins the vast expanse of the *llanos*, the low-lying and marshy cattle lands of the centre-south of the country where innumerable rivers make their way down from the Andes to the Orinoco. The *llanos* stretch down to the Colombian frontier and beyond, and eventually reach the tributaries of the Amazon in Brazil.

Barinas spreads out in extensive fashion from its crowded bus station, mostly with single-storey buildings, and I put up at a small hotel in the Plaza Zamora, beside the San Domingo river. The name of the square recalls Ezequiel Zamora, the revolutionary leader of the federal forces in the 1850s, who won a great victory in 1859 not far from here, at the battle of Santa Inés. Zamora has long been one of the heroes from whom President Chávez draws his inspiration. The *llanos* were the scene of many of the other fratricidal battles of the nineteenth century, and in these latitudes Simón Bolívar gathered the plainsmen together for his spirited and successful attack on the Spanish forces in Colombia in 1819.

This is provincial Latin America at its most appealing, only eight hours from the capital city by bus, but light years away by most other measurements. 'There's little to do or see here,' says the guidebook, and that's how it should be. I soon discover an open-air restaurant serving barbecued chicken and yucca, and the regional beer from Maracaibo. The walls are covered with utopian murals in lurid colours, with exotic birds flying out of the forest and over a great expanse of water, and the evocative songs of the *llaneros* pour out from an ancient juke-box.

Yet modernity is not altogether absent. Behind the immense statue of Bolívar in the central square stands a gigantic communications mast, tucked in behind the state governor's relatively humble palace. The statue was designed to command all it surveys from a great height, but was wholly dwarfed by this essential element of the contemporary world. Even my hotel, appropriately called the Hotel Internacional, receives several dozen television programmes plucked from the air, only four of them being generated in Venezuela. The disparity between the respect accorded to the historical figure of Bolívar, and the reality of a twenty-first-century world with technological trappings that were unimaginable two centuries ago, is one of the reasons why some educated Venezuelans still have doubts about the course on which President Chávez has embarked. Invoking the thoughts and ambitions of Bolívar today can seem rather, well, quaint.

Barinas is the home state of the president; his father has been the governor here since November 1998, a supporter of his son's political movement. Chávez the president was actually born a few miles away, in the village of Sabaneta, but he came to school in Barinas and was stationed here for some years in the army. It seemed an appropriate place to start.

Chávez was born on July 28, 1954. His parents, Hugo de los Reyes Chávez and Elena Frias, were both schoolteachers, but they took an active part in political life. His father had long been involved in the educational politics of the state, being enrolled at one stage in the social-Christian party, Copei. Politics seems to run in the blood, for the president's elder brother, Adán Chávez, a professor at the university of Mérida, was a member of the Constitutional Assembly in 1999. The president's second wife, Marisabel Rodríguez, was also a member of this Assembly.

Chávez was first married to Nancy Colmenares, a girl from Barinas, and the couple had a boy, Huguito, and two girls, Rosa Virginia and María Gabriela, who were university students during his first years as President. With Marisabel, who already had a son, Raúl, he has a daughter: Rosa-Inés. One significant characteristic of Latin American political life is the family, almost tribal, relationships that often exist at the top. Adán Chávez was to become minister in charge of agrarian reform and then ambassador to Havana.

Recent history still lies close to the surface in this region, and the Chávez family is itself the heir to some of the rebellious traditions of the nineteenth century. The great-grandfather of Chávez's father was the guerrilla chief Colonel Pedro Pérez Pérez. Ezequiel Zamora summoned this Colonel Pérez to join his Sovereign Army of the People in the 1840s and to fight with them against the landed oligarchy. The son of Colonel Pérez, in turn, was another legendary figure, General Pedro Pérez Delgado, known as Maisanta, who rebelled in 1914 against the dictatorship of General Juan Vicente Gómez. At the turn of the twentieth century, Maisanta had hitched his star to the fortunes of General Cipriano Castro and had settled in the *llanos* as Castro's man in Sabaneta. He married a local woman, Claudina Infante, and with her, he had two daughters. One of them, Rosa, was the grandmother of Hugo Chávez.

Maisanta subsequently organised a guerrilla movement against Gómez in the *llanos*, but he was captured and imprisoned. His lands were confiscated and he died in prison, but his son continued the struggle. Chávez was told stories by his grandmother of how soldiers had arrived at their farm with machetes, to slaughter the peasants and to burn down all the barns and buildings. He was also told, such were the enduring political hatreds of the region, that Maisanta was an assassin, best forgotten. Only later, when an adult, did Chávez understand that his great-grandfather would be better described as a freedom fighter.

This local and personal history had a considerable impact on the youthful Hugo, and he was to ponder it again in later years when stationed as a young officer in Barinas and at other points in the *llanos*. Maisanta and Ezequiel Zamora, as archetypal soldier-revolutionaries, have remained, alongside Bolívar, as his principal heroes to this day.

4

FROM BARINAS TO CARACAS: THE IRRESISTIBLE FLIGHT FROM THE COUNTRYSIDE

When I first interviewed Hugo Chávez in 2000, he was standing in the garden of La Casona, the presidential residence in Caracas, with his back to the house, gazing out towards the small forest of bamboo and palms that fringes the far end of the lawn. Since he is on television most days of the week, making impromptu speeches, greeting protocol visitors at the Miraflores palace, or glad-handing his way through a shanty town, everyone knows what he looks like. They are familiar with his pugilist's face, his generous lips, his beaming grin, and the almost imperceptible asthmatic tick of his mouth as he takes a breath or is caught searching for a word in mid-rhetorical flow. He always appears decisive, and radiates confidence and optimism.

Yet alone on the green lawn he appeared more vulnerable, a monochrome and ambiguous sculpture dressed in a grey suit. He stood absolutely motionless for several minutes, as though gaining strength to face the long day ahead, and seemingly oblivious of the arrival of a stranger. Finally he turned round and walked across the grass to greet me.

He is a master of the surprise gesture and the rhetorical flourish, with a considerable sense of theatre. I was reminded for a moment of *Yo el Supremo* (I the Supreme One), the great Paraguayan writer Augusto Roa Bastos's novel about José Gaspar Rodríguez de Francia, the ascetic Robespierrean president of Paraguay in the early nineteenth century who isolated his country for thirty years from the globalising currents of his time and laid down the solid foundations of its economic development. Chávez has a similar messianic streak.

The damp heat of the early morning, the lush colours of a tropical garden, and the verandah columns of a building designed as a replica of a colonial hacienda house of the eighteenth century, all conspired to create the illusion of a time warp. Our lengthy conversation – much of it devoted to his ambitious plan to stimulate development in the countryside – seemed to have a timeless quality to it, as though recalling that this was an issue that presidents and colonial viceroys in Latin America had been wrestling with for centuries.

In an interview, Chávez becomes a cross between an after-dinner raconteur and a university lecturer giving a tutorial, sometimes telling long stories about distant events, sometimes analysing current problems. José Vicente Rangel, his vice-president, had told me that Chávez was 'a head of state quite unlike any other'. While 'most of them have a laconic style and keep a low profile, Chávez is quite the opposite: he accepts a challenge in any area; he really enjoys permanent confrontation; he is an extrovert and an excellent communicator, and he likes polemic and seeks it out'. Would I be a sufficiently stimulating interviewer, I wondered. Rangel also said that Chávez was much more of an intellectual than people think, with great creativity. 'He is a pragmatic romantic, a mixture of passion with calculation.'

On that first occasion, we were in tutorial mode, and Chávez delved for my benefit into the history of Venezuela in the twentieth century, explaining how the exploitation of oil in the 1920s had led to the collapse of the rural economy. This in turn had brought an end to Venezuela's old 'balanced and harmonious model', whereby the cultivation of coffee, sugar and cocoa in the country had marched in step with the industrial development of the towns. 'The government simply gave up on the countryside, and what the history books call the peasant exodus began.' Chávez emphasised that 'this was not because the peasants wanted to leave, but because the rural areas were abandoned by the government'.

He used a personal example close to home. 'This is something that I have felt ever since I was a child; I never wanted to move away from my home village, but I had to go; I was drawn into the city by a centripetal force.' The aim of his policies, he explained, was 'to make this force go in the opposite direction'.

Once he had finished sixth grade at school in Sabaneta, he had to leave his home village, to go first to Barinas and then to Caracas. He explained the causes of his move, an explanation that lies at the heart of what he thinks is wrong with the country's development – and what he plans to put right.

'If I wanted to continue studying, which I did, since my father was a teacher, then I would have to go to Barinas, which was a larger town, the state capital. But if there had been a secondary school in Sabaneta, I wouldn't have had to go.'

When it came to further education, Barinas had no university. 'All my brothers had to travel to the university in Mérida, and I had to come to Caracas, to the military academy. Those who didn't leave, stayed behind and stagnated.'

The same forces affecting education had also influenced the provision of health care in Sabaneta and Barinas. 'People who needed attention had to go to Barquisimeto or Caracas. Even our local sportsmen had to leave. Peasants left when they lost their land to the great haciendas. There was a massive exodus.'

The military were subject to the same centripetal force, dragging them to the city. When he was in the army, he said, there was 'always a struggle with the *muchachos* who came from the rural areas to do their obligatory military service.'

'They were brought to the cities, to the barracks in Caracas, and of course when they saw the city – when they set out on a day off – and saw everything that the city has to offer, they didn't want to return to the country. For there they would have no land and no work, nothing, just a shack to go home to. Military service was another factor that helped to force people into the towns.'

Venezuelans have been migrating over many years, Chávez pointed out, to the narrow centre-north coastal strip of the country. 'Eighty per cent of the population is now concentrated here,' he said. All he wanted to do, he claimed, was to reverse the trend. The principal aim of his revolution was 'to occupy the geographic space of the country in a more harmonious and balanced way'.

In his first year in office, Chávez proposed a bold scheme to move hundreds of thousands of people from the crowded cities of northern Venezuela to new economic centres in the sparsely populated east and south of the country. He planned to develop 'integrated' agro-industrial projects in these empty lands, and he hoped that these would cajole people living in the shanty towns to start a new life in the rural areas. While some early reports suggested that most people wanted to cling to their urban shanties, others suggested that some were thrilled by the prospect of being provided with land and new homes – and the possibility of a fresh start.

Politicians and urban planners have argued for years about what to do with the gigantic urban conglomerations of Latin America, the old capital cities housing millions of people for whom there are few real homes, not much food, and little work. To move urban dwellers back to the country is a tall order, flying in the face of historical experience and of what is now believed to be possible, for few people hanker after the grinding life of the peasant. Yet to populate the rural areas with the country's own population, rather than to bring in fresh settlers from outside, is an ambition that goes back at least as far as the proposals of Simón Rodríguez, Bolívar's tutor, in the early nineteenth century. Chávez's utopian schemes have a venerable lineage.

PART TWO: PREPARING FOR A BOLIVARIAN REBELLION

5

THE DEVELOPMENT
OF A MILITARY CONSPIRACY

Chávez first enrolled as a soldier at the age of seventeen, and he often claims that it was his enthusiasm for baseball that persuaded him to join the army. He was to become one of the army's champion players, though eventually he showed a greater propensity for politics than for sport. He entered the military academy in Caracas in 1971 during the first presidency of Rafael Caldera, the founder of Copei, at a time when some of the future supporters of his government were abandoning the guerrilla struggle in the hills. Caldera was to pioneer the pacification of the country after the revolutionary insurrection of the 1960s, permitting former guerrillas to re-enter civilian life, albeit after a decent interval.

The political thinking of the young Chávez was influenced by his early love of history, sparked off by his family's particular experience, but soon he was to acquire fresh insights into contemporary affairs. In 1974, while still a cadet, he travelled to Peru with a dozen other young soldiers. They had gone to participate in the international celebration of the 150th anniversary of the battle of Ayacucho, held on the Andean battleground outside the old colonial town. The battle, in 1824, had marked the liberation of Peru from Spanish rule by the forces of Bolívar and Sucre.

In more recent years, after 1968, Peru had been the scene of a radical experiment in government conducted by the armed forces. General Juan Velasco Alvarado, an unusually progressive officer, had seized power in Lima in 1968 and embarked on a radical programme of reform, supported by revolutionaries within the armed forces and by some of Peru's left-wing parties. This was Chávez's first acquaintance with a radical military regime, and Peru, evocatively for him, was a country where Bolívar still had an honoured name.

Chávez and the other Venezuelan cadets were each given a small memento by President Velasco, a booklet of speeches called *La Revolución Nacional Peruana*. He still recalls the visit, the booklet, and the enthusiastic support that the Peruvian cadets gave their president. The Peruvian experiment has remained an important influence on his political thinking.

In 1975, a year after his trip to Lima and Ayacucho, Chávez graduated from the military academy as a sub-lieutenant, receiving his sword of command from the hands of President Carlos Andrés Pérez at the annual passing-out parade on July 5, the anniversary of Venezuelan independence in 1811. President Pérez was the man he was to try to overthrow sixteen years later, in February 1992.

Chávez spent the next two years based in Barinas, joining a counter-insurgency battalion stationed there since the guerrilla war of the 1960s. In 1976, the battalion was sent to Cumaná to help crush a fresh guerrilla outbreak, organised by a group within *Bandera Roja*, or Red Flag, one of the ultra-leftist groups that had remained faithful to the guerrilla strategy of the 1960s. At this stage, according to his own account, Chávez began to feel some sympathy for the guerrillas that his battalion was supposed to be fighting. He also became aware for the first time, he says, of how the generalised corruption in the political world was percolating through into the armed forces. Officers would raid their budgets and pilfer military equipment for their own personal use.

In 1977, at the age of twenty-three and with only two years' experience as a lieutenant, Chávez decided to form his own revolutionary armed group. He gathered together a few friends to dream of revolution, calling their group the *Ejército de Liberación del Pueblo de Venezuela* (ELPV), the Liberation Army of the Venezuelan People.

'What was the purpose?' he was asked years later by Gabriel García Márquez, the Colombian novelist. 'It was very simple,' Chávez told him.

'We did it to prepare ourselves in case something should happen.' This was doubtless but the youthful enthusiasm of a 23-year-old, and, as he recalls, 'we hadn't the least idea at that time what we were going to do'. But it was an important pointer to the future.

Soon afterwards, he encountered another young officer, Jesús Urdaneta Hernández, with similarly radical attitudes. They soon became close friends, and Chávez told Urdaneta how he had been disappointed by his experience in the army and how he had formed a small revolutionary group. 'I'm not going to go on like this in the army all my life,' he said.

Chávez then suggested that perhaps the two of them should try something different. 'Why don't we create a movement within the army,' he said, rejecting the possibility of organising a guerrilla movement. 'We're not going to join the guerrillas, that's all over and done with, and anyway our outlook and our education don't fit with them.'

What he had in mind, he revealed to Urdaneta, was something entirely different. They would organise 'a movement within the armed forces'. General Urdaneta, as he later became, was to remain a faithful ally of Chávez, playing a central role in the first cabinet as the head of the secret police, the Dirección de Servicios de Inteligencia y Prevención, the DISIP. One of his many jobs was to root out the Cuban exiles and the Israelis who had been employed there over many years.

Chávez was transferred in 1978 to a tank battalion in Maracay, and two years after that, pursuing his interests in baseball, he was moved back to the military academy in Caracas – as the chief sports instructor. He remained there for five influential years, from 1980 to 1985, eventually graduating from sports to culture and becoming a tutor in history and politics. The authorities underestimated the impact that this intelligent and charismatic tutor would have on his students at the academy.

During this period his political ambitions hardened into a firm belief that his generation of military officers would at some future date be called upon to run the country. The 1970s had been the glory years of 'Venezuela Saudíta', when Venezuelans were led to believe that they might soon inhabit a rich and developed Western country, but in the early 1980s, they were finally replaced by the harsh reality of devaluation and indebtedness, leading to a worsening spiral of poverty. The civilian leaders began to look increasingly incompetent and vulnerable. The government of Carlos Andrés Pérez in the 1970s had lived off the immensely increased revenues of the post-1973 oil boom, and the petrodollar loans it brought in its train; his successors in the 1980s had nothing so substantial at their command.

Finally, in 1982, Chávez began to organise a serious political conspiracy. Assembling two other military officers, lecturers at the military academy, he created a political cell within the army, calling it the *Movimiento Bolivariano Revolucionario – 200* (MBR-200), the Bolivarian Revolutionary Movement. The '200' was added to mark the year-long celebrations that were taking place at that time to record the 200th anniversary of the birth of Bolívar in July 1783. The two other officers were Felipe Acosta Carles, and Chávez's friend Jesús Urdaneta. Whilst Urdaneta survived to play an important role in the Chávez government, Acosta was killed during the *Caracazo* rebellion in 1989.

On December 17, 1982, the revolutionary officers swore an oath underneath the great tree at Samán de Güere, near Maracay, repeating the words of the pledge that Simón Bolívar had made on the slopes of the Monte Sacro in Rome in 1805, when he swore to devote his life to the liberation of Venezuela from the Spanish yoke:

'I swear before you, and I swear before the God of my fathers, that I will not allow my arm to relax, nor my soul to rest, until I have broken the chains that oppress us ...'

The Bolivarian Revolutionary Movement started more as a political study circle than as a subversive conspiracy, but as the young officers examined the history and the contemporary problems of their country, they began thinking in terms of some kind of *coup d'état*. They knew that they would have to overthrow the existing political system, for they believed that Venezuela's version of 'democracy' was a sham. Chávez explained his reservations about the existing system when interviewed by Agustín Blanco Muñoz in June 1999:

What has been called the democratic system in Venezuela has not differed much in recent years from what came before: the dictatorship of Marcos Pérez Jiménez; the three years government [of *Acción Democrática*] between 1945 and 1948; the governments of Isaías Medina and López Contreras; and even the government of Juan Vicente Gómez, which takes us back to 1908. Everything has basically remained the same; it's been the same system of domination, with a different face – whether it's that of General Gómez or of Dr Rafael Caldera. Behind this figure, this caudillo, with a military beret or without it, on horseback or in a Cadillac or a Mercedes Benz, it's been the same system – in economics and in politics – and the same denial of basic human rights and of the right of the people to determine their own destiny.

Chávez and his friends, from their position in the military academy, were well placed to recruit other young and discontented officers to their cause. In March 1985, they were joined by Major Francisco Javier Arias Cárdenas, a former pupil at a Catholic seminary who had returned from a postgraduate course in Colombia. Arias Cárdenas came from Zulia, and was destined to play an important role in the coup attempt that was eventually made in February 1992. He had many friends in the civilian left, and later, in the 1990s, he was to join one of the smaller radical parties, *La Causa R*, and was elected as governor of his home state. He was once perceived as the most prominent intellectual within the Chávez movement, though he lacked Chávez's authority and charismatic charm.

Encouraged by Chávez, the participants in his Bolivarian Revolutionary Movement sought historical endorsement for their project in the ideas of three significant figures, known, although not well, to every Venezuelan schoolchild: Ezequiel Zamora, the *llanos* leader with whose story Chávez had been familiar since childhood; Simón Bolívar, the Liberator of Venezuela and much of Latin America; and Simón Rodriguez, often remembered as Bolívar's tutor though a man with an infinitely more interesting career than that simple fact would suggest.

From the start, the conspirators had a left-wing slant to their project. Soon they were using the language of the civilian left that some of them had acquired when studying at the Universidad Central in Caracas. An interesting and unique characteristic of the Venezuelan military in the 1980s was their relationship with the civilian world. Junior officers were sent to study social sciences in Venezuelan universities, and, as they moved about in civil society, many young officers found themselves making contacts with the survivors of the guerrilla movements of the 1960s.

As the revolutionary-minded officers made their way slowly up the military hierarchy, they began to consider when they might be in a position to stage a revolutionary coup. The year 1992 looked the earliest and most suitable moment, since at about that time they might expect to be given command of troops. In the meantime, they became known as the MACATE organisation, short for 'Mayores, Capitanes and Tenientes' – the ranks they held. Later their group was called COMACATE, when some of the more senior officers became *comandantes*.

It would have been difficult to keep such an organisation secret, and military intelligence, the Dirección de Inteligencia Militar, the DIM, eventually got to hear of what was happening. The DIM knew about the radical lectures being given in the military academy, but they did not know what kind of conspiracy was afoot, or how widespread it had become. They knew that they were dealing with some of the most competent, popular, and promotable young officers in the army, and to discipline them, or to sack them, would have caused serious disaffection within the ranks.

Chávez was clearly known to the military authorities as a potential subversive, and their initial solution to this problem was to transfer him as far away from Caracas as possible. In 1986, he was removed from his influential position in the military academy and transferred to Elorza in the state of Apure, a distant point on the frontier close to Colombia.

6

BANISHED TO ELORZA:
EXPERIMENTS IN CIVIL-MILITARY
COOPERATION

I travelled to Elorza on a small local bus, a twelve-hour journey from Barinas. The road is appalling, with a metalled surface that has long since disintegrated. Elorza lies almost due south of Barinas, and the road crosses two of the great tributaries of the Orinoco, the Apure and the Arauca. A bridge over the Apure links Ciudad de Nutria with Bruzual, and one day in the future President Chávez – faithful to his first utopian dreams – plans to turn these remote villages into the heart of a great new development plan for the *llanos*.

Elorza lies even further south, on the far side of the Arauca river, over another fine bridge. With a hotel, a main street, and a military base outside the town, this is rural Venezuela. The shops are run by Syrians, the restaurants by Colombians, and a mixed group of indigenous people – Cuivas and Yaruros – live on the outskirts of the village. The mighty Arauca storms past its northern edge. Chávez is still remembered by people here with great affection, for he put their village on the map. I settled down to a meal of beef and yucca, and talked to the restaurant owner, a refugee like many other local residents from the violence in Colombia, a few miles away across the border. He had moved here from Tolima, and found Venezuela relatively peaceful compared with the horrors of the endless Colombian civil war.

Chávez, as a lieutenant, had commanded a motorised division at the base down the road, but he used his years here to try out some of the ideas that were later to inform his political and social programme for the country. He encouraged experimental schemes of cooperation between soldiers and civilians, and soon the radical lieutenant at the Elorza base had become hugely popular throughout the Apure region. At first providing military support for social and economic development in the area, he soon widened the focus of his activities, moving into the life of the community through the organisation of historical pageants and through encouraging the collection of oral history records.

Someone must have forgotten his past activities or lost his file, for in 1988, in the final months of the presidency of another *Acción Democrática* politician, Jaime Lusinchi, Chávez was brought back to Caracas – to work in the presidential palace at Miraflores. He became an assistant to the national security council. Finally he was on his way up, and he was sent that year on an official visit to Central America, then at the height of the contra war in Nicaragua and the counter-insurgency campaigns in Guatemala.

In Elorza, Chávez had been isolated from his brother revolutionaries in the army. Now back in Caracas, he was better placed to continue the conspiratorial planning of his Bolivarian Revolutionary Movement. It was not before time. The following year, in February 1989, the city of Caracas exploded in an unexpected and unorganised rebellion. Chávez had always hoped that something like this might 'turn up', yet when it did so his Bolivarian conspirators were not remotely prepared.

7

FEBRUARY 1989 (1):
REBELLION IN CARACAS,
THE *CARACAZO*

Guarenas is a soulless satellite town, some thirty kilometres east of Caracas, where thousands of the capital's service workers have established their homes. The first signs of trouble here began early on the Monday morning – February 27, 1989. People travelling in to the city by bus discovered that the fares had doubled that morning, and they began spontaneously to protest. Trouble soon flared in Petare, further in, and by mid-morning it had spread, via television, to the major cities of the country: to Maracay, Valencia, Barquisimeto, Ciudad Guayana, and Mérida.

Buses were overturned and burnt, but this was just the initial stage of the revolt. Within hours the rebellion had become more generalised, with widespread looting and the destruction of shops and supermarkets. Gangs of young people from the suburbs, both poor and angry, invaded the commercial centre of Caracas and moved on to the privileged residential areas of the wealthy under the slopes of Mount Avila, close to the heart of the city. Rioting and looting continued unchecked throughout the night and the following day. The disturbances developed into a prolonged and mighty rebellion – the *Caracazo* – and it was soon followed by days of brutal military repression.

Lieutenant Chávez was lying in bed that Monday morning with a contagious illness; indeed, the doctor at the Miraflores palace had told him to go home lest he risk infecting the entire presidential household. During all their years of plotting, the young officers of the Bolivarian Revolutionary Movement had often discussed the possibility of a popular explosion that they might be able to turn to their advantage. Yet when it actually happened, they were in no way ready, and some among them were obliged to participate in the repression.

The impact of the urban revolt, both on the general population and on the soldiers involved, was to have a dramatic effect on the political developments of the subsequent decade. Indeed the contemporary history of Venezuela begins with this cardinal event, for it persuaded the officers involved in the Bolivarian conspiracy to accelerate their plans.

The year 1989 was an important date for most of the rest of the world as well. The fall of the Berlin Wall in the autumn, and the subsequent collapse of the pro-Soviet governments in Eastern Europe, were quickly perceived as the harbinger of the end of the entire Communist era. In the same way, the *Caracazo* marked the beginning of the end of Venezuela's *ancien régime*. The people had taken to the streets just thirty years earlier, in January 1958, and had paved the way, under the direction of the Patriotic Junta, for the overthrow of the dictatorship of General Pérez Jiménez. Now they were doing it again, almost by accident, to indicate their desire to get rid of their corrupt and bureaucratic government with its democratic facade. Yet whereas the uprising in 1958 had been organised, purposeful and politically inspired, the *Caracazo* of 1989 was anarchic, chaotic, and leaderless.

Such a spontaneous explosion took the government's intelligence operations entirely by surprise. The efforts of the militarised secret service, the DISIP, had been devoted for many years to infiltrating the political groups of the ultra-left, yet such groups had all but disappeared by the end of the 1980s. They played no role in promoting the *Caracazo*. The DISIP had never troubled itself to monitor the capacity for autonomous rebellion brewing in the *ranchos*, or shanty towns, of the suburban areas of the city. Military intelligence, the DIM, was by all accounts better informed. It knew that something was up, and had warned the government that February 27 might well be a difficult day. Yet its warnings either failed to get through to the Miraflores palace, or were simply ignored.

'There were riots in the suburb of Guarenas on the first day, and the police didn't intervene,' I was told by Heinz Sonntag, a sociology professor at the *Centro de Estudios de Desarrollo in Caracas*, who made a study of the *Caracazo*. 'They didn't do so on the following day either. The National Guard was then ordered in, but they refused to enter the *ranchos*. The government turned to the military.'

Soldiers now moved in to the shanty towns, and cordoned off the high-rise state housing blocks (the creation of the Pérez Jiménez era in the 1950s). They shot anything that moved. 'The official figure of those killed was 372, but the more probable figure is over two thousand – in Caracas alone.' Thousands were wounded.

It is Sonntag's belief that 'the repression was meant as a warning to the poor, so that they wouldn't do it again'. It worked for a long time, he recalled. 'People grew afraid.' The event cast a long shadow over the 1990s, perpetuating a climate of hopelessness and political apathy that only began to be dispelled by the election of Chávez in 1998.

President Carlos Andrés Pérez had only taken office at the beginning of February. This was his second term, and he knew the ropes – he had been President before in the 1970s – but he was unprepared for this popular explosion. Holding a meeting of his council of ministers at midday on Tuesday February 28, he decreed a state of emergency, a constitutional device that involved the imposition of martial law and the suspension of all civil liberties. The army imposed a night-time curfew.

The immediate cause of the rebellion was the rise in the price of petrol, part of the new, neo-liberal, economic 'packet' that Pérez had announced ten days earlier, on February 16. The petrol price had been scheduled to increase by 100 per cent on Sunday February 26, but precisely in order to avoid the trouble that suddenly blew up in its face, the government had envisaged a staggered increase in bus fares. Bus owners were to be allowed to put up fares by 30 per cent on the first working day after the petrol price increase, the fateful Monday, while a further 30 per cent increase would be permitted three months later.

Many bus owners, of course, passed on the increase to their passengers on the very first day, putting up the fares by 100 per cent to cover their own increased costs. This was the cause of the inevitable explosions of dismay among impoverished commuters, customarily short of money at the end of the month. A particular burden fell on students, whose normal half-price concessions were withdrawn.

Within a few days, the terrified and terrorised city had returned to some kind of normality. The poorer parts of the capital nursed their wounded and nourished a terrible grievance against the regime. Hundreds of bodies were buried in unmarked graves. The richer parts reinforced their steel fences and their security arrangements, and congratulated themselves on a lucky escape.

Yet the most significant and immediate impact of the *Caracazo* was on the armed forces charged with the repression. While some of the soldiers involved in shooting down their fellow citizens doubtless felt ashamed at the actions they had been ordered to take, the group of politically motivated officers associated with Chávez and the Bolivarian Revolutionary Movement felt aggrieved that the moment – and the opportunity they had been half expecting – had passed them by without any possibility of action. Their contacts with civilian groups, including some of the left-wing parties and some of the survivors of the guerrilla groups of the 1960s, had provided them with no warning of what was to happen.

Many of the principal military conspirators were in Caracas during the *Caracazo*, but they all had different experiences of the events. Chávez himself was out of action, in bed, but two of his close associates, Francisco Arias Cárdenas and Felípe Acosta Carles, were ordered out into the *ranchos* to take part in the repression. In an unexplained incident, Acosta was shot dead. Some people, including Chávez, believe that the DISIP was aware of Acosta's participation in the military conspiracy, and it is possible that he was killed by the secret police rather than by rioters. The same people think that Chávez was lucky to have been at home that week.

Later, in an interview with Angela Zago, Arias Cárdenas revealed his rage that the revolutionary movement in which he was involved had not been ready 'to stand side by side with the people in a civilian–military rebellion'. He felt that the army was on the wrong side in this war, and he made herculean efforts to try to ensure that his soldiers did not fire on the crowds. He was appalled by what he saw:

As soon as I arrived at the place that was to be my centre of operations, I realised that the officer from whom I had taken over had already been firing against the tower blocks, in an absolutely irresponsible and inhuman fashion. I also heard stories of the excesses committed by the political police, the DISIP.

I immediately gathered my troops together and said: 'Hands up those who belong to the Country Club!' I looked at their expressions of surprise, and saw that they all remained motionless and silent. I repeated my request: 'Hands up those who live in Alto Prado, in Lagunita Country Club, or in Altamira!' Nobody moved.

He had been referring to the wealthiest and most exclusive suburbs in Caracas.

Then I said, well that means that we all come from the shanty towns and the poor parishes like this one. The people who live here are like us, they are the people, our brothers; that means that no one must fire without authorisation; no one must shoot unless we are attacked.

Chávez returned to his duties in the presidential palace at Miraflores some weeks later. On his way in, he was stopped by the palace guards who, though not part of his conspiracy, were aware that something was in the wind. 'Look here, major,' one of them asked him, 'is it true about the Bolivarian Movement? We'd like to hear more about it; we're not prepared to go on killing people.' These were soldiers from the presidential guard, Chávez recalled, people trusted by the government. The conspiracy was clearly gathering pace, and the moment for decisive action could not be long postponed.

Yet the authorities were now on his track. At the end of the year, on December 6, 1989, the day on which new state governors were to be elected, Chávez and a number of army majors of his seniority were summoned to appear before the army high command. They were accused of plotting against the government, and of planning to assassinate the president and senior officers on Christmas Day. The information was false, and, since nothing definite could be proved against them, the authorities could take no action. It was decided that most of the subversive majors should be posted to different and distant places around the country. Chávez was given permission to enrol at the Simón Bolívar university in Caracas and began to work towards a master's degree in political science. Any coup attempt would have to be postponed.

Some eighteen months later, in August 1991, after following a course at the staff college, Chávez was given command of a parachute battalion based at Maracay. At last, with command of troops, he was in a strong position to take the action for which he had so long prepared.

8

FEBRUARY 1989 (2):
THE NEO-LIBERAL 'PACKAGE' THAT
DESTROYED THE PÉREZ GOVERNMENT

One afternoon in 1990, a year after the *Caracazo*, I called on President Carlos Andrés Pérez in the little white nineteenth-century building in the centre of Caracas that they call the Miraflores palace. Pérez liked to meet foreign journalists and he was always extremely genial. I asked him how someone so closely involved with a specific form of statist economic development in the 1970s could have turned head over heels in the 1990s and embraced the economic doctrines of the International Monetary Fund (IMF) that he had for so long opposed, especially since the fierce cuts he had imposed in 1989 had led directly to the *Caracazo*.

Pérez admitted that the *Caracazo* had been an unpleasant shock, and he agreed that his new policy had brought serious problems in its train. He also recognised that it had led to a rise in the cost of living:

> The decisions I made were extremely difficult, and in general they are still quite unpopular. People resent the harsh measures we have taken. The people's anguish is being expressed through demonstrations and protests, but we must understand that these are unavoidable. There was no other way out.
>
> Times have changed quite a lot in these last fifteen years. The economy has become more global and better organised, and economic relations must be conceived differently. With this globalisation of the economy, our people will understand better the need for foreign investment.

Venezuela was now in desperate need of such investment, the president said, since rent from oil was no longer sufficient to power the economy. Even in the case of oil refining, once thought of as an area of exclusive investment by the state, he now thought that it would be necessary to negotiate 'the participation of foreign capital'.

Pérez was equally downcast about the future role of the state itself. Lessons had been learnt, he said, about the inherent tendency of state institutions to degenerate. His government was planning to abolish 'all those elements where corruption would have been possible', though understandably he made no reference to his own role in the phenomenon. With a free exchange rate for the bolívar, and the abolition of licences for foreign trade operations, he hoped that corruption would simply wither away. 'The best thing for us,' he said with the enthusiasm of a convert, 'is to reduce the intervention of the state to a minimum.'

Much of the political rhetoric of Chávez in the 1990s and subsequently was directed against 'neo-liberalism', against the programmes of economic reform imposed on Latin America by the government in Washington, and willingly accepted by Pérez. These programmes were made possible largely as a result of US control over financial agencies such as the IMF and the World Bank, but also because Latin American economists and politicians, in significant numbers, had been successfully converted to the new American doctrines.

Although Chávez makes a general complaint against these programmes – he always refers to the phenomenon as 'savage' neo-liberalism – his particular arguments hark back to the dismal experience of Venezuela during the years after 1989. His chief target has been the policy turn-around introduced by Pérez that led directly to the *Caracazo*, and was to lead later, in 1993, to the downfall of Pérez himself.

As noted in the previous chapter, the rise in the price of petrol, and consequently of bus fares, that was the immediate cause of the Caracas rebellion was itself part of a more extensive change in economic policy undertaken by the government earlier in the month, swiftly dubbed *el gran viraje*, 'the great turn around'.

The policies of neo-liberalism unleashed on Latin America (and elsewhere) in the 1990s are often and usefully defined as the 'Washington

Consensus', a ten-point programme originally devised and codified in 1989 by John Williamson, formerly an IMF adviser in the 1970s. The programme, deemed appropriate in Washington, was directed essentially at countries with large foreign debts, forced on them by international banks in the 1970s and 1980s. Its purpose was to so reform the internal economic mechanisms of debtor governments in Latin America (and elsewhere) that they would be in a position to repay the debts they had incurred, usually from American banks.

Venezuela, with its large accumulation of debt, that had been rashly borrowed at high interest rates by a succession of corrupt and incompetent governments, was a prime target for the reforms of the Washington Consensus. Some reform was clearly necessary if foreign investment was to continue. Yet the specific reforms had a serious downside. While taking into account the requirements of the foreign banks, they effectively ignored the needs of the poorer inhabitants of the debtor countries. In practice, of course, the reforms embraced a far wider agenda than the problems of a handful of international banks.

John Williamson, the codifier of the Washington Consensus, explained his terms at a conference on the subject in 1994. He claimed to have identified 'ten areas where policy-makers and scholars in "Washington" could arguably muster a fairly wide consensus as to the character of the policy reforms that debtor countries should pursue'.

Couched in the cool language of imperial economists, his programme might seem innocuous enough. Yet in practice the terms demanded of the debtor countries spelt out a new form of colonialism. The advantages granted to US-based transnational companies under the neo-liberal programme went far beyond a simple policy of debt recovery.

The 'ten areas' of the Washington Consensus defined by Williamson involved debtor governments agreeing to enforce the following reforms:

1. guarantees of fiscal discipline, and a curb to budget deficits;
2. reduction in public expenditure, particularly in the military and in public administration;
3. tax reform, aiming at the creation of a system with a broad base and with effective enforcement;

4. financial liberalisation, with interest rates determined by the market;
5. competitive exchange rates, to assist export-led growth;
6. trade liberalisation, coupled with the abolition of import licensing and a reduction in tariffs;
7. a welcome to foreign direct investment;
8. privatisation of state enterprises, leading to efficient management and improved performance;
9. deregulation of the economy;
10. protection of property rights.

This was the programme of economic reform that the Pérez government felt called upon to impose on Venezuela in February 1989. An ideological blank page himself, the president accepted the prevailing wisdom without a qualm. Surrounding himself with a crowd of young US-trained economists, schooled in the disciplines of the Chicago School, he announced his new economic 'packet' two weeks after the official inauguration ceremonies.

To the two principal figures in his government responsible for the reform programme, the terms of the Washington Consensus were meat and drink. Moisés Naím, the development minister, and Miguel Rodríguez, the minister of planning, were young whizz-kids from the Massachusetts Institute of Technology and from Yale. They were cut from the same cloth as Vaclav Klaus in Czechoslovakia and Lescek Balcerowicz in Poland, the economists who were to spearhead the free-market drive into Eastern Europe in the 1990s.

These men had all drunk deeply at the wells of neo-liberalism, and all shared a familiarity with the world of academic think-tanks, university lecture halls, and international financial institutions. These were the shock troops of the new economic fundamentalism. Yet at the same time, they had an Achilles' heel. They suffered from a marked lack of knowledge or understanding of the political sphere in their own countries. The economics was self-evident, they thought, the politics could take care of itself.

During the last months of the regime of President Jaime Lusinchi, which had lasted from 1984 to 1989, everyone in Caracas had been aware of a looming economic crisis. This came to a head in January 1989, and Lusinchi's last act as president was to suspend repayment of the foreign debt. After twenty years of profligate spending and unparalleled corruption, the foreign reserves were about to run out. In the aftermath of that decision, people speculated about the policies the new Pérez government would be likely to promote when he took over in February. Pérez was remembered as the man in charge during the palmy days of 'Venezuela Saudíta' in the 1970s, when the country had appeared to be impossibly rich. The population had voted for his return to the presidential palace largely in the improbable belief that he might work his magic a second time.

Pérez kept the country waiting. As president-elect, he spent some weeks visiting the principal countries of OPEC – Saudi Arabia, Kuwait, and Algeria – suggesting perhaps that he planned to revive Venezuela's participation in the international politics of oil. When finally he returned to Caracas, his mind had been made up. He had decided, to most people's surprise, to embrace the revolutionary neo-liberal policies of the hour, which had not yet grown at that time into the new orthodoxy of the 1990s. Quite possibly, he could see no other way forward.

There would be a drastic revision in the role and the size of the old Venezuelan state, such a dominant participant in the economics and politics of the previous half century. State enterprises would be privatised. The government would no longer seek to generate employment and economic growth through its own drive and impetus, but instead would rely on 'the accelerated expansion of the private sector'. It would 'liberalise' prices and interest rates, and abolish the variable exchange rates.

Miguel Rodríguez was the principal author of this programme of structural change. Some years later, when out of office, he proudly outlined what it had consisted of. He had fulfilled the terms of the Washington Consensus down to the last dot and comma, producing a programme that went entirely contrary to everything that most Venezuelans had long believed in and held most dear:

The programme was comprehensive in its design. It included complete trade reform, elimination of all trade restrictions, and reduction of tariffs to a narrow band; elimination of all exchange controls and adoption of a free float that would permit an exchange rate compatible with the development of non-traditional exports; price liberalisation; the restructuring of the public sector with widespread decentralisation and privatisation of parastatal enterprises; a comprehensive tax reform; a new policy to set public sector prices at efficient levels; the restructuring of the financial sector, featuring liberalisation, increased competition, and strengthening of the regulatory framework; modernisation of labour legislation, including the creation of pension funds and the restructuring of the social security system; elimination of restrictions to foreign investment; restructuring of the external debt; an overhaul of the policy of external financing; and a new social policy that would eliminate the system of massive generalised subsidies (many of which went to the rich) in favour of targeted subsidies directed to the poorest segment of the population.

This was the new economic strategy unleashed on Venezuela in February 1989, and, to crown it, Pérez announced with some satisfaction and relief that his economic team had secured something from Washington in exchange: a loan from the IMF for US$4,500 million, to be made available over a period of three years. In earlier and happier times, when claiming leadership of the Third World in the 1970s, Pérez had denounced the economists of the IMF as 'genocide workers in the pay of economic totalitarianism'. Now he was having to go on all fours to beg for money from an institution he had once described as 'an economic neutron bomb' that 'killed people but left buildings standing'.

The *Caracazo* served to slow down his ambitious plans. In the first year, not a single state enterprise was privatised. Pérez signed a decree favouring privatisation in August 1989, but the Congress was unable to agree on the definition of the 'basic and strategic enterprises' that were to remain in the public sector. Many congressmen were happy to drag their feet, but the time lost was not used by Pérez to prepare the country for the changes to come. For by 1990 it was clear that, whatever the temporary and peculiar hiccups of the process, Venezuela was now participating fully in the global revolution in economic thought. The recipe was the same as in Prague or Warsaw, although the local conditions might be rather different.

When I interviewed Miguel Rodríguez that year, I found the minister sitting in his shirt-sleeves under the obligatory portrait of Bolívar and talking into two phones at once. Young economists may lack political experience, but Rodríguez was clearly enjoying the exercise of power, relishing his intellectual superiority and his capacity not to suffer fools gladly.

He thought it was unfortunate that the country had grown accustomed to cheap oil and cheap electricity, 'sold to the consumer (in the case of electricity) far below cost'. His adjustment programme, he said, was 'going to achieve efficient pricing in the public sector in a very short period of time'. He believed – with the elegant disdain of a technocrat – that the time had come to be tough. When I murmured something about the *Caracazo*, he dismissed it with a wave of the hand: 'It's not the man in the street who complains about an increase in petrol prices, it's the politicians, and two or three agitators in the universities and the high schools. The people understand these things.'

His main concern was the slow speed with which the government was getting its programme through the Congress. Delay deprived the government of the initiative, he said; it allowed the opposition to regroup, and inertia to set in. He knew that both he and Naím were unpopular with the ruling bosses of *Acción Democrática*, and the lack of political support for their programme from the governing party was a serious drag on the impetus for economic reform. The Young Turks wanted to move quickly; the bosses urged caution.

In the long run, the Young Turks' lack of political understanding created the conditions for a military coup, and caused the downfall of their president. The political crisis that resulted from their economic programme had two outcomes that no one had remotely envisaged at the outset.

Spurred on by the horror of the *Caracazo*, Colonel Chávez redoubled his efforts to prepare his Bolivarian Revolutionary Movement for action, and in February 1992, he set out to do what the ruling group in *Acción Democrática* was able to perform a year later: to overthrow the president.

Within three years, before Pérez's term as president had run its course, his party had resolved to throw him to the wolves. Pérez was impeached by Congress on charges of corruption in 1993, removed from office, and placed under house arrest.

In February 1996, when he was still under guard at home, I talked to him again. He had lost the trappings of office, but in his mountain eyrie above El Hatillo outside Caracas he still gave the impression of a man awaiting the call of a people clamouring for his return.

'Venezuela is suffering from a tremendous structural crisis,' he said from the far side of his huge desk. 'One of the reasons for the crisis is that the parties are in crisis – they have been for some time. In Copei, the structure of the party was in the hands of a man – Rafael Caldera – who wouldn't allow anyone to be a candidate for the presidency except himself.'

Pérez was equally critical of his own party, *Acción Democrática*: 'It's a party, unfortunately, that has been gobbled up by clientelism and the party machine. I was excluded from it, but I continue to have the support of the people who vote for it. Indeed that's why I'm imprisoned here, to keep me isolated, so that I don't have access to my political base. These limitations on my activity are serious, for I cannot hope to have a direct influence on what's going on.'

Pérez was right about Venezuela being in a state of crisis, though he was unable to recognise that he was the man largely responsible for what had happened. The people were not clamouring for his return, but for his head – and in February 1992 he had nearly lost it.

9

THE DEBATE BETWEEN MILITARY AND CIVILIAN REVOLUTIONARIES

The road from Chavez's home town of Barinas to the university city of Mérida is one of the great scenic routes of Latin America, winding up from the heat of the Orinoco plains to the limpid atmosphere of the Andean valleys, while zig-zagging through forests and around water-falls. I found a *por puesto* in the Barinas bus station, and waited for it to fill up. The *por puesto* is a taxi or small bus that only leaves when its complement of seats is entirely taken up. Soon after we had eventually got going, the engine of the minibus phuttered to a stop, and nothing that the driver could do would persuade it to revive. We all got out and stood around in the road for an hour or so before another bus arrived to rescue us, and to take us on and up, through the clouds and over the mountain pass to Mérida.

Mérida is an Alpine town, spread along a broad valley and sur-rounded by green mountains. Not much remains of the old colonial structure, but it still retains the charm of a small university town, where the youthful student population crowds the streets in the morning and evening and at the lunch hour. This is the intellectual heartland of Venezuela, an oasis of peace and calm after the urban nightmare of Caracas. People come here on holiday to charge their batteries, and the professors here at the Universidad de los Andes usually stay put, regard-ing Caracas as Babylon.

Mérida has always been a leftist centre, and after the collapse of the guerrilla movements of the 1960s many former guerrillas came to live in and around the town. Some of the guerrilla survivors regrouped in the 1970s in the *Movimiento al Socialismo* (MAS), while others joined the *Partido Revolucionario Venezolano* (PRV), an organisation set up by Douglas Bravo, the guerrilla leader in Falcón state, after his break with the Communist Party in 1966. The PRV was a legal political organisation, and one of its supporters at the university in Mérida was Adán Chávez, the colonel's elder brother, and a professor in the science faculty. In the early 1980s, Adán Chávez perceived that it would be useful to organise a meeting between Bravo, his revolutionary friend, and Hugo, his revolutionary brother.

Douglas Bravo recalls the meeting which seems to have taken place in 1982 or 1983. 'The movement involved in these initial discussions with Chávez was the PRV.' Bravo says that he talked with Chávez and 'with other officers' who had been participating 'in the revolutionary structure we were preparing'. Their purpose was to construct 'a civilian–military movement, with the long-term aim of preparing a revolutionary insurgency'.

In an interview with Alberto Garrido, Bravo gave a fairly full account of what was being considered. 'We did not envisage an immediate uprising, we were all clear about that, both the military and the civilians … ' Both sides agreed that unless there was a significant political development in the country – 'a sense of expectation in the mass of the people' – nothing much would happen until the military conspirators were senior enough to have command of troops. This would not happen before the year 1992, when most of them would be aged about forty.

As it happened, the *Caracazo* of February 1989 proved to be the 'significant development' among the mass of the people that they had been half expecting, although neither the civilians nor the military were prepared for it.

Throughout the political and economic crisis of the 1980s, a number of civilian and military groups had been circling around each other, making spasmodic contact. A wide spectrum of civilian groups hostile to Venezuela's corrupt and inadequate political system were happy to make contact with subversive officers in the armed forces.

Chávez's Bolivarian Revolutionary Movement was by no means the only politicised grouping within the armed forces at that time. There was a subversive cell in the navy, about which little is publicly known, except that it was not connected with the group led by Admiral Hernán Grüber that organised the second coup in 1992. There was also a group in the air force, developed by Lieutenant William Izarra, a revolutionary officer with Trotskyist leanings who had studied at Harvard.

In the early 1980s, at the time when Chávez was organising his Bolivarian Revolutionary Movement in the army, Izarra had formed a revolutionary cell in the air force and called it the Alianza Revolucionaria de Militares Activos (ARMA), the Revolutionary Alliance of Active Service Officers. Like Chávez he held meetings with civilian politicians; with Teodoro Petkoff of MAS, and with José Vicente Rangel, both of whom had once been presidential candidates of the left. Nothing concete emerged from these discussions.

Izarra later joined up with Chávez after the 1992 coup, and was put in charge of the international relations of Chávez's Fifth Republic Movement (MVR). In November 1998, Izarra was elected as a senator, but after disagreements with Luís Miquilena in December 1998, he parted company with Chávez, resigning his senate seat in May 1999 to set up his own party, the Movimiento de Democracia Directa. Later he returned to the Chávez fold, and his son, Andrés Izarra, became a significant player too.

Chávez was always convinced of the need for civilians to be involved in his project. He had been influenced in the 1970s by the military revolution in Peru, and he well understood from his reading of its history that the eventual failure of General Velasco's government was a result of its lack of civilian participation, which had led in turn to a lack of popular support. Both Chávez and Admiral Grüber believed that civilian support was necessary for the eventual success of their 'military interventions', and that well-selected civilian political groups should be involved from the start.

Chávez did not limit his discussions with civilian revolutionaries to Bravo's group. He also established a relationship at an early stage with the political leaders of *La Causa R*, the leftist organisation then active in

Caracas and Bolívar state, and met its founder, Alfredo Maneiro, shortly before his death in 1983. Maneiro was another of the charismatic revolutionaries who emerged from the guerrilla struggle of the 1960s.

The supporters of *La Causa R* were among those who might cooperate with a military rebellion, and Chávez had an idea how they might be used. He had been intrigued by the organisation set in place by the left-wing military government of General Torríjos in Panama. Torríjos, and subsequently Manuel Noriega, had organised a kind of civilian paramilitary grouping, known as the Dignity Battalion, capable of acting in support of the military.

Chávez had seen this battalion undergoing training in Panama, and had been impressed by its apparent capacity to act as an irregular unit, blocking roads and performing other tasks, in association with more regular insurrectionary forces. He approached the leaders of *La Causa R* with this project:

> We made suggestions over the years to these people that they should form 'dignity battalions', made up of civilians from the shanty towns, and led by genuine community leaders. We provided material about different weapons, and we gave classes in the use of arms, though we couldn't provide them with arms for obvious reasons. We were under permanent surveillance.

Nothing much developed from these embryonic contacts that Chávez made with *La Causa R*, and they seem to have left him with doubts about their capacity to deliver. Chávez feared that some leftist groups were simply hoping that a tactical alliance with the military would help to hoist them into power, while he perceived that others were unhappy, in their heart of hearts, about the idea of relying on military men to prosecute the revolution.

Any discussion between civilian leftists and potentially revolutionary officers raised disruptive questions. More important than the issue of what role civilians might play in the unfolding of a military coup was the question of the kind of participation they might expect to have in a subsequent government. This was not an academic argument. Much of the left in Venezuela had felt historically betrayed by what had happened after the civilian–military uprising organised by the Patriotic Front of 1958. The hopes of the people then had been defrauded. Many subsequently took part in the guerrilla war of the 1960s to try to recover what they believed they had been cheated of.

After the *Caracazo*, when Bravo resumed contact with Chávez, Bravo claims that Chávez began to detach himself from 'the revolutionary elements' with whom he had once been in contact. After several disagreements, the last meeting between the two men took place in October 1991, four months before the coup that Chávez was to make in February 1992, and they made a final attempt to iron out their differences. According to Bravo's account:

> We met to talk about the plans for the uprising … We said that first of all there should be a civil action, like the general strike organised by the Patriotic Junta on January 23 [1958]. The military action would come later. This was so that civil society should have an active participation in the revolutionary movement. But that was exactly what Chávez did not want. Absolutely not! Chávez did not want civilians to participate as a concrete force. He wanted civil society to applaud but not to participate, which is something quite different …

Bravo recounts one rather damaging story of an incident in that period:

> Some 20 or 25 guerrillas were assembled, and Chávez brought his action plan for a military coup. The coup bore no resemblance to the idea we had previously discussed with him that the civilian population should take an active part … As a result, when he announced his plan, one of those present at the meeting said: 'José María – that was his name in clandestinity – I can see all the military units that will be mobilised, from Maracaibo, from Valencia, from Carora, from Barquisimeto, from Yaracuy, from Maracay, from Caracas, but where are the rest of us, the civilians, where do we fit in to this plan?' Chávez replied firmly: 'Civilians get in the way. We shall summon them when we get into power.'

Bravo argues that this was not just a tactic on Chávez's part: 'It was his political position.'

Breaking off relations with Bravo, Chávez continued to hold meetings with other old revolutionaries from the PRV, notably with Kléber Ramírez, a former guerrilla who had become an adviser to Colonel Arias Cárdenas. Both men had been educated in a Catholic seminary, and had much in common. Ramírez played a role in the preparations for the coup of February 1992, but was eventually blamed, probably unfairly, for unwittingly betraying the earlier plan to stage the coup in December 1991.

One problem associated with the strategy of permitting civilian involvement in a military coup, though not perceived by Chávez in the early stages, was that civilian revolutionaries rarely had the kind of hermetic discipline associated with military conspiracies. The more civilians became involved in the plans of the Bolivarian Revolutionary Movement, the greater the risk of discovery.

Chávez eventually became disillusioned with many of the old leftists, and they with him. Later he reflected on the adverse impact that the guerrilla strategy of the 1960s had on the country's political development:

> One of the unfortunate effects of the guerrilla war in Venezuela was the isolation of political leaders who might otherwise have contributed to the development of a different mentality and outlook in the country. Many of them remained in the mountains, or jumped into the opposite camp. I think that this isolated and cut off an entire generation that might have created new political currents.
>
> There has been a huge leadership vacuum – in the workers' movement, among the peasants, in the shanty towns, and in the whole of society. Given this historical situation, we have to dedicate ourselves to transforming the collective consciousness through action. We have to fill the vacuum, summoning up a new leadership ...

This analysis, with its all too accurate description of much of the Venezuelan left, was not dissimilar to that of Alfredo Maneiro and *La Causa R*. While Chávez did not secure much action or support from the old guerrilla leadership, their views undoubtedly influenced his thinking.

10

THE 'MILITARY INTERVENTION' OF CHÁVEZ, FEBRUARY 1992

In the early hours of the morning of Tuesday, February 4, 1992, five army units led by Colonel Chávez moved by road into Caracas. Chávez was the commander of a parachute regiment based at Maracay, some fifty miles from the capital. His purpose was to detain President Carlos Andrés Pérez, and to arrest the high command of the armed forces. Orders were then to have gone out to garrison commanders throughout the country to obey the edicts of the new government.

One unit attacked the defence ministry, another advanced on La Carlota, the military airport inside the city, while a third moved towards the Miraflores palace. Chávez himself drove to the Historical Museum, near the palace, where plans had been made to install communications equipment. From there, he would direct the countrywide operation that he had unleashed.

President Pérez was out of the country, but contacts within the palace had informed the conspirators that he was scheduled to return that day, arriving at Maiquetía airport, close to the port of La Guaira. 'The idea was to detain Pérez at the airport,' Chávez later explained to Agustín Blanco Muñoz, 'and to take him, via the motorway, to the Historical Museum; our boys had organised a commando at the airport that would have captured him, but they were unable to enter, for it had been put under guard since midday.'

The conspiracy had in fact been betrayed the previous day, though the authorities were unaware of the details of the rebellion or of its dimensions. General Fernándo Ochoa Antich, the defence minister, knew that something was up, and went in person to meet President Pérez at Maiquetía, organising a small force to be mobilised there from the National Guard and the marines.

'The second attempt', Chávez continued, 'was to have been in the motorway tunnel, blocking the road with a burnt-out car; but there were too many guards, and our forces were insufficient. Afterwards our plans included taking him at his house at La Casona, where there was a serious attack, but the forces of the Disip fought back. Pérez arrived there, but a few minutes before it was surrounded, he made off to the Miraflores palace. When he got there, our tanks attacked, but he escaped through an unguarded entrance.'

Chávez and the principal conspirators of his Bolivarian Revolutionary Movement had always hoped that the year 1992 would be a suitable time to launch a *coup d'état*. As they had expected, they were all promoted to regimental command in the course of 1991. As mentioned earlier, Chávez took over the parachute regiment in Maracay in August 1991; Jesús Urdaneta and Joel Acosta Chirinos received their regiments a week earlier. Francisco Arias Cárdenas, who worked in intelligence and had always managed to keep a low conspiratorial profile, had been given an artillery regiment in Maracaibo the previous year.

Chávez realised that the military authorities were aware of some of his activities, though not of their extent. As mentioned in Chapter 7, in December 1989 he and others had been hauled before an inquisition of senior generals who believed him to be organising a coup, but he had escaped unscathed. He now knew that he needed to act swiftly. His initial plan was to stage a coup in December 1991, but the details appear to have been betrayed, possibly by his civilian collaborators.

In February 1992, the agreed strategy was to advance on Caracas and to capture the president and the senior generals. If the conspirators failed to detain the president, their insurrectionary movement would be stillborn. Chávez knew that about 10 per cent of the armed forces were firmly on his side. But if President Pérez was not captured in the first hours, and remained free to give orders to the forty battalion commanders likely to remain loyal, the government would inevitably win.

'We had been on the alert since Thursday, January 30,' runs Chávez's own account. A final meeting had been held on the Sunday, at a petrol station on the Panamerican highway, with the Bolivarian conspirators in the air force, Francisco Visconti Osorio and Luís Reyes Reyes.

> I remember that on Sunday, 2 February, almost at midnight, our people rang me from the Miraflores palace and told me, in code, the date and time of the return of Pérez. That was the moment that we began to activate the operation, and on the Monday we woke up and started getting people on the move.

Chávez said goodbye to his children and his wife, leaving her a cheque and cash that he had taken from his bank account in Maracay.

By the evening of Monday, February 3, the conspirators were in control of the barracks at Maracay, Maracaibo, and a number of other cities, an essential preliminary to the advance on Caracas. But an exchange of telephone messages with other military bases, conducted in simple code, revealed that all was not well:

'I can't make it.'

'The party's today, send me the whisky.'

'No, we can't send the whisky, we couldn't get the money.'

'OK, don't send me anything.'

The conspirators did not realise at the time that they had already been betrayed. Earlier on that Monday, at midday, a captain in the military academy in Caracas, detailed off by Chávez to seize its senior officers, decided to tell the director what was afoot. The military high command now knew they were faced with a coup attempt, but they did not know where it would come from. They had just twenty-four hours to find out, and to regain control of the country.

At 8 p.m., Chávez's column of soldiers loaded into a fleet of hired buses and began to move on Caracas from Maracay. Chávez himself arrived at his designated position at the Historical Museum at 1 a.m. He had hoped to direct operations from within the museum, but was greeted with a rude surprise. His troops came under machine-gun fire. For the first time he was forced to recognise that his plans had been betrayed. By means of some adroit arguing, he gained entry to the museum, persuading the colonel in charge that his men had come to reinforce the position. But when he got inside, he found that the communications equipment he was expecting to use had not been delivered. Out of touch with rebellious units in the rest of the country, he was now alone and isolated.

Elsewhere in the capital, a group of soldiers had attacked the presidential palace, but they proved unable to break through. The situation of the conspirators was now critical, and deteriorating. Reinforcements were blocked on the outskirts of Caracas, the air force generals in the conspiracy decided that it was too risky to allow their planes to take off, and a civilian group that was supposed to seize the television and radio stations failed to do so. The conspirators were facing disaster.

In the aftermath of the coup, considerable debate arose within the ranks of the military conspirators about the role of the civilian supporters. In Valencia, it seems, civilians supporting the coup arrived at the barracks and were indeed given weapons and vehicles; they helped to seize the city. In Caracas and Maracaibo this did not happen. According to Chávez:

> The civilians didn't show up. I had a lorry near Miraflores filled with guns to be handed out to the civilians. Although it's true that we didn't control the media, and were unable to appeal for popular support, it's also true that there were people who knew that that was the night of the operation, people who knew the password, 'Páez-Patria', to ask for weapons. But they didn't show up. We are not the only ones to blame. There were people who knew about the operation in advance, and they simply didn't come.

Early in the morning of February 4, President Pérez appeared on television. He announced to a startled nation that a military rebellion had occurred in Maracay and was now in the process of being crushed.

Watching the broadcast, Chávez realised that his coup had failed. At nine o'clock, he decided to surrender.

At this stage something rather extraordinary occurred. To avoid further bloodshed, Chávez asked to be allowed to speak on television so that the colonels who had seized barracks and cities in other parts of the country might also peacefully surrender. Individual officers, like Arias Cárdenas in Maracaibo, were still in control of their regions, but since the plot had failed in Caracas, there was no chance of countrywide success.

Chávez's appearance on television lasted for just over a minute. Its unexpected result was to turn him from a largely unknown colonel into a national figure. One minute of air time, at a moment of personal disaster, converted him into someone perceived as the country's potential saviour.

His broadcast was directed principally at the parachute regiment in Aragua and the tank brigade in Valencia. These two forces had successfully occupied their towns, and were showing no signs of wishing to surrender. Chávez perceived that if they did not do so, there would be a bloodbath. He spoke confidently, and without notes:

> First I want to say good morning to all the people of Venezuela, but this Bolivarian message is directed specifically to the courageous soldiers of the parachute regiment of Aragua and the tank regiment of Valencia.
>
> Comrades: unfortunately, for the moment, the objectives that we had set ourselves have not been achieved in the capital. That's to say that those of us here in Caracas have not been able to seize power. Where you are, you have performed well, but now is the time for a rethink; new possibilities will arise again and the country will be able to move definitively towards a better future.
>
> So listen to what I have to say, listen to comandante Chávez who is sending you this message, and, please, think deeply. Lay down your arms, for in truth the objectives that we set ourselves at a national level are not within our grasp.
>
> Comrades, listen to this message of solidarity. I am grateful for your loyalty, for your courage, and for your selfless generosity; before the country and before you, I alone shoulder the responsibility for this Bolivarian military uprising. Thank you.

Two phrases from this short broadcast made a particular impact. No one in Venezuela had ever heard a politician apologise for anything before. In spite of the political and economic failures of recent years – the devaluation of the currency, the bank collapses, the trials for corruption, the economic decline – no one in a position of power had ever said sorry, or accepted any portion of blame. And now here was a military officer saying he accepted responsibility for something that had gone wrong. This was something entirely new.

The other phrase that caught the popular imagination was 'for the moment', *por ahora*. As mentioned earlier, this was read by most people optimistically, as a sign that Chávez would return to the struggle at some later date. His revolutionary project of overthrowing the government had been thwarted, but it would be revived. Chávez himself recalls that the words he uttered simply slipped out; he had no ulterior motive in saying *por ahora*. For years afterwards, the phrase was his trademark, an implicit promise that he would return.

The coup was over, and the leading conspirators were safely behind bars, but the country had been dramatically changed: the formerly monolithic institution of the armed forces was now seriously divided, and the great mass of the population was lining up solidly behind the coup leader.

Politicians had to adjust their discourse to this new reality. At an emergency session of the Congress, held immediately after the coup, former president Rafael Caldera made a powerful speech that came within an inch of endorsing it. His words were certainly read as such by the population. He was re-elected as president two years later, in December 1993, regarded by many people as the only significant political figure who had understood the mood of the country.

Caldera's speech firmly put the blame for trouble in the armed forces on the shoulders of President Pérez and on his neo-liberal economic programme. He uttered a number of home truths:

> We must recognise – though it hurts to say so but it's the truth – that we have found no evidence in the popular classes, among the great bulk of non-political Venezuelans, of any enthusiasm, or any immediate and

selfless decision, to take action that might have put a stop to this threat to constitutional order.

I must say to the President of the Republic, speaking from this tribune with a great sense of responsibility, that he has the principal responsibility to make the immediate changes that the country is demanding, though of course it depends on all of us as well.

It is difficult to ask people to sacrifice themselves in a struggle to defend liberty and democracy, when you know that democracy and the rule of law have not been able to provide them with food, or to prevent exaggerated increases in the cost of living; they have not been able to put a stop to the terrible round of corruption that has eroded the institutional legality of the country, as everyone has seen with their own eyes. This is not something that can be hidden.

A military coup, whatever form it takes, must be censured and condemned; yet it would be naïve to think that this was an event in which a handful of ambitious men threw themselves rashly into an adventure, on their account, without being aware of the wider implications of their action. There was a set of circumstances here, a backcloth to these developments, which is the serious situation in which the country finds itself. If this situation is not dealt with, the future may yet hold unpleasant surprises for us all.

Caldera was not quite alone in giving a speech that was read as a coded message of support for the coup. His speech was followed by one from Aristóbulo Istúriz, a former leader of the teachers' union and a Congressman from *La Causa R*. Like Caldera, Istúriz was rewarded for his outspoken views by the electorate: he was later elected as the mayor of Caracas (and was subsequently the vice-president, supporting Chávez, of the Constitutional Assembly in 1999, and the minister of education after that).

Fourteen soldiers were killed during the coup, and fifty were wounded; some eighty civilians caught in the cross-fire were also wounded. More than a thousand soldiers were subsequently detained.

For some months there was considerable debate about the role of the defence minister, General Ochoa Antich. Chávez had known him for many years, and there were many allegations that the defence minister had had something to do with the coup. These were never proved, but some people believed that he had moved rather slowly against officers known to be conspiring. In the incestuous world of the Venezuelan political elite, it was well known that his brother, Enrique Ochoa Antich, was on the left. Enrique was a prominent member, and later the secretary-general, of the MAS, which would throw its weight behind Chávez's presidential campaign in 1998. A decent if bumbling man, General Ochoa was subsequently transferred from the defence ministry to become minister of foreign affairs, and was eventually banished to Mexico as ambassador. But in February 1992, it fell on his shoulders to enquire into the state of the armed forces. Why had there nearly been a successful coup? What could be done to prevent a coup happening again?

11

THE FAILED *COUP D'ÉTAT* OF
ADMIRAL GRÜBER, NOVEMBER 1992

With Colonel Chávez behind bars after his 'military intervention' of February 1992, the coup attempt later the same year seemed almost like a coda to the first, though it was considerably more violent. On November 27, a second effort was made to capture President Pérez, and the Miraflores palace was bombed from the air. Heavy fighting took place, both in Caracas and in Maracay, and more than 170 people were killed.

The chief organiser of the coup was Admiral Hernán Grüber Odremán, assisted by air force General Francisco Visconti Osorio, a member of Chávez's Bolivarian conspiracy whose planes had failed to take off in February. Both men were later to play a political role in the Chávez government in 1999, Grüber as the governor of Caracas, and Visconti as a member of the Constitutional Assembly.

Admiral Grüber was not a natural rebel. Born in Upata in 1940, he came from a long-established German immigrant family, farming land in the state of Bolívar once owned by the Franciscan missionaries of Caroní. He joined the navy in 1958, while his brother, Roberto, joined the army and eventually rose to be a general. Grüber took part in the suppression of the left-wing guerrillas in Lara and Anzoátegui in the 1960s, and subsequently was appointed to senior positions in frontier areas, notably on the Colombian border at Puerto Páez.

In the aftermath of the February coup, considerable discussion had taken place within the government and the armed forces about what might happen next. What was behind the conspiracy? How far had it spread? What measures could be taken to stop the rot?

In March, General Ochoa, the defence minister, summoned Admiral Grüber for a private discussion. They were joined by another senior naval officer, Admiral Luís Enrique Cabrera Aguirre. At issue was the continuing groundswell of discontent within the military. One particular grievance, high on the agenda, was the way in which junior and low-grade officers had been promoted to senior rank at the whim of civilian politicians, disregarding all established procedures.

A version of the meeting written up by Grüber was clearly designed to enlist sympathy for his cause. Yet it gives a chilling account of the extent of the dissatisfaction within the armed forces, and the outspoken way in which senior officers were prepared to voice their preoccupations to their indecisive political masters.

General Ochoa told the two admirals that he was concerned about the situation inside the armed forces. He perceived that it was 'still very delicate'. He had heard 'accounts of serious discontent among middle-ranking and junior officers', he said, and he wanted to know what the two admirals thought was going on.

'Look,' replied Admiral Cabrera, 'you must understand that the senior ranks have lost all credibility and trust. It's that simple. The subalterns no longer believe in their generals and colonels.'

'How can you be so certain?' asked Ochoa. 'Do you put them all in same camp?'

'From generals and colonels who have all been promoted as a result of carrying the bags of some senator or other,' replied Cabrera, 'what can you expect?'

'So what should be done?' asked Ochoa, turning to Grüber.

'You want me to tell you?' Grüber replied pithily (and this of course is his own highly coloured account). 'The entire high command should be asked to resign. They should be retired immediately, and replaced by officers with genuine military qualifications.'

'But that would lead to chaos,' objected Ochoa.

'Look,' Grüber went on, 'the chaos will get worse as the military discontent accumulates. How is it possible that in the Soviet Union they could sack their defence minister and other high officials when a young German pilot landed his plane on Moscow's Red Square, while in Venezuela the army commander still keeps his job after half his forces have taken part in a rebellion, and everyone pretends that nothing has happened?'

It was a good question, but General Ochoa took no action. He could neither sack the high command, nor discipline the junior officers who were clearly plotting another coup. Like a rabbit caught in the head-lights, the entire government was paralysed, unable to act.

Ochoa did manage to set in train the preparation of an academic survey of the situation within the armed forces, for he wanted to get a clear overview of the dimensions of the dissent. Admiral Cabrera was handed this important task, and was provided with a team of univer-sity researchers. They interviewed a large number of senior politicians and generals, both in retirement and in active service, and they also sent questionnaires to 5,000 servicemen stationed at the most important gar-risons in the country, at Aragua, Táchira, Zulia, Monagas, and Caracas.

Their report, signed by Cabrera, was ready by the middle of July. It revealed the existence of five serious complaints about the condition of the armed forces and about the state of the nation, and made a number of comments and recommendations. Some of the complaints were about conditions of service: the inadequate nature of the health service within the armed forces; the ineffectiveness of the social security system; and the 'poor' perception of the system of promotions and of the pro-vision of compensation for the loss of seniority. Other complaints indicated a more general (and thus less remediable) discontent: a lack of leadership; and the culture of corruption, both political and military, that permeated the country at the highest level.

The chief of the general staff, General Iván Jiménez Sánchez, received the report and took note of it. He even promised that he would set up a commission to ensure that its recommendations were implemented. Inevitably, perhaps, given the political stasis in the country, the report was shelved.

In August, with no guarantee that any reforms would be made in the wake of the February coup, and with no attention paid to the July report, Admiral Grüber's group began to plot a new coup. Those included in his conspiracy were Cabrera from the navy, Visconti from the air force, and a number of civilian contacts, chiefly from *La Causa R*. Grüber's group also enjoyed the support of the surviving members of Chávez's Bolivarian Revolutionary Movement, directed from Chávez's cell in the Yare prison. The group called itself the 'July 5 Movement', in homage to the independence struggle and Venezuela's national day.

More time seems to have been spent on planning events after the imagined success of their coup than on thinking how they might make the actual uprising more effective than the previous one. The initial political plan was to form a Council of State, with both civilians and officers, and with a civilian as president. The council would last for a year or so, and try to reorganise the country. The model was that of the Patriotic Junta of 1958, though they had also read up what happened on the occasion of Rómulo Betancourt's coup against General Medina Angarita on October 18, 1945, when a 'revolutionary junta' had been installed in the Miraflores palace.

Their plans were subject to innumerable delays, and several key plotters lost enthusiasm as the weeks went by. Elections, for governors and mayors, were due in December, and the conspirators realised that their actions might be misconstrued if their coup were to occur during or after that event. They decided that they would have to act quickly, in November. Admiral Grüber, whose pseudonym was 'Julius Caesar', describes in his memoirs how the decision was taken 'to cross the Rubicon'.

On November 25, he put the final touches to his preparations, making a video recording of the speech that he planned to have broadcast to the nation on the day of the coup. He practised before the cameras, and the technicians seemed satisfied with the result.

Two days later, on the morning of November 27, he arrived at his headquarters to preside over what he hoped would be a well-organised coup. Yet as before, in the case of the Chávez coup, there were serious errors and omissions, with important participants failing to keep their promised appointments. Worst of all was the failure of the communications equipment. Like Chávez before him, Grüber had no means of keeping contact with the officers in other parts of the country. He too was destined to be isolated and out of touch.

There was one difference. This time, the conspirators had managed to seize a television station, and Grüber pinned his hopes on a civilian uprising. If his video were to be shown on television screens across the nation, calling for support for his programme of national reconstruction, he fondly imagined that the masses would rise up and support his rebellion.

Disaster struck again, and no one seems to know quite how it happened. Instead of the measured and recorded tones of the admiral announcing a *coup d'état* and calling for popular support, a series of conflictive images flickered across the television screen. Masked men appeared, and promptly embarked on a round of looting reminiscent of the *Caracazo*; occasional bursts of rhetoric could be heard from the voice of the imprisoned Colonel Chávez.

It seems that the videos had been switched, or perhaps the operator had picked up the wrong one to put in his machine. No one subsequently claimed responsibility for what went wrong. The television-watching nation, preparing to go to work, did not know whether to laugh or cry. They certainly had no intention of going out into the streets to support a revolution organised in such an incompetent way.

Later in the morning, as he had done in February, President Pérez appeared on the screen to announce that all was well, and at midday Admiral Grüber surrendered. At that very moment, an air force plane passed over Caracas, making a supersonic bang. Grüber's video that was never shown had mentioned a flypast, as the signal for the people to take to the streets. Now, nobody moved. General Visconti wisely embarked his air force conspirators onto a Hercules cargo plane and set off across Colombia to seek sanctuary in Peru. At the prisons of Yare and San Carlos, a fresh group of failed military conspirators joined Colonel Chávez behind bars.

12

THE PATRIOTIC FRONT OF
CIVILIAN REVOLUTIONARIES

Colonel Chávez and Admiral Grüber did not act alone. The planners of the two attempted coups in 1992 had both envisaged a revolutionary change in government that would be made by soldiers acting in alliance with civilian groups. They had looked essentially to the forces of the Venezuelan left, with its long tradition of encouraging, and participating in, military subversion. Most coup attempts in the previous half century, notably in 1944 (against Medina Angarita), in 1958 (against Pérez Jiménez), and in 1962 (against Rómulo Betancourt), had taken place with the participation of civilians.

In the wake of the *Caracazo* of February 1989, a group of civilian activists anxious to take advantage of the popular explosion had sought to renew this tradition. They came together to form a new Patriotic Front, a political device that crops up from time to time in Venezuelan history when people of goodwill across the spectrum get together to try to change the course of events during troubled times. A Patriotic Front had played an important role in the downfall of Pérez Jiménez in 1958, and in the more distant past a similar front was created in the 1850s, in the days of Ezequiel Zamora.

The Venezuelan elite has often liked to think of their country as 'a democracy', yet this democracy has been a comparatively new development. Venezuela has been no stranger to military rule, and was run by military dictators during the first half of the twentieth century, and for much of the nineteenth century as well. With such a history, it is hardly surprising that politicians should seek to involve the military in their plans, and the left has been no exception to this rule. 'Venezuelans are so accustomed to make the army the arbiter of their political contests', wrote Rafael Caldera in the 1970s, 'that at any moment the most varied groups, for the most dissimilar ends, attempt to involve the army in new adventures to change our political reality.'

During the Second World War, the government of General Isaías Medina Angarita enjoyed the support of the Communist Party, and the military coup that overthrew this government in 1944 was organised by the civilian politicians of *Acción Democrática*, including Rómulo Betancourt, and, in a junior capacity, Carlos Andrés Pérez. In 1958, the military government was overthrown by the Patriotic Front of the time, a group within the left that conspired with sections of the military. The left then gave warm support to the presidential campaign of Admiral Wolfgang Larrazábal. Finally, in 1962, during the leftist guerrilla campaign against Betancourt's regime, civilian leftists were intimately involved in two military revolts at Carúpano and Puerto Cabello.

The new Patriotic Front that assembled after the *Caracazo* in 1989 was presided over by Luís Miquilena, the leader of the busdrivers' union in Caracas in the 1940s, and one of the great survivors of the Venezuelan left. He became the chief political adviser of Colonel Chávez and, in 1999, when over eighty, the President of the Constitutional Assembly. He finally parted company from Chávez at the end of 2001.

The participants in the Patriotic Front were all interested in the creation of a political alliance between civilians and the military, and much of the internal debate aroused in Venezuela since the advent of the Chávez government has concerned the legacy of this civil–military relationship. Taxed with the criticism that his government owes its origin to a failed military coup, albeit one that took place some years before he was elected president, Chávez often recalls that the progressive government of General Medina Angarita, for which he has some affection, was overthrown by a coup organised by Betancourt and *Acción Democrática*, a political grouping for which he has always had undisguised contempt. Betancourt, of course, is fondly remembered by his supporters as 'the father of Venezuelan democracy', yet his route to power was via a military coup.

Luís Miquilena is a living witness to the arguments of that era. 'There was a certain process of political development in Venezuela,' he recalls, 'which began with the replacement of the dictatorship of Juan Vicente Gómez by General López Contreras; this later moved forward considerably with Medina Angarita, who opened the doors to democracy.'

General Medina ruled Venezuela during the boom years of the Second World War, when the Allied powers were keen to secure their supplies of Venezuelan oil. He obtained important concessions from the foreign oil companies, and was supported by the Communist Party. A positive memory of his government is still firmly upheld by sections of the left. Yet his otherwise rather progressive policies were not supported by the oil workers, whose union rights were restricted in order to ensure that strikes did not interfere with wartime production. *Acción Democrática*, supporting the rights of the workers, soon became the dominant political force in the oilfields. Fearing that the Communists might make common cause with Medina Angarita's chosen successor, Betancourt and *Acción Democrática* decided on a coup in October 1944.

Miquilena, who likes to describe himself as 'a fighter for social rights who took an active part in the trade union struggle', had taken a benign attitude towards Medina Angarita, though unlike the orthodox Communists at the time he did not wish to support his government actively. When it was under threat, however, he was actively hostile to the military uprising against it. 'I played my part in support of Medina, against the uprising of *Acción Democrática*, to try to prevent this military action from succeeding.'

Medina Angarita was overthrown yet, as Miquilena points out, the coup proved a mixed blessing for its organisers. Betancourt and *Acción Democrática* (and their president, Rómulo Gallegos) enjoyed the fruits of their coup for a brief spell of three years, from 1945 to 1948, but their government was then itself overthrown in 1948 by Pérez Jiménez, who ruled for a decade. '*Acción Democrática* was forced to endure the disastrous consequences of the coup during a dictatorship that lasted for ten years, and ensured the absence of all civil liberties.'

To understand the history of today, these detours into the obscurities of the past are almost inevitable. The trajectory of Miquilena, a politician with a long history of dissent, is particularly illuminating, for although eventually disillusioned he was the man who helped to revive the tradition of socialist nationalism that lies at the heart of the Chávez project. In 1944, when still a union leader, Miquilena formed part of an anti-Stalinist Communist group known as the *Machamíques*, at a time when the orthodox Communist Party had joined forces with Medina Angarita. It had done so towards the end of the war, under instructions from the United States Communists led by Earl Browder (and by extension from America's ally in Moscow, Joseph Stalin). Moscow wanted no actions that would upset its Western ally.

Miquilena and the Machado brothers, Gustavo and Eduardo, both Communists, were opposed to this position (hence the name *Machamíques*). They thought that policy should be made in Venezuela, not in Moscow – and still less in the United States. Miquilena helped to set up a new anti-Stalinist communist party in 1946, called the *Partido Comunista Venezolano Unitario*. His party was known at the time as '*los negros*' (the blacks), because in the distribution of election colours (essential in a largely illiterate population) the orthodox Communist Party had secured the colour red.

The chief organiser of '*los negros*' – and the pioneering creator of socialist nationalism in Venezuela – was Salvador de la Plaza, a history lecturer at the Universidad Central in Caracas (he died in 1970 at the age of 74). This forgotten figure, known to his students as 'the red monk', is one of the intellectual authors of the project of Hugo Chávez. Indeed it is impossible to understand the historical roots of Chávez's success without reference to the powerful anti-Stalinist communism of De la Plaza and Miquilena that was to influence important sections of the Venezuelan left in the years after the 1940s. Miquilena was the most significant spokesman of this tradition, though it touched some of the other participants in the Patriotic Front of 1989.

In addition to Miquilena, the core of the Patriotic Front's membership consisted of Douglas Bravo; Manuel Quijada, a lawyer involved in the military rebellions of 1962; Lino Martínez, another former guerrilla fighter; and Lieutenant William Izarra.

The Patriotic Front issued a series of pamphlets, called *Three Decades of Frustration*, which made a certain impact in the newspapers. Among its more concrete proposals was one for a constitutional assembly to be held to prepare a new constitution, a recommendation that eventually became an essential plank in the political programme of Chávez. Yet the membership of the Patriotic Front was too diverse and too politically divided to last out the year, and Chávez later described it as 'stillborn': 'A Patriotic Front cannot be invented; you cannot assemble a hundred distinguished figures and say "We are the Front." I don't believe in that.'

Yet the composition of the Patriotic Front of 1989 was an important pointer to the years ahead, for several of its members were to become key supporters of the Chávez government in 1999. Another of the civilian leftists involved was Pedro Duno, a philosophy professor at the Universidad Central in Caracas, and always an influential figure on the left. Duno, who came from a military family, kept up his contacts within the military over the years. He died in November 1998 just after being elected senator for Miranda state as a supporter of Chávez. Writing in *Ultimas Noticias* on June 23, 1991, two years after the *Caracazo*, he had prepared the intellectual ground for a new coup:

> Venezuela is a country in an advanced state of collapse, whose characteristics of corruption and pillage, incompetence, irresponsibility and cynicism, define the gloomy panorama of the present. In this bleak situation it is being suggested that the armed forces should intervene. Since it is impossible to use the force of reasonable argument, or of law, or of rights, or of the constitution, because the state and the government provide no guarantees, then it will be justifiable to use the reasonable argument of force, the *ultima ratio*.

Just over six months later, on February 4, 1992, Colonel Chávez took him at his word.

13

LATIN AMERICA'S EXPERIENCE OF RADICAL MILITARY REBELLION

Years ago, in 1974, I went to visit General Omar Torríjos, the military ruler of Panama. I flew to his seaside dacha by the shores of the Pacific and we spent all day talking. There were just four of us: the head of the secret service, the rector of the university, Torríjos and I. The general lay in his hammock for most of the day, in a shaded patio overlooking the sea, sometimes talkative and sometimes taciturn. Much of the time we talked about peasants and land reform, and about what had happened in the rural areas of China and Chile, of Vietnam and Peru, and Cuba. Torríjos was a great admirer of Castro, but he said he didn't agree with everything being done in Cuba. 'They should have left the peasants with a little piece of land they could call their own.'

As Graham Greene was to find, it was difficult not to be captivated by this enchanting figure, the complete antithesis of the Latin American officer in dark glasses. Torríjos had seized power in 1968, and was to rule Panama for thirteen years until he was killed in an air crash in 1981. He had a radical programme of reform, chiefly related to the Canal Zone, the chunk of Panamanian territory that the Americans had expropriated in 1903. The Canal Zone had subsequently been directly controlled by the United States Department of Defense, later the Pentagon, and used for the construction of an inter-oceanic canal and innumerable military bases. But Torríjos's political programme went beyond the nationalist issue of the canal. He rebelled against the corruption of the political elite, and he pushed through a land reform to try to benefit the peasants.

The history of Latin America in the 1970s and 1980s was so dominated by the eruption of military dictatorships of the right that it is easy to forget the existence of another tradition. For on many occasions, in the nineteenth as well as the twentieth century, radical officers have appeared with the interests of the people at heart, ready to do battle on their behalf with local landlords or foreign capitalists. Manuel Isidoro Belzú in Bolivia, Ezequiel Zamora in Venezuela, Luis Carlos Prestes in Brazil, Marmaduke Grove in Chile – there is a long and infinitely fascinating list.

When members of the old Venezuelan political elite come together to discuss the Chávez phenomenon, they like to examine the examples of countries where military rule was imposed on civilian societies by left-wing nationalist officers – both in Latin America and elsewhere. The favoured foreign examples are Kemal Atatürk in Turkey and Gamel Abdul Nasser in Egypt, with occasional references to Charles de Gaulle in France. Closer to home, the 'usual suspects' under consideration are Omar Torríjos in Panama, Juan Velasco Alvarado in Peru, and Juan Domingo Perón in Argentina. The government of Colonel Chávez, it is always assumed, is going to take one of these roads.

Although democracy rather than military rule became the dominant practice in Latin America in the 1990s, this was not always so. Few have been the periods in the continent's history in which military officers have not played a pivotal role, though most have come from the right rather than the left.

The ruling elites of the continent have always held ambivalent views about their armed forces. On the one hand, they are remembered as the essential and historic bulwark against the rebellious indigenous Indian population whose lands were stolen by settlers over the centuries. In this context, the soldiers appear as the saviours of the nation to whom the descendants of the settlers are expected to register their eternal gratitude. Since the descendants of the indigenous population now people the inflated and explosive urban shanty towns of the continent, and continue to pose a similar, though different, threat to the heirs to the settler class, gratitude to the armed forces remains high on the agenda.

On the other hand, while the military may be useful or even essential to the ruling elites, they are also perceived to represent an inferior social class that is always held in low esteem. Officers are often the butt of endless jokes. The excesses of the military dictatorships of the 1970s and 1980s gave the military everywhere a bad name, and the political elites of the twenty-first century, whether of ancient lineage or newly emerging from the universities, tend to regard the armed forces as a necessary evil, best kept corralled in their barracks. This view was reinforced by the government of the United States in the 1990s, in complete contradiction to earlier American policies which favoured strong military dictatorships over effete civilian regimes.

The Americans used to fear that democratic governments would be dominated by nationalists, leftists, or social democrats, people insufficiently mindful of American economic or strategic interests. This was often the case. Throughout the 1970s and into the 1980s, the United States was content to see much of Latin America fall under conservative military rule, and often actively encouraged the process. A pattern begun in Brazil in 1964 was continued in Chile in September 1973, when General Augusto Pinochet overthrew the elected government of Salvador Allende. The tradition was sustained in Bolivia and Uruguay in the 1970s, and reached a low point in March 1976 with the coup in Argentina by General Jorge Videla, who overthrew the government of María Estela, the widow of General Perón.

These regimes were noted for their flagrant disregard for human rights, but the generals enjoyed the warm support of successive governments in Washington. The firm stand of the military in support of the traditional economic interests of the United States, and their rigidly anti-Communist position in the Cold War, overrode any doubts about their domestic repression. The tough, centralised government provided by the military, which forbade workers from uniting in trade unions, was much appreciated by foreign capital.

In the 1990s, however, with the development of a new kind of neo-liberal economics that had no need of military government, and with an end to the strategic emergency imposed by the Cold War, Washington began to favour democracy. The trademark dark glasses of the military dictators were no longer in fashion.

Yet there was an alternative tradition, and Colonel Chávez had always taken an interest in the experience of General Torríjos and General Velasco of Peru. He had met the son of Torríjos who had taken part in a military training course in Venezuela, and he had read some of the political material relating to the transformations in Panama that Torríjos junior brought with him. Some of yesterday's rhetoric by Torríjos is echoed by Chávez today.

Interviewed in August 1975, Torríjos had justified his *coup d'état* on the grounds that the Panamanian National Guard, which he led, had been transformed into 'the wage slaves of the oligarchy':

> Our mission was to maintain the status quo, with blood and thunder, with timely military deployment, or with a *coup d'état*. I was forced to take part in acts of repression, indeed I got sick of so much repression. As a direct result, the National Guard decided to rebel, to de-colonise the country. Above all, we wanted to solve the problem of the canal, which for the Panamanians was almost a religion.

As was to happen in Venezuela, the Panamanian officers had rebelled against what they perceived as the incompetence and corruption of the civilian rulers:

> We were the sentries of the oligarchy until the mistakes of the politicians became so serious that there was no prospect of rectification. A generation of young officers, graduates of the Panamanian Military School, decided not just to organise a *coup d'état*, but to do away with the entire system of apparent 'democracy' in the country. People had grown accustomed to mixing up politics with their economic activity, using their democratic freedom in much the same way as women use cosmetics.

In 1979, Torríjos succeeded in wrenching a new canal treaty from the United States government of Jimmy Carter, and the Panama Canal was eventually handed over to the Panamanians twenty years later, in December 1999. But Torríjos did not live to see this cardinal event; as already mentioned, he was killed in an air crash in August 1981. His successor, Manuel Noriega, handled matters with less diplomatic aplomb, and in 1989 suffered the indignity of an American invasion – Operation Just Cause – in which more than 1,000 Panamanians were killed. He was captured, accused of drug smuggling and money laundering, and is still serving a lifetime's sentence in a US prison.

As influential as Torríjos in the political formation of Colonel Chávez has been the nationalist experiment of the Peruvian military during the government of General Velasco between 1968 and 1976. Chávez had visited Peru as a young cadet in 1974, at a time when Velasco's Revolutionary Government of the Armed Forces was already in sharp decline. He claims to have been influenced by the Peruvian example, though the Peruvian experience actually bears little comparison with the project on which he has embarked in Venezuela – nevertheless, a few of its lessons might still be learnt.

As in Venezuela and Panama, a group of intelligent Peruvian officers, unhappy about corruption and the state of the country, had been discussing the possibility of a military intervention. Some of them had been influenced by their experience in France during the Algerian war. As in Venezuela, these officers held their country's principal political party – Apra in Peru, *Acción Democrática* in Venezuela – in great distrust, partly because of its overtly anti-nationalist and pro-American position. As in Venezuela, the Peruvian officers had had experience of an anti-guerrilla war and were more aware than civilian politicians of the abject conditions of the population in the rural areas.

When they seized power in 1968, the Peruvian military announced their intention of building a new order that would be 'neither capitalist nor communist'. Their particular concern at that moment was the corruption of the civilian regime of Fernándo Belaúnde Terry, the devaluation of the currency, and a clause in a government contract signed with a US oil company, Standard Oil, that appeared contrary to the national interest. Inflation, low by Latin American standards, but unusually high for Peru, was running at 19 per cent.

The reformist zeal of General Velasco derived in part from his experience in crushing the Peruvian guerrilla movements of the 1960s. His first-hand knowledge of the sufferings of the rural population of the Andes, which the guerrillas of Hugo Blanco and Luís de la Puente Uceda had sought to redress, led him to adopt much of the guerrilla programme as his own. Velasco was an officer of high intelligence, influenced by the example of General de Gaulle in France, where he had served as a military attaché in the years immediately after the end of the Algerian war.

Velasco nationalised the foreign oil companies, expropriated the sugar haciendas, and carried out an extensive land reform; he made Quechua, the language of the Andes, an official language of the country. He also expropriated the conservative newspapers and encouraged worker participation in the management of state industries. To the annoyance of Washington, he re-established diplomatic relations with Cuba and engaged in a growing bilateral trade with the Soviet Union.

In retrospect, as Richard Webb, the governor of the Peruvian central bank in the successor regime, has recalled, Velasco's economic programme was not quite as radical as it once had seemed:

> The military regime carried out deep social, institutional, and economic reforms, many of them applauded by the Washington consensus of the time. Indeed much of the reform agenda, in particular the land reform, the educational reform, and the reinforcement of the planning mechanisms, seemed to come straight from the books of the earlier Alliance for Progress and from standard World Bank prescriptions of the time.

The Velasco government suffered from two fundamental flaws: after a period of initial enthusiasm, it lacked popular support; and it tried to carry out a revolution on borrowed money. These two flaws, implicit from the start, proved the cause of its downfall. The government had no civilian presence; it was entirely composed of officers; and it never reached out to sectors beyond the immediate beneficiaries of Velasco's reforms. The lack of money was even more serious. By 1976, Peru had exhausted its foreign reserves, and had to seek a foreign loan from a consortium of American banks. The conditions imposed were impressive: a wage freeze, devaluation, and budget cuts in the public sector; the abolition of the right to strike; the sacking from the government of its more prominent radical members; an end to the ban on oil contracts with foreign firms; and the sale of state companies to the private sector.

Not surprisingly, the regime ran into deep trouble. After Velasco's death in 1977, there was severe rioting and a prolonged police strike. Perceiving the depths of public hostility, his conservative successor, General Francisco Morales Bermúdez, was persuaded to abandon the entire project and to return the country to civilian rule. After fresh elections in 1980, Belaúnde Terry, the politician so rudely deposed in 1968, was re-elected president, and soon the memory of the military revolution was rubbed out.

The military governments of Peru and Panama have often been derided by journalists and political scientists. Both Velasco and Torríjos set off with high hopes of redeeming the conditions of the poor and 'standing up' to the local big power in the Americas. Both were serious and intelligent leaders possessed of considerable charisma. Their deaths were mourned as a national catastrophe. They could not be faulted for their ambition, yet they were unable to sustain the revolutionary programmes they had put in train.

Colonel Chávez follows in their footsteps, but with a different agenda and having learnt from their mistakes. He is an elected president, not a military dictator. He knows that you cannot make a revolution on borrowed money, and he recognises that the armed forces cannot rule on their own. They need the support of the great mass of the people.

PART THREE:
RECOVERING THE REVOLUTIONARY
TRADITIONS OF THE NINETEENTH CENTURY

14

THE LEGACY OF SIMÓN BOLÍVAR, THE LIBERATOR

Wherever you go in Venezuela, and in much of Latin America, an image can always be found of Simón Bolívar, the 'Liberator' of Venezuela (and of a large part of the continent) from Spanish rule. It may be a statue in a town square, a painting in a minister's office, or a scribble on a wall: you can never entirely escape from the noble brow, the slightly supercilious curve of the smile and, if the artist is honest, the sallow complexion of the skin that indicates a *zambo*, a man of mixed race.

Traditional Venezuelan histories have always emphasised Bolívar's aristocratic origins rather than his black heritage. Yet Bolívar stood up for the rights of Venezuela's large community of black slaves. During the fight for independence, he sought assistance in 1816 from President Alexandre Pétion, black ruler of the free slave republic of Haiti. Pétion agreed to help if Bolívar would promise to liberate the slaves of Venezuela. Bolívar had freed the slaves on his own estates, but he could make no impact on the slave-owning class of Venezuela, and slave freedom did not finally come until 1854.

The secular cult of Bolívar has survived unchanged in Venezuela over many generations. Successive presidents and generals, the corrupt, the idle, and the patriotic, have all bowed down in homage to the Liberator. Chávez has been no exception, having erected the example and the thoughts of Bolívar almost to the level of an ideology, and renamed the country the 'Bolivarian Republic' of Venezuela.

This is not an exercise in mindless nationalism. His purpose is not just to venerate a figure to whom most of his predecessors have only paid lip service, but also to rescue the historical character and achievements of the Liberator from the accretions of myth and fable.

He has not been alone in this. A similar task has been undertaken by several writers in recent years. One internationally famous effort was the novel about Bolívar, *The General in his Labyrinth*, written by Gabriel García Márquez and first published in 1989. This was a fictional account of the final months of the Liberator's life, in 1830, when he was already out of power and his life's work appeared to have crumbled around him. The novel gave a human dimension to the conventional bronze statue.

Another influential book within intellectual circles in Venezuela and Colombia was *El culto a Bolívar* by the Venezuelan historian Germán Carrera Damas. This also made a stab at demystifying Bolívar's career, and was not well received by the senior officers at the military academy in Caracas. Chávez warmed to this rewriting of received history and used the debate about Bolívar's role in the past in the classes he taught at the academy in the early 1980s, seeking to recover some of the characteristics of the Liberator that might be of political value in the present. His aim was to draw on the country's historical traditions to help lay out a pattern for the future,

Research into Bolívar's career was of particular service to Chávez in his examination of a possible role for Venezuela in the affairs of the continent. Most Latin American politicians have long recognised that their nation states are too weak to operate on their own. This has been the common view in the continent for many decades, and provided the political push behind the drive towards economic integration. Bolívar had faced a similar problem, drawing the conclusion that a continent-wide crusade against Spanish imperial rule would be necessary, uniting Latin America against the outside power.

Chávez has sought to do something similar, re-igniting the Bolívarian dream and seeking the political unification of Latin America on a new basis: the internal integration of each country. His eventual aim is to hold a great conference of the 'Bolívarian' states, those liberated by Bolívar, to replicate the one that Bolívar organised in Panama in 1826. Chávez has long argued that 'a valid project for the twenty-first century' would be 'to bring together ... the Balkanised countries of Latin America'.

Bolívar is not the only figure that Chávez has resurrected from the nineteenth century. In the 1980s, in discussion with his closest military friends, he began to rescue the thoughts and writings of other Venezuelan protagonists, notably Simón Rodríguez and Ezequiel Zamora, and all were soon included in the pantheon of his embryonic revolutionary movement. In the process, he found himself participating in the historical debate that had been going on within the Venezuelan left since the 1960s.

The original view of the Marxist left, in Venezuela as elsewhere, was one of extreme hostility to Bolívar. Taking their cue from the writings of Marx himself, most Marxist writers perceived the Liberator as a typically bourgeois figure whose actions had only served the interests of the emergent imperial power of the time. Bolívar, according to this reading, had secured independence from Spain with British support, and had handed over the continent to exploitation by English capitalism. For years, this caricature portrait of Bolívar as an imperialist stooge effectively precluded the left from examining his more positive characteristics. It was impossible for anyone on the left to perceive him as a revolutionary model for the twentieth century.

In the course of the 1960s, in Venezuela, this view had already begun to change. The guerrilla movements had given their military units the names of heroes from the past: José Leonardo Chirinos, the leader of an eighteenth century slave revolt in Coro; and Ezequiel Zamora, the leader of the peasantry in the *llanos* in the nineteenth century. Later, when some of these groups split away from the orthodox Communist Party, they began to re-examine what they had learnt about the past, with a view to creating an ideology of the left with a heavier dose of nationalism – just as Chávez was to do in subsequent years.

Among their number was Douglas Bravo, commander of the 'José Leonardo Chirinos' guerrilla group in Falcón state. Bravo claims today that his expulsion from the Communist Party, in June 1965, was partly due to his arguments in favour of the ideas of the heroes of the nineteenth century: Bolívar, Simón Rodríguez, and Ezequiel Zamora among them. Their notions ran directly contrary to Soviet orthodoxy.

Bravo formed a new political party in April 1966, the *Partido de la Revolución Venezolano* (PRV), infused with the ideas of these figures from the past. He recalls that his party's chief ideologue, Pedro Duno, published a document in 1969 entitled 'Marxism-Leninism-Bolívarianism'. Duno's aim was to 'nationalise' the ideology of the Latin American left. As well as reviving the figure of the Liberator, Bravo's party was also attracted to the key idea of Simón Rodríguez that 'America should not slavishly imitate, but should seek to be original.'

When Chávez started to organise his military conspiracy in the 1980s and made his first contacts with the revolutionary left, he found that they were already talking the same language. The resurrection of Bolívar as an important and necessary forerunner of any future radical revolution was accepted by the leftists that he met.

Although Bolívar is widely recognised as one of the great figures of the nineteenth century, few people outside Latin America retain anything more than a few anecdotal details about his life and work. He is probably most famous for the sad reflection made at the end of his life that he had 'ploughed the sea'. Since his life is such a significant presence in Chávez's political project, and is mentioned so frequently in his rhetoric, it may be useful to include here a brief account of his life and achievements.

Born on July 24, 1783, in Caracas, Bolívar died in Colombia before he was fifty, on December 17, 1830. The principal leader of the Latin American rebellions against the Spanish empire, he fought for the liberation of Venezuela and Colombia, as well as Ecuador, Peru, and Upper Peru (Bolivia); his campaigns spanned a period of more than ten years. He fought backwards and forwards across Venezuela, up and down Colombia, and then made an inspired march down the Andes into Ecuador and Peru. Not since the battles of the first generation of *conquistadors* in the sixteenth century had a single general covered so much ground with such far-reaching results.

Bolívar was also something of an intellectual. Widely read in the classics and the recent emancipatory literature of pre-revolutionary

France, he maintained a voluminous correspondence that reveals a man of sharp wit and observation. Many of his 'open letters' and speeches are models of the advanced political thought of the time.

He was also a man of harsh and uncompromising views, often cruel and unpredictable in his actions. He made many mistakes, both tactical and strategic, and his entire project was frequently on the verge of collapse. He firmly believed that he was in charge of an anarchic continent that would benefit from strong leadership. Arrogant and almost certainly insufferable, he had no doubt that he himself was that necessary leader.

Bolívar's parents died when he was young, and he lived for a while in the house of his tutor, Simón Rodríguez, who will reappear in the next chapter. Bolívar travelled as a young adult to Europe, first to Spain between 1798 and 1801, and then to France and Italy between 1804 and 1807. Stimulated by the revolutionary atmosphere of the time, he devoured the works of Voltaire and Rousseau, and, returning to Venezuela in 1807, he devoted himself to his country's embryonic and clandestine independence movement.

An uprising occurred in Caracas on April 19, 1810, and forced the resignation of the Spanish ruler. A revolutionary junta assumed power in the city, and sent Bolívar to England to secure British support for their regime. Arriving in London in July, at the height of the Napoleonic Wars, Bolívar failed to interest the British government in the fate of his country, but he had some success in persuading the exiled Francisco de Miranda to return with him to Caracas, to take command of the revolutionary forces. Miranda, who had fought in the ranks of the French Revolution, had made an earlier attempt in 1806, to organise a rebellion against Spain.

On his return to Caracas, Bolívar joined the republican army and was given command of the strategically important port city of Puerto Cabello. Venezuela's independence was formally declared on July 5, 1811, after a republican Congress had gathered in Caracas in March to draft a constitution for the newly independent country.

Ten years of fighting lay ahead, for the Spaniards refused to accept this republican rebellion in Caracas, still controlling much of the rest of the country – and the continent. Their counter-attack was not long in coming, presaged in March 1812 by a serious earthquake which destroyed much of the city. The Catholic Church, loyal to Madrid and hostile to the republican regime, soon made political capital out of the disaster, just as prominent clergymen were to do after the terrible mudslide disaster in Caracas and Vargas state in December 1999.

The republican forces were weak and ill-armed, and divided among themselves. Soon they were on the defensive: the Spaniards recaptured Puerto Cabello when Bolívar was looking the other way; and Miranda attempted to make peace with the Spanish commander in Caracas. Denouncing Miranda as a traitor, the republicans handed him over to the Spaniards. He was taken in chains to Spain, and died in prison in Cadiz.

Bolívar, meanwhile, had escaped by sea from Venezuela and arrived at the port of Cartagena in New Granada (now Colombia), then an enclave under the control of independent republicans. There he published the first of his great political statements, the Cartagena Manifesto, calling for the destruction of Spanish power in Venezuela as a prelude to continental unification, and demanding that it be replaced by strong centralised government:

> Government must prove to be formidable and ruthless, without regard to law or constitution, until peace is established. I believe that our enemies will have all the advantages as long as we do not unify our American government. We shall be inextricably caught in the web of civil war, and be shamefully beaten by that little horde of bandits which pollutes our country.

Taking him at his word, the republicans in Cartagena chose Bolívar to be the commander of an expeditionary force that would secure the liberation of Venezuela. Embarking on a three-month campaign, he defeated the Spanish army in several battles, and recaptured Caracas on August 6, 1813. The reconvened Congress gave him the title 'Liberator'.

It was a fleeting victory, for the republican forces did not hold Caracas for long. With the end of the Napoleonic Wars in Europe, the Spaniards sent fresh troops out to Latin America, and in General José Tomás Boves they had a skilled and ruthless commander, able to mobilise the Indians and peasants of the *llanos* into a fighting force capable of matching those of Bolívar. Boves captured Caracas a year later, in July 1814, exacting exemplary punishment and closing the first chapter in the history of the independent Venezuelan republic.

Bolívar escaped again to Cartagena, and in December he captured Bogotá. But the arrival of a fresh Spanish army from Europe brought new defeats, and in May 1815 he was obliged to escape to the British island of Jamaica. Here he wrote, in his 'Letter from Jamaica', a visionary plan for the future of Latin America, embracing the entire continent, from Argentina and Chile to Mexico:

> We are a macrocosm of the human race. We are a world apart, confined within two oceans, young in art and science, but old as human society. We are neither Indians nor Europeans, yet we are a part of each other.

Bolívar tried to return to Cartagena, but since it had fallen again into Spanish hands, his ship sailed to the independent black republic of Haiti. Arriving at Port au Prince on January 1, 1816, he was welcomed by President Pétion, who agreed to provide him with arms and ammunition, and allowed him to recruit sailors for his invasion fleet.

Launching an attack on Venezuela from Haiti was always going to be a risky operation, and it proved a disaster. Bolívar's fleet captured the island of Margarita, but in July it was repelled from the mainland at Carúpano and at Ocumare. Bolívar retreated to Haiti to prepare a second expedition, and he returned to the Venezuelan mainland at Barcelona at the end of the year.

The war against Spain now entered a new phase. In April 1817, Bolívar sailed round the coast to the delta of the Orinoco. Advancing upriver, he established his headquarters in July at Angostura (now Ciudad Bolívar). Here he made contact with republican leaders in the *llanos*, notably with José Antonio Páez and Francisco de Paula Santander from the Colombian border. Bolívar's forces now fought in the *llanos* over a long, two-year period, until they were ready to launch an attack on Spanish-held Colombia.

Finally, in 1819, his army forces climbed the mountain passes from the *llanos* into what was still the Spanish viceroyalty of New Granada. The royalist officers could not believe that the republican assault would come from this direction. Unprepared, they were defeated at the battle of Boyacá on August 7. Bolívar entered Bogotá three days later, while the Spanish viceroy escaped to the sea at Cartagena. Colombia was in the hands of a republican army.

Leaving General Santander in charge in Bogotá as the vice-president for New Granada, Bolívar retraced his steps, climbing back down the slopes of the Andes, and sailing down the Apure to the Orinoco. He arrived at his old base at Angostura in December, and summoned the Congress to tell it of his triumphs:

> The union of New Granada and Venezuela is the goal that I set for myself even in my earliest fighting days. It is the desire of all the citizens of both countries, and would give the assurance of South American freedom.

Soon Ecuador was to be thrown in for good measure. The Angostura Congress appointed Bolívar as the president and military dictator of the new state, to be called the Republic of Gran Colombia. It was designed to be a federation of the old Spanish 'departments' of Venezuela and New Granada (Colombia), and Quito (Ecuador).

For several months there was a truce, but in June 1821, Bolívar's men advanced north from the Orinoco and defeated the Spanish army at the battle of Carabobo. The way was now open to Caracas, and Bolívar arrived there in triumph. The liberation of Venezuela was complete. A new Congress assembled in September on the border, at Cúcuta, to draft a constitution and to formally elect Bolívar as president.

Bolívar was now the ruler of the joint republic of Venezuela and Colombia, with a duty to be the liberator of Latin America. He did not linger long in Caracas. He had wider ambitions. He had sent one of his officers, General Antonio José de Sucre y Alcala, south that year to assist in the liberation of Ecuador. Sucre had gone to the Pacific port of Guayaquil, and was now in need of assistance.

Again leaving Santander in charge in Bogotá, Bolívar marched south in December 1821 along the mountain road towards Quito, the capital of Ecuador. His military campaign against the forces of Spain had still not finished. While Bolívar advanced from the north, Sucre advanced inland from Guayaquil in the west. Sucre's forces defeated the Spanish army at the battle of Pichincha on May 24, 1822, and Quito fell the following day. Bolívar arrived three weeks later, on June 16, and then moved down to Guayaquil.

The three territories of Gran Colombia were now liberated from Spanish rule. Argentina and Chile were also free, conquered by republican forces from Argentina led by General José de San Martín. Only Peru remained under Spanish control.

San Martín had marched into Lima from the south, and proclaimed Peruvian independence, but Spanish soldiers still controlled the cities of the Andes. San Martín travelled up the coast to Guayaquil to seek Bolívar's help in what would be the final attack on the Spanish army. The two generals met there on July 26, 1822, to discuss their requirements. San Martín needed assistance to defeat the Spaniards and to regain control over his own divided Argentinian forces stationed in Lima. Bolívar proved reluctant to take his side in this endeavour, and San Martín returned to Lima without receiving the support he had hoped for. Resigning all his positions, he left for exile in Europe, never to return.

A year later, in September 1823, Bolívar travelled down to Lima to prepare the final defeat of the Spanish army in the Andes. Assembling a fresh army, he defeated the Spaniards at the battle of Junín in 1824. The campaign finally came to an end on December 9 when the Spanish viceroy surrendered to Sucre at the battle of Ayacucho.

Sucre pursued the remnants of the Spanish army south along the Andes and into the country of Upper Peru, which, finally liberated in April 1825, was given the name Bolivia, in honour of the Liberator. Spanish Latin America was finally free from Spanish rule.

Bolívar moved on towards the Potosí mountain in Bolivia, pausing to be addressed by the mayor, José Domingo Choquehuanca, of a small village on the frontier:

You are the man of destiny. Nothing that has happened in the past bears any resemblance to your accomplishments. To imitate you, it would be necessary once again to liberate a world. You have created five republics, an achievement which, in its unprecedented demand for their development, shall lift your image to a height never yet reached by any human being. Your glory will grow with the centuries, as the shadows grow when the sun is setting.

Gerhard Masur, Bolívar's biographer, thinks that this speech must be apocryphal, but since it is a legend that is now encrusted in Venezuela's history, as well as being one of Chávez's favourite quotations, it deserves a place in this story.

Bolívar spent the remaining months of 1825 in Bolivia, returning at the end of the year to Lima, to be elected President of Peru in August 1826. His far-flung empire was now too large to be controlled by one general, as insoluble political problems arose in each separate state. Bolívar's dream of teaching Europe a lesson remained undimmed: 'Let us show Europe that America has men capable of emulating the glory of the heroes of the ancient world,' he told Sucre, as he ordered him to take charge of Bolivia.

Yet there was dissension in Peru, soon to be followed by war between Venezuela and Colombia. His two generals, Paez and Santander, quarrelled, and the ambitious project of a united Gran Colombia evaporated in 1828. The union of the two countries was split asunder, and Peruvian forces invaded Ecuador in 1829 in an attempt to capture Guayaquil.

Bolívar made one final effort to secure the political union of Latin America, at a Congress of Spanish-speaking states held in Panama in 1826. There were many absentees, and only Peru and Gran Colombia, and representatives from Mexico and Central America, took part. Political union was on the agenda, and the states present agreed to plan for a joint army and navy, but all such concrete schemes were stillborn. All that remained of the Congress of Panama was an enduring vision of what might one day be. Bolívar died of tuberculosis in December 1830, near Santa Marta in Colombia, on his way into exile in Europe.

'America is ungovernable,' he said at the end. 'Those in the service of the revolution have ploughed the sea.'

Hugo Chávez does not share Bolívar's pessimism. 'The contradictions in Bolívar's thought are not the determining factor,' he argues. 'What we can see in the period of history between 1810 and 1830 are the outlines of a national project for Spanish America.' That project was taken up again on occasion, notably by Ezequiel Zamora a quarter of a century after Bolívar's death. Chávez now plans to put it back onto the continental agenda.

15

ROBINSON CRUSOE AND THE PHILOSOPHY
OF SIMÓN RODRÍGUEZ

Hugo Chávez often refers to the 'Robinsonian system', and I thought at first that perhaps he was thinking of the work of the late Joan Robinson, the distinguished Cambridge economist with whom Latin American intellectuals were certainly familiar in the 1960s and 1970s. Then, inevitably, I thought of Robinson Crusoe, the fictional hero of Daniel Defoe, who hailed originally from York and lived for 'Eight and Twenty Years all alone in an uninhabited Island on the Coast of America, near the Mouth of the Great River of OROONOQUE'.

That turned out to be nearer the mark. The political and economic thinking of Chávez does indeed derive in part, by a circuitous route, from the story of Robinson Crusoe, and the impact that it made on Simón Rodríguez, a young Caracas schoolteacher in the 1790s. Rodríguez was first the teacher and later the close friend of Simón Bolívar, and the radical philosophy both men espoused, one influencing the other, lies at the heart of the Chávez project for Venezuela and for Latin America. Rodríguez was so struck by the story and character of Robinson Crusoe that he changed his name to Samuel Robinson.

The life and works of Simón Rodríguez, who was born in Caracas in 1769, are almost unknown outside Latin America, and his writings have never been translated into English, yet he had influence in several countries, living and working in Venezuela and Colombia, in Bolivia and Chile, and in Peru and Ecuador. He was a schoolteacher and an educational philosopher, a man with unorthodox ideas about education and commerce far in advance of his time. He also had a passionate belief in the need to integrate the indigenous peoples of Latin America, and the black slaves brought from outside, into the societies of the future independent states. Two hundred years later, his words and ideas have a contemporary ring – and have been resurrected by Hugo Chávez.

Daniel Defoe's story about Robinson Crusoe's adventures was based on the true-life adventures of Alexander Selkirk, who was marooned on Juan Fernández island in the Pacific. Defoe simply changed the island to one in the Atlantic, off the Orinoco river. The book was first published in London in 1719, and translated into French and Dutch the following year. It must eventually have been available on the banks of the Orinoco itself, in Venezuela, although it is possible that Latin Americans first read the German version of the story written by Joachim Heinrich Campe. *Robinson der Jüngere* by Campe was first published in Hamburg in 1769, and was destined to become one of the most famous German books of all time. It was written under the influence of Rousseau's *Émile, or Education*, which had suggested that *Robinson Crusoe* was a most excellent book for children in that it taught them to learn as Robinson had done, by doing.

Whichever version of the story arrived in Caracas, it was read by Simón Rodríguez, the teacher in charge of the town council's primary school. Among his young pupils, and at one stage his lodger, was Bolívar, the orphaned son of a wealthy land-owning family.

Rodríguez's first primary school soon ran into trouble with the city fathers. He had written and published a long memorandum suggesting that his school should be not just for the children of wealthy whites, but for the children of blacks and *pardos* (those of mixed race) too. This concern with the underclass remained with him all his life, and caused him endless pain and trouble. He was a hundred years ahead of his time. Years later, when working in Bolivia in the 1820s, he was to insist that the children of Indians should be provided with free education in the public schools he was setting up. The authorities soon found an excuse to close them down.

Dismissed by the Caracas council, Rodríguez became involved in the early independence movement of 1797, organised by Manuel Gual and

José María España. When this premature revolt was crushed, Rodríguez was forced into exile. He sailed across the Caribbean to Jamaica, arriving a couple of years after the British colonial government had crushed a great rebellion of maroons. In Jamaica he learned English. He thought of his new home as 'the island of Robinson Crusoe' and, anxious to shake off his own Spanish antecedents, he changed his name from Simón Rodríguez to Samuel Robinson. He kept the pseudonym for a quarter of a century, throughout the years he remained outside the continent.

Leaving Jamaica, he travelled on to the United States, and then to Europe. 'I stayed in Europe for more than twenty years,' he wrote years later when asked to describe his peregrinations. 'I worked in a laboratory as an industrial chemist where I learnt a thing or two; I joined a number of secret societies of a socialist nature ... I studied a little literature, I learnt a few languages, and I taught in a primary school in a small village in Russia.'

Samuel Robinson might well have been an interesting but forgotten footnote in the intellectual history of Latin America had his path not crossed for a second time that of Simón Bolívar. The two men, teacher and pupil, met again in Napoleon's Paris in 1804, and travelled together to Italy. Through his friendship with Robinson, Bolívar met Alexander von Humboldt, the German scientist who had explored the Orinoco; his tutor also gave him the writings of the Enlightenment to read. Years later, when fighting in Peru, Bolívar wrote of his feelings for his 'Robinson':

> I love this man madly. He was my teacher and my travelling companion; he is a genius. He has an extraordinary wit, and a talent for learning and criticism ... He is a teacher who instructs through entertaining, and a writer who instructs through example. He means everything to me. When I used to know him, he was worth the world. He would have to have changed a lot for me to be mistaken in my judgement.

While in Rome, in August 1805, these two independent-minded Venezuelans climbed the slopes of the Monte Sacro, the hilly promontory above the river Aniene north-east of Rome, where a bottling plant still dispenses *acqua santa* from an ancient spring. Here Bolívar took a romantic oath, swearing to devote his life to the independence struggle of Latin America. Long after Bolívar was dead, Rodríguez recalled the words of the oath and wrote them down, doubtless with some fictional embellishment. They remain deeply ingrained in the Venezuelan psyche, learnt by schoolchildren and committed to memory by Venezuelan soldiers performing their military service. When Chávez came to organise a conspiracy of his own in the 1980s, it was to the words of Bolívar, remembered by Simón Rodríguez, that he turned:

> I swear before you, and I swear before the God of my fathers, that I will not allow my arm to relax, nor my soul to rest, until I have broken the chains that oppress us ...

Bolívar returned to South America in 1806, to take up the challenges of the independence struggle. Samuel Robinson remained behind, still intrigued by Napoleon's Europe. He set off on further travels, visiting and living in Italy and Germany, Prussia and Poland, and Russia. Somewhere along the way he must have joined the 'secret societies of a socialist nature' that he writes about.

Eventually, in 1823, he abandoned his Russian school and arrived in London. There, in the house in Grafton Way that had once belonged to Francisco Miranda and was still occupied by Miranda's widow, he met the philosopher and poet Andrés Bello, another exile from Venezuela. Bello, who was also an educationalist, encouraged him to return home now that Latin America's independence was almost secured.

Samuel Robinson, by then aged fifty-four, sailed back across the Atlantic, landed at the Colombian port of Cartagena, and changed his name back to Simón Rodríguez. Travelling on to Bogotá, he received news from Bolívar, who was then engaged in the conquest of Peru: 'Oh, my teacher, my friend, my Robinson, you are in Colombia, you are in Bogotá, and you have not told me!' Bolívar urged him to hurry down to meet him in Lima. The two old friends were reunited in Lima in 1824, shortly after the battle of Ayacucho which settled the fate of the Spanish empire in Latin America.

We do not know exactly what they discussed, though we do have a very clear picture of how the ideas of Simón Rodríguez developed in the years after his return to Latin America from Europe. His European experience had convinced him that America would have to try to do things differently. In one of his first books, published in 1828, he wrote about the need for difference, and this has become one of the keys to the thinking of Hugo Chávez:

> Spanish America is an original construct. Its institutions and its government must be original as well, and so too must be the methods used to construct them both. Either we shall invent, or we shall wander around and make mistakes – *O inventamos o erramos*.

In April 1825, Rodríguez joined Bolívar on an expedition across the Andes into the newly named country of Bolivia. From Lima, they passed through Arequipa, Cuzco, Tinta, Lampa, Puno, and Zepita; once in Bolivia, they travelled on to La Paz, Oruro, Potosí and Chuquisaca (later to be called Sucre, after the victor at Ayacucho).

Bolívar decided that the country to which his name had been given was a place that would benefit from the talents of Rodríguez. He appointed him to be the Director of Public Education and Director-General of Mines, Agriculture and Public Roads. The two friends then separated – Bolívar returned to Peru, while Rodríguez remained in Bolivia. Rodríguez was soon at work in Chuquisaca on the formation of a technical school for local children, Indians as well as whites. Years later, he outlined the extraordinarily ambitious and far-sighted plans he had tried to implement in Bolivia:

> My project at that time was a well-thought-out scheme designed to colonise America with its own inhabitants. I wanted to avoid what I feared might eventually happen one day; that's to say, the sudden invasion of European immigrants with more knowledge than our own people; this would result in them being enslaved once again, and subjected to a worse

tyranny than that of the old Spanish system. I wanted to rehabilitate the indigenous race and to prevent it from being entirely exterminated.

Tragically for Bolivia, the conservative citizens of Chuquisaca rejected the imaginative schemes of Rodríguez out of hand. They had only with reluctance accommodated themselves to republican rule. Soon some of the worst fears of Rodríguez were realised. The old land-owning class remained in place, and summoned fresh immigrants from Europe. These took their turn at slaughtering and destroying the indigenous peoples, notably during the rubber boom at the end of the nineteenth century. Rodríguez's revolutionary project – the education of the Indians – might have changed the subsequent history of Bolivia, but it was not to be.

Even in Venezuela, the post-independence governments encouraged white immigration from Europe on a huge scale, long before the white settlers had come to terms with the country's aboriginal inhabitants. More than a million European immigrants came to Venezuela after the end of the Second World War in 1945.

Rodríguez set up his school in Chuquisaca and then left on a trip to Cochabamba, where he hoped to establish a new school on the same model. His passion for the education of the Indians was deeply rooted in his appreciation, almost unique at that time, of the role that the underclass played in the country's development. He wrote in 1830 of the debt that could never be repaid:

The scholars of America have never revealed the fact that they owe their knowledge to the Indians and the blacks; for if these scholars had had to plough and sow and reap, and to gather up and prepare everything that they eat and wear and use and play with during their valueless lives, they would not know so much …

They would have been working in the fields, and would have been just as brutish as their slaves; they would have been working with them in the mines, in the fields behind the oxen, and on the roads behind the mules, in the stone quarries, and at hundreds of tiny workshops where they make ponchos and coats, and ropes, and shoes and cooking pots.

Rodríguez knew of the hostility of the whites; he had encountered it thirty years earlier in his school in Caracas. Now it was to affect him again. When he returned to Chuquisaca from Cochabamba, he found that his school had been closed down on the orders of President Sucre, the former general of Bolívar.

Sucre was under pressure from the local Bolivian elite. He complained that Rodríguez was a hopeless organiser and had failed to keep his school within budget. This certainly may have been true. But the real cause of the closure was the racist attitudes of the Chuquisaca authorities, and the white parents who did not like their children to be educated with Indians. Rodríguez later explained what had happened to the school:

> A lawyer named Calvo destroyed my establishment in Chuquisaca, saying that I had exhausted the treasury in order to maintain whores and thieves, instead of devoting my efforts to giving a polish to decent folk.
>
> The whores and the thieves were the children of the real owners of the country, that is, the *cholitos* and *cholitas* who used to run around in the streets and would by now have been considerably more 'decent' than the boys and girls of Señor Calvo.

Depressed by the reception he had received, Rodríguez resigned all his posts in Bolivia and retreated to Lima, perhaps in search of Bolívar. The two men never met again, and there is some suggestion that letters written by Rodríguez to Bolívar never got through to the Liberator. For some years, he sustained himself, and the Bolivian *cholita* he had made his wife, by establishing a candle factory in Ecuador.

Then, in 1834, perhaps summoned by Andrés Bello, he left Ecuador for Chile. There he lived and worked for many years, first in Concepción and later in Valparaiso. He set up technical schools, teaching his pupils to read and write, and then showing them how to make bricks and tiles, and candles – learning through doing. He is often remembered for causing a scandal by his method of teaching anatomy. Since there were no spare corpses, he would himself appear naked in the classroom.

After ten years in Chile, in 1843, he returned to Ecuador, living in the small town of Latacunga. There, in 1847, he set down his views on labour and trade:

> The division of labour in the production of goods only serves to brutalise the workforce. If to produce cheap and excellent nail scissors, we have to reduce the workers to machines, we would do better to cut our fingernails with our teeth.

Rodríguez died in 1852. The year before his death, he wrote of his belief in the desirability of an agrarian revolution:

> If the [Latin] Americans would like the political revolution that the weight of events has created, and whose survival the force of circumstance has permitted, to bring genuine benefits, they must make a genuine economic revolution and they must start in the rural areas: from there the revolution should move on to the industrial workshops. In this way, daily improvements will be observed that could never have been obtained if a start had been made in the cities.

Rodríguez had one further thought:

> The Americans must conquer their reluctance to join together to achieve something, and their fear of seeking advice before moving forward. He who does nothing will never make mistakes; yet it is far better to wander around and make mistakes than to go to sleep.

It is not difficult to see why a revolutionary like Chávez, anxious to revive a nationalist discourse in the age of globalisation, should have wished to resurrect the life and writings of this extraordinary man. Simón Bolívar, one of Chávez's other heroes, was much in debt to the old friend he called Samuel Robinson. And so are we all today.

16

EZEQUIEL ZAMORA INVOKES
'HORROR A LA OLIGARQUÍA'

The third exemplary figure recovered by Hugo Chávez from the troubled history of Venezuela in the nineteenth century is that of Ezequiel Zamora, leader of the federal forces in the civil wars of the 1840s and 1850s. Zamora was a provincial radical, a trader who became a soldier and a strategist. He had a far-reaching programme of land reform for the benefit of the peasants, a passionate hostility to the land-owning oligarchy, a project for combining soldiers and civilians in his struggles, and a desire to fulfil the Bolivarian dream of uniting his troops with like-minded forces across the border in Colombia. The aims of this nineteenth-century revolutionary all fit neatly into Chávez's own programme.

Zamora has sometimes been claimed by the left in Venezuela as an early socialist. There is some evidence to suggest that this charismatic soldier, this 'General of the Sovereign People' as he described himself, who was originally a provincial shopkeeper, acquired considerable knowledge of the revolutionary upheavals in Europe in his time through his brother-in-law, Juan Gaspers, an immigrant from Alsace. Zamora was certainly familiar with the slogan of 'liberty, equality, and fraternity', which he used from time to time, and he was well informed about the European events of 1848. Socialist or not, he was unquestionably a progressive liberal, and a man with advanced opinions for his time and place.

Like Douglas Bravo and the guerrilla movements of the 1960s, who named one of their guerrilla fronts in honour of Zamora, Chávez had long been attracted to Zamora's radical programme, and would discuss it during his lectures at the military college in Caracas in the 1980s. He had been familiar with the story since childhood, for the final campaign of the soldier–revolutionary in 1859 was fought across the territory of Chávez's home state of Barinas.

Little survives in writing of Zamora's ideas, but oral traditions collected by Chávez personally, when stationed at Elorza in the *llanos*, sustain the received wisdom that this was a man with a strong sense of solidarity with the rural poor. His appeal to the insurgent peasantry was based on three slogans, often recalled by Chávez:

Tierra y hombres libres; Land and free men;

Elección popular; General elections;

Horror a la oligarquía! Hatred towards the oligarchy.

For many years after his death, and the victory of his conservative opponents, the name of Zamora was held in low esteem. The local oligarchy, says Chávez, never forgave Zamora for the action he took against their interests when he sacked the town of Barinas. He ordered that the building holding the archives of land titles should be burnt to the ground. He wanted the land seizures of the peasants to be freed from retrospective legal action by the landowners.

Rómulo Gallegos, writer and once briefly president of *Acción Democrática*, muddied the republican waters by comparing Zamora with José Tomás Boves (1782–1814), the uncompromising leader of the *llaneros*, the cowboys of the Orinoco, who fought with the Spanish royalists against Bolívar in 1814, and captured Caracas from the republicans. In his novel *Pobre Negro*, published in 1937, Gallegos describes how Zamora had once been welcomed by the village crowds: 'It is Boves who is coming back, said the old men, and he now calls himself Ezequiel Zamora. Like Boves, he knows how to sweep the people along with him ...'

The strength of Boves lay in his capacity to mobilise the oppressed classes, the slaves and the Indians, against the republicans. According to José Ambrosio Llamozas writing in 1815:

From the start of his campaign he revealed the nature of the strategy he was following and from which he never diverted: it was based on the destruction of all the whites, while rescuing and preserving and flattering the coloureds … The houses and the goods of those who were killed or exiled would be handed out to the *pardos*, who would also receive title to the land.

This was *horror* to the *oligarquía* indeed! When Boves finally captured republican Caracas in July 1814, he destroyed the town, forcing Bolívar to escape into exile in Jamaica. Boves did not long survive: he was killed later in the year.

Zamora was a popular leader, and he certainly proclaimed 'hatred towards the oligarchy', but there is no evidence that he mounted the kind of uncompromisingly racist campaign favoured by the *llanero* cowboy. Yet he certainly bequeathed a conflictive legacy. The state of Barinas, once known as Zamora state, was later renamed by local landlord politicians who disliked seeing Zamora commemorated in this way. Zamora's statue in the Plaza Zamora in Barinas was taken down and thrown into the San Domingo river that runs alongside the square.

All this was part of the family history of Chávez. He recalls that in 1960, at the age of six, he used to listen to the stories told him by his grandmother, Rosa Chávez, in her house in Sabaneta. She in turn would remember the stories that she had been told in the 1920s by her grandfather, a man who had accompanied Zamora on his march through Barinas in 1859. Here, at Santa Inés, Zamora had secured his greatest victory. Outside Sabaneta, Zamora had crossed the river Bocono at a ford, and here the youthful Chávez would go with his father to fish and to swim. Sometimes he would go with his schoolfriends to the battle-field of Santa Inés itself, always in the hope of finding old bayonets in the sand.

The battle of Santa Inés was Zamora's 'masterpiece', writes Malcolm Deas, a historian at Oxford, 'an elaborate affair of entrenched ambuscades'. Deas argues that Zamora's 'reputation as an egalitarian reformer rests on little more than an extraordinary *don de gente*, a gift for getting on with all classes, just as his military ascendancy came entirely from ability in the field'. Yet there is no doubt that Chávez is right to claim Zamora as a visionary radical with the needs of the peasants at the heart of his programme for transforming the country's rural economy. Among his concrete proposals that have survived is his four-point plan for the peasantry:

1. the five leagues around each village or town, at all points of the compass, to be set aside for common use;
2. the system of assessing rents on agricultural land to be abolished;
3. the wages of labourers to be fixed in accordance with their work;
4. ten milking cows to be farmed out by the landowners on common land, to provide free milk each day to the homes of the poor.

Whatever the specific proposals in his programme, Zamora has remained in popular legend as one of Venezuela's most dashing leaders of the nineteenth century. He was not as bloodthirsty as Boves, but he had a similar capacity to mobilise people for action, as indeed does Chávez.

Zamora was born in February 1817 in Cúa in Miranda state. His father had died in the wars of independence, and his family moved to Caracas when he was quite young. Zamora subsequently returned to the *llanos*, and earned his living there as a cattle dealer for some years before opening a general store in Villa de Cura.

He became an outspoken supporter of the liberal cause in the epoch of Antonio Leocádio Guzmán, the founder of the Liberal party, and a powerful opponent of the landed oligarchy grouped around the figure of José Antonio Páez, the great long-surviving conservative caudillo who had fought with Bolívar. After a typically fraudulent election in his home town in 1846, Zamora launched an attack on the forces of the landowners, allying himself with one of the great native leaders of the *llanos*, José Rangel, 'el Índio'.

Zamora and Rangel organised the local peasants and slaves into a scratch force, and called it the Army of the Sovereign People, but they were defeated at the battle of Laguna del Piedra in 1847. Zamora and Rangel were captured and sentenced to death. Rangel was killed with blows from a machete, but Zamora was reprieved and given a ten-year prison sentence. Escaping near Maracay, on his way to the prison at Maracaibo, he found work as a labourer on an hacienda until he was granted an amnesty the following year.

He then enrolled in the Liberal Army of José Tadeo Monagas, and continued the fight against the landowners. In 1849 his troops brought Páez in chains to Caracas, and in 1851 he became the military commander in Coro. In 1854, when the slaves were finally granted their freedom, Zamora campaigned, albeit unsuccessfully, against the provision of compensation to the slave-owners.

The landowners' defeat was only temporary, and soon they came back, led by President Julián Castro. Zamora and other liberal leaders went into exile in the Caribbean, but in October 1858, a group of exiles formed a Patriotic Junta and planned a rebellion. They were to be led by General Juan Cristóstomo Falcón, whose sister Zamora had married.

Zamora returned to the mainland, making a successful attack on Coro in February 1859. His subsequent campaign in the west was to last until his death, ten months later, at the battle of San Carlos. His greatest success, at Santa Inés in December 1859, caused the government forces led by Pedro Ramos to retreat to Mérida, leaving the states of Coro, Barinas, and Portuguesa in the hands of the federal forces.

Chávez frequently refers to the battle of Santa Inés in his speeches (and he was thrilled to discover on a visit to Havana that Fidel Castro knew all about it). When urging the citizen to vote 'yes' in the referendum campaign for the new constitution, held on December 15, 1999, Chávez made a speech describing the battle ahead, and compared his own position with that of Zamora:

> At the battle of Santa Inés, Zamora pretended that his troops were retreating, allowing those of the 'no' camp to advance and to take Barinas without firing a shot. Zamora, from the 'yes' camp, had prepared an ambush, launched a counter-attack, and hit them with a terrific blow, pursuing them as far as Mérida.

Chávez's aim was to repeat Zamora's success at the referendum, as indeed he did.

Chávez also claims Zamora as a link in the chain that connects the project of Bolívar with the programme that he wishes to pursue. Zamora is seen by Chávez as following in the footsteps of Bolívar, pursuing the goal of Latin American unity through an integral alliance with Colombia:

> In Zamora you will find the same Bolivarian geo-political thinking about the unity of Latin America; he had tried to link up his forces with those who were fighting for the Federation in Colombian territory across the Apure river. On May 19, 1859, in a proclamation to the peoples of Barinas and Apure, he described 'the new era of the Colombian Federation that was now opening up, that had been the final wish of our Liberator, the great Bolívar'.

Zamora has one further characteristic that Chávez has invoked. In a painting of Zamora by José Ignacio Chaquett, after the battle of Santa Inés, and one that has sometimes been copied by Chávez, the warrior-hero is depicted in profile wearing two hats, one placed rather unusually on top of the other. One is an ordinary bowler (*sombrero*), the other is a military cap (*képis*). For Zamora, the purpose of his outfit was to symbolise the unity of the people and the armed forces in their efforts 'to make the Revolution'. In his aim of restructuring the relationship between civil society and the armed forces, Comandante Chávez tries to maintain this tradition.

Zamora's legend survives today in the couplets of a military song from the era of the Federal wars. These were written down by and put to music by Domingo Castro, a musician in his army:

> El cielo encapotado anuncia tempestad,
> Y el sol tras de las nubes pierda su claridad.
> !Oligarcas temblad, viva la libertad!
> Las tropas de Zamora al toque de clarín,
> Derrotan las brigadas del godo malandrín.
> The overcast sky warns of the storm to come,
> While the sun behind the clouds loses its bright shine,
> Oligarchs tremble, long live freedom!
> The troops of Zamora, at the bugle's sound,
> Will destroy the brigades of the reactionary scoundrels.

In an account of Zamora's great battle at Santa Inés, Román Martínez Galindo complains that today's generation of Venezuelan children are overly influenced by television, and television from the United States at that. Martínez laments the fact that they are 'more familiar with "the conquest of the West", "the annexation of Texas", or "the American civil war between the north and the south"' than they are with the war of the *federales* in nineteenth-century Venezuela. Zamora's story, he suggests, is 'an episode in our history of singular importance, written by our nearest forebears, which we ought to know about if we really want to know who we are'.

Martínez Galindo expresses the hope that one day 'the talented film-makers of Venezuela will decide to rescue us from the cowboy movies of colonialism, from the Marines and the Green Berets ... and we shall be able to see the General of the Sovereign People at the cinema, playing his bugle at the front of his troops as they sing: *!Oligarchas temblad!*'

PART FOUR:
ORGANISING THE OVERTHROW OF
THE *ANCIEN RÉGIME* BY PEACEFUL MEANS,
1992–1998

17

YARE PRISON AND THE SEARCH
FOR POLITICAL ALLIES

For his part in organising the coup attempt of February 1992, Colonel Chávez was given a long prison sentence. In practice, he was only locked up for two years, from February 1992 to March 1994. Imprisoned first in San Carlos, he was moved later to San Francisco de Yare. He was well treated in prison, looked after in a manner befitting a distinguished officer. He was allowed to be interviewed on radio and television, and to receive many visitors, some of whom were to play an important role in his political formation, and later in his government. He also had time to read and to think, and to consider more fully the nationalist foundations of his political philosophy.

While Chávez was still in prison, a number of dramatic events took place on the national stage. President Carlos Andrés Pérez, who had survived the two military coups of 1992, was finally removed from power in June 1993 by what was, in effect, a congressional coup. He had lost the support of the old guard in *Acción Democrática*, his own party. Ganging up against him in Congress, they accused him of corruption, and, with two of his ministers, he was forced to resign from office. He was replaced for what was left of his term by Ramón J. Velásquez, a distinguished historian.

When fresh presidential elections were held in December 1993, Colonel Chávez called on his supporters to abstain, and many of them did so. The voting pattern was of little comfort to the established parties. When Pérez had been elected in December 1988, a quarter of the potential voters had abstained. In December 1993, the abstention rate rose to 40 per cent, a rather larger percentage of the electorate than the miserable 30 per cent that actually voted for the eventual winner, former president Rafael Caldera.

The political strength of the old parties was crumbling. The economic crisis, the *Caracazo*, the two attempted *coups d'état*, and their own internal dissensions were paving the way for catastrophe. Almost for the first time in Venezuelan politics, the four principal candidates received a similar slice of the vote. Claudio Fermín for *Acción Democrática* received 23.60 per cent, Oswaldo Alvarez Paz for *Copei* received 22.73 per cent, and Andrés Velásquez for *La Causa R* received 21.95 per cent. Only Caldera, with 30 per cent, managed to edge ahead, and everyone recognised that he owed his victory to his famous speech to Congress in February 1992, in which he virtually legitimised the Chávez coup. By innate political skill or by simple good fortune, Caldera had conducted his campaign as an independent, forming a group called Convergencia which was allied with the *Movimiento al Socialismo* (MAS). Once the founder of Copei, he had abandoned his old party, and they had abandoned him.

Although Caldera was the winner by a short head, he did not have anything resembling a majority in Congress. His government was hamstrung from the start, and he was obliged to beg for support from Luís Alfaro Ucero, the leader of *Acción Democrática*.

Political scientists began to talk for the first time in terms of the 'messianic' nature of Venezuela's political culture. Caldera was seen as the magician of the moment, rather as Pérez had been in 1988. Caldera was the man who might put the country back together again, against all the odds. Later in the 1990s, so desperate had the political situation become that miracle candidates appeared on all sides. One was to be Irene Sáez, the former beauty queen who became mayor of the Caracas district of Chacao. Another was to be Colonel Chávez.

New forces were now emerging in the country. One important feature of the election of 1993 was the large vote of *La Causa R*, the radical workers' party in Bolivar state, whose programme had already had some influence on Chávez. This now became the third largest force in the country after the two main parties. The two largest parties together got fewer votes than the two smaller, and more recent, configurations, Caldera's Convergencia (which included the Movement to Socialism) and *La Causa R.*

The two left-wing parties were now significant players on the national stage. The Movement to Socialism decided to jump in with Caldera, while *La Causa R* decided to wait awhile. Both were eventually, after serious splits, to support Chávez.

The Movement to Socialism is a small but intellectually significant political organisation that has followed most of the ups and downs of comparable socialist movements in Europe, oscillating between 'euro-communism' and social democracy. A large proportion of the intellectual left in Venezuela has moved in or out of MAS during its thirty-year existence, and its fierce internal dissensions have provided most of the raw material for what passes in Venezuela for political debate.

Established early in the 1970s by former members of the Communist Party, some of whom had fought in the guerrilla movements of the 1960s, its most articulate spokesman and several times presidential candidate was Teodoro Petkoff. Disenchanted with the guerrilla struggle, and disillusioned with Communism by the Soviet invasion of Czechoslovakia in 1968, Petkoff slowly slid to the right politically, though his actions were always informed by a strong moral sense of what it was right to do at any given moment. During the crisis of the 1990s, he thought it was his job to steer the MAS towards Caldera's rather abject minority government. Petkoff himself played a key role in that government as the minister of planning, pushing through a number of neo-liberal reforms. He was joined in this endeavour by Pompeyo Márquez, another well-known former Communist and MAS supporter, who became Caldera's minister for frontiers.

President Caldera acknowledged his political debt to Colonel Chávez, which had given him the edge over other candidates, and he gave orders early in his presidency for those involved in the two military coups of 1992 to be released. Chávez came out of prison on Palm Sunday, March 27, 1994.

During his time in prison Chávez, like Caldera, had been looking around for political allies. He had renewed his contacts with a number of civilian figures he had encountered before the coup. Luís Miquilena was a frequent visitor, of course, as well as others from the Patriotic Front formed in 1989. Chávez also talked to people from the MAS and from *La Causa R*, but he seems to have drawn the line at *Bandera Roja* (Red Flag), a *groupuscule* that still championed the armed struggle and had some claim to be an heir to the guerrillas of the 1960s. Chávez never had much time for the ultra-left:

> Groups like them appear to have given themselves the holy mission of proclaiming themselves to be the only revolutionaries on the planet, or at any rate in this territory. And those who don't follow their dogmas are not considered genuine revolutionaries. I have never talked for more than five minutes with a single leader of *Bandera Roja*.

Although Petkoff was working with Caldera, another prominent figure in the MAS, Jorge Giordani, had become a regular visitor to the Yare prison. A radical economist, he had studied at the Institute of Development Studies at the University of Sussex in the days of the late Dudley Seers. He was now a professor at the Universidad Central in Caracas and at Cendes, and the economic guru of the MAS. He had refused to support Caldera and was now to become one of Chávez's principal economic advisers. Many of the half-formulated economic ideas of Chávez came from his interaction with Giordani, who became minister of development in the Chávez government in 1999, in charge of Cordiplan, the ministry of economic planning and coordination.

The MAS was not synonymous with Petkoff by any means, and when the possibility of a Chávez presidency emerged over the horizon in 1998, Giordani and a majority of the MAS supported Chávez. Petkoff was still a minister in Caldera's government, and had no desire to jump ship. He was also clearly in complete disagreement with the political proposals of Chávez in almost every sphere. But the rest of his party signed up with Chávez.

When asked why MAS had supported his presidential bid, Chávez noted that the leadership had been rather reluctant, but had been put under pressure from the rank and file. Interviewed by Agustín Blanco Muñoz in June 1998, he claimed that the membership had probably supported him for quite a long time:

> When I came out of prison at Yare, during the extensive journeys that I made through the country, the people from the MAS were always there, always hoping to talk. I'm sure that most of the political base of the MAS, the political structure that exists all over the country, were always on our side, and had never agreed with the strategy of supporting the [Caldera] government, and even less with the subsequent decisions taken by the leadership ... I think that they were able to put sufficient pressure on the leaders of the party to enable them to make a decision that was more in line with the party's roots: its original projects of social justice, equality, freedom, democracy, and the democratic revolution. Those were the slogans that I used to hear when I was a schoolboy in Barinas at the time when the MAS was born. That was about the same year, in 1971, that I joined the army.

Chávez made the acquaintance of another intriguing political operative in the early 1990s, a historian from Argentina called Norberto Ceresole. A man with roots on the left, Ceresole had subsequently moved to positions more closely identified with the right, and Chávez's early connections with Ceresole often used to be cited to indicate the reactionary nature of his views.

Ceresole claimed to have been a member in the 1970s of the Montoneros, the Peronist guerrilla group that sprang to prominence during the government of Juan Domingo Perón in the 1970s and that of his widow, Isabel. Subsequently Ceresole was to argue in favour of the military coup against President Isabel Perón in 1976 by General Jorge Videla, and to claim that the human rights organisations that criticised the excesses of Argentina's 'dirty war' were part of a 'Jewish plot' against the nation. Ceresole was the author of many books. One of them, *La conquista del imperio americano*, published by Al-Andalus in

Madrid in 1998, contains a powerful denunciation of 'the Jewish financial mafia' behind American capitalism.

Ceresole was undoubtedly useful to Chávez at this early stage because of his well-established historical interest in 'progressive' military governments. As a radical Peronist, Ceresole looked back to Nasser and Ataturk, and he had also written books in support of the Peruvian Velasco Alvarado and the Panamanian Omar Torríjos. Ceresole had a number of connections with Arab governments that were to prove extremely useful. Yet a continuing friendship with this controversial Argentinian might have proved embarassing, and when Chávez became president, Ceresole was conveniently spirited out of the country. He returned to Buenos Aires where he died a few years later.

Ceresole had been a useful mentor at a particular moment. Ultimately more significant was the friendship that Chávez established with Fidel Castro soon after leaving prison. Chávez travelled to Havana in December that year; nearly a decade later, in a speech at the Social Forum in Porto Alegre in January 2003, he recalled that first visit:

> Fidel surprised me by meeting me at the airport from where we headed to the University of Havana for a meeting with the students … As the Bolivarian ideology was taking shape, I had a few points to make. I remember that, in answer to my words, Fidel said: 'the struggle for dignity is called Bolivarianism in Venezuela; in Cuba, this struggle is called socialism'.

Castro was always alert for potential allies on the mainland. Hugo Chávez was not to disappoint him. (See Appendix A, p. 277.)

18

POLITICS IN GUAYANA AND
THE RISE OF *LA CAUSA R*

Ciudad Bolívar, once called Angostura because of the narrowness of the Orinoco here, is a tiny colonial town perched high above the river on its southern shore. A tree-girt walk borders the river, with railings to prevent anyone falling victim to the crocodiles that were once such a feature of this strategic waterway. Walter Raleigh came here to Angostura, and so too did the German scientist and traveller Alexander von Humboldt, recovering for several weeks after a bout of fever.

Simón Bolívar was also based at Angostura, in the years before the town was renamed in his honour. He came here first in 1816 before his dramatic advance through the Andean passes to Colombia. Then in 1819 the Congress that he had assembled from the liberated peoples of the lands of the Orinoco and the shores of the Caribbean appointed him to be the president and military commander of the new state of Gran Colombia.

'Fortunate the citizen,' said Bolívar at the opening of the Angostura Congress, 'who, under the protection of arms, calls on national sovereignty to exercise its unrestricted will.' President Chávez was to quote the same words when he summoned a new Constitutional Assembly to draft a new constitution 180 years later, in 1999.

Angostura, Ciudad Bolívar, was once an important trading centre on the Orinoco, but today basks in the glory of its forgotten history. It still retains some significance as the capital of Bolívar state and as the gateway to the plains of the lower Orinoco and the eastern region of

Guayana. Beyond the town, a great motorway leads on to Ciudad Guayana, the centre of Venezuela's largest planned industrial complex, an area with a heroic, pioneering feel, reminiscent of the Soviet Union in its heyday. This is the powerhouse of Venezuela, a place where the state assumed responsibility for the development of heavy industry, and for the energy provision deemed necessary for a modern economy.

You might think that because Venezuela has so much oil it would have been content to build oil-fired power stations. But this is not so. Ambitious governments long ago decided to sell oil on the foreign market, and to develop hydro-electric power at home for local industry. The Guayana region now contains the second largest hydro-electric complex in the world, on the Caroní river at Guri. Only the Itaipú dam on the River Paraná, on the border between Brazil and Paraguay, is larger. Here too are the excavations of the immense iron mountain of Cerro Bolívar, the huge steelworks run by *Siderúrgica del Orinoco* (Sidor), and the embryonic aluminium industry. All these were set up and run by the all-powerful state.

To serve and manage these gigantic enterprises has required a huge labour force, attracted to the region from all over the country, and not surprisingly, the region has become famous for its radical politics. A powerful workers' movement, independent of the unions of the previous governments and developed over a period of thirty years, has furnished President Chávez with strong support.

Ciudad Guayana is the birthplace of *La Causa R*, a political organisation unique to Venezuela. Originally set up in the early 1970s, *La Causa R*, or Radical Cause, developed in 1997 into *Pátria Para Todos* (PPT), the Fatherland for Everyone, an integral part of Chávez's governing coalition. The PPT has provided the government with several of its most important ministers, and many of its most lucid ideas.

La Causa R was founded in the 1970s by Alfredo Maneiro, a guerrilla fighter of the Communist Party in the previous decade. Maneiro's group, like Teodoro Petkoff's MAS, had split away from the Communist Party in 1970 at the end of the guerrilla war. Maneiro, born in 1939, had been a member of the central committee of the party and a guerrilla commander on the eastern front. When the party splintered in the late 1960s, he was close to the Chinese position in the Sino-Soviet dispute, an attitude radically different from that of dissidents like Petkoff who were moving towards European-style social democracy. One of Maneiro's disciples was Pablo Medina, a labour organiser and an early and prominent civilian supporter of Chávez. Medina was elected to the Constitutional Assembly in 1999, but subsequently joined the opposition.

Maneiro's group participated in the formation of MAS in January 1971, but soon moved off in a new direction. Maneiro had been highly critical of the old Communist Party of the 1960s, and not just because of its ideology. He began to question the desirability of political parties themselves, and soon he had formulated an ideological position hostile to these organisational constructs. In a collection of articles, *Notas Negativas*, published in 1971, he outlined the political position of a new left-wing nationalist group he called Venezuela 83. It was the forerunner of the movement known as *La Causa R*.

The figure '83' was a reference to the year 1983. At that time, then more than a decade ahead, the foreign oil companies operating in Venezuela would be required, according to the terms of a treaty signed in 1944, to hand over their concessions to the Venezuelan state. This was an event which Venezuelan nationalist opinion looked forward to with keen anticipation. (In practice, President Carlos Andrés Pérez, ever the populist demagogue, was able to advance the date to 1976, the year when the oil companies were finally nationalised.)

Maneiro's political aim – a highly original one – was to canalise the protest movements of the people without the creation of a party political structure. The historian Margarita López Maya has described his project thus:

He said it was necessary both to create a political framework for the extraordinary and spontaneous mobilising capacity of the masses, and to participate in the infinite and varied forms of a popular movement; but this had to be done in the firm belief that the masses themselves would decide on their own political direction. Instead of starting with a given political structure, it was important to trust in the capacity of the popular movement to take on the task of producing a new leadership from within its ranks.

With this interesting and innovative political philosophy formulated and in place, Maneiro and his group decided to concentrate on three particular areas of popular mobilisation where the necessary vanguard leadership might eventually emerge. One was the student movement based at the Universidad Central in Caracas, an effervescent political organisation housed in the magnificent modernist buildings of Carlos Raúl Villanueva. With strong roots dating back over the generations to 1918, 1928, and 1958, as well as to 1968, the university had been associated for many years with the left. A second area of popular protest was the western Caracas suburb of Catia, with a mixed population of nearly a million people and considerable traditions of popular struggle.

Political activity on both these fronts – in the university and in Catia – was initially successful but eventually proved politically unrewarding. *La Causa R* concentrated its efforts on the third area chosen by Maneiro, the workers' movement in Ciudad Guayana associated with the state steel industry Sidor, *Siderúrgica del Orinoco*. A long strike there had left the workers highly politicised and critical of the government unions, controlled by *Acción Democrática*. Here the Maneiro philosophy was tested and found to be satisfactory.

The great public works of Ciudad Guayana – the Sidor steel works and the great dams on the Caroní river – were the fruit of decisions taken much earlier, in the 1950s, in the era of General Pérez Jiménez. The former dictator, a figure everyone preferred to forget, lived in exiled retirement in Spain until he died in September 2001 at the age of eighty-six. In the Miraflores palace in Caracas, a row of presidential portraits moves without any gap from Rómulo Gallegos (overthrown in 1948) to Rómulo Betancourt (who took power in 1958). Pérez Jiménez, who ruled in the ten years in between, became a non-person, removed from history. Yet he took many of the fundamental decisions that were to affect the Venezuelan economy for fifty years, decisions of such dimension and implication that no subsequent president ever had the courage or the opportunity to reappraise them until the 1990s.

Luís Miquilena, one of Chávez's earliest political advisers, had an interestingly ambivalent attitude towards Pérez Jiménez. Although a victim of the repression at that time, Miquilena later had an appreciative view of his achievements:

> The dictatorship had a rather more developed idea of what the country could be than the supporters of *Acción Democrática* had at that time. Pérez Jiménez established the foundations of our development – and I can say that with the authority of someone who was imprisoned for seven years during his rule. During that time, the steel industry was developed, and the principal roads in the country were laid down, indeed there was a plan and a concept of what the country ought to be that had never existed before.

These ideas, Miquilena claimed, were important, and they were only recovered 'when Chávez presented the idea of a establishing a new country by taking the democratic road'.

Venezuela's industrial development, envisaged by the Pérez Jiménez government, should have been a straightforward task. With cheap iron and bauxite, cheap electricity, and cheap transport on the Orinoco (as well as the proximity of a large market in the United States), the way forward appeared simple and attractive. Yet the state enterprises of Ciudad Guayana were to become the cause of endless economic headaches to successive governments, and, as with the Soviet Union, the disadvantages of state capitalism became increasingly apparent over the years.

The powerful state development agency in the area, the *Corporación Venézolana de Guayana* (CVG), became a state within a state, corrupt and bureaucratised. Industrial development had been financed from the rent from oil, but when the oil price collapsed in the 1980s, the economic ruin of the Guayana region became increasingly apparent.

On the surface, everything remained much the same. Great motorways plunged across the land, the vast steelworks at Sidor remained hard at work, the Pharaonic construction of the Guri dam was in full functioning order. Yet an examination of the books revealed the extent of the ruin. Money from oil revenues was channelled through to the political party in power in the region – in league with the unions (themselves a branch of a political party) – permitting gross overmanning. Huge debts were incurred without any thought as to how they might be paid off. Sidor employed six thousand more men than was economically justifiable. The hydro-electric plant at the Guri dam could not survive if it did not charge an economic price for the electricity it was producing. Other industrial plants required substantial fresh investment, and little was now available from the state. New money would have to come from the foreign investor, and that in turn would demand greater efficiency and more competition – a sea-change for state-coddled Venezuela.

Suddenly the workers of the region began listening to the spokesmen of *La Causa R.* Pablo Medina had been sent to Sidor as an activist years before, in January 1972. The climate for political activity then appeared propicious. The new city of Ciudad Guayana had become a magnet for unorganised migrant workers from all over the country, and the growth potential for a creative union organisation was rapidly made evident. Medina worked at the steelworks on the night shift; during the day he produced a newspaper, *El Matancero*, highly critical of the dominant *Acción Democrática* union.

The account of these early activities by Margarita López Maya describes how Medina's newspaper moved into areas of political struggle that had previously been neglected:

> *El Matancero* battled against the corruption of traditional unionism, and it also fought for the right of workers to democratic participation in union decisions that affected them – something previously unknown in the region – as well as in decisions concerning conditions and safety at the workplace – subjects never touched by other union leaders.

An early recruit to the cause, fulfilling Maneiro's ambition that a new leadership should arise from specific struggles, was Andrés Velásquez, a skilled electrician who later became a presidential candidate of the left. After five years of sustained political activity, in 1977, another recruit, Tello Benítez, secured an elected position in the steel-workers' union, Sutiss, the *Sindicato Unico de los Trabajadores de la Industria Siderúrgica y Similares*.

After nearly a decade of political work, the activists associated with *El Matancero* made a momentary breakthrough. At union elections in 1979, the *Matancero* slate, headed by Velásquez, won a controlling stake in the Sutiss union. It was a pyrrhic victory. Two years later, in 1981, Sutiss was 'intervened' by its parent federation, *Fetrametal*, an organisa-tion controlled by *Acción Democrática*. Velásquez and Benítez both lost their jobs at the steelworks. *La Causa R* was now at a low ebb, and soon its founding father was gone. Alfredo Maneiro died in November 1982, at the early age of forty-five.

Several more years elapsed before Sutiss was able to regain its inde-pendence, and the *Matancero* slate won again in 1988. The tide was turning, and for the first time *La Causa R* came to national prominence. In the congressional elections of 1988, three LCR candidates for deputy were successful. In December 1989, some nine months after the *Caracazo*, Andrés Velásquez was elected as the governor of Bolívar state. Three years later, in December 1992, he won again, and another LCR activist, Aristóbulo Isturiz, a prominent figure in the teachers' union, who had given veiled support to the Chávez coup, was elected mayor of Caracas. And in the presidential elections of December 1993, Velásquez won 22 per cent of the national vote. It was an extraordinary triumph.

The programme of Velásquez in 1990 provides some indication of the national ambitions of *La Causa R* at that time, and it also gives a flavour of the ideas that were later to inform Chávez's government.

According to the account by Margarita López Maya, it had four principal guidelines: the practice of democracy was to be understood not just in terms of elections, but in the actions of government itself; corruption was to be rooted out; and in the provision of services – especially in health, education, and social security – competence and transparency were to be secured.

The fourth guideline, which referred specifically to the development of the Guayana region, outlined criteria rather different from those conceived at the time by the Venezuelan state:

La Causa R rejected a strategy of sustaining the mega-projects involved in the export-oriented industry of primary products (iron, aluminium, and bauxite); and aimed instead on the downstream activities on the Orinoco, concentrating on medium-scale manufacturing industry that would transform raw materials within Bolívar state itself.

There were to be no more mega projects for which the state could no longer guarantee financing, and a lot more medium-scale enterprises that could be locally sustained. This is the intellectual legacy that *La Causa R* has bequeathed to the government of Hugo Chávez. Some writers have suggested that *La Causa R*, with its emphasis on workers and on unionism, bears some resemblance to the leftist *Partido de los Trabalhadores* of President Lula in Brazil. In practice, a more satisfactory parallel is with the Green parties in Europe, particularly in Germany. *La Causa R* is not in any way a traditional leftist party.

In the aftermath of the Chávez coup of 1992, *La Causa R* secured the support of one of its most prominent recruits, Francisco Arias Cárdenas, once the companion of Chávez in the Bolivarian Revolutionary Movement, and the officer who seized Maracaibo during the coup attempt. Arias Cárdenas was a native of the state of Zulia and in the 1996 elections for state governors he was elected to his home state as the candidate of *La Causa R*.

This was probably the high point of what had once been Maneiro's organisation. *La Causa R* subsequently became swamped by the spring tide of the Chávez phenomenon. Like all political movements in Venezuela, it was confronted with unexpected decisions. Should it support Chávez for president or reject him?

In February 1997 *La Causa R* divided into two different groups: a small rump remained with the name *La Causa R*, while a new and larger organisation came into being called *Patria Para Todos* (PPT), Fatherland for Everyone.

The division brought Andrés Velásquez into conflict with Pablo Medina. Velásquez remained with *La Causa R*, supported by Ana Brunswick, the widow of Alfredo Maneiro. Medina, supported by Aristóbulo Istúriz, Ali Rodríguez Araque and Alberto Müller, formed the PPT, and together they threw their weight behind the presidential campaign of Hugo Chávez.

The PPT became an important component of the *Polo Patriótico* alliance created to support the presidential bid of Hugo Chávez in 1998. At least five of its members were to play influential roles in the first years of the Chávez presidency. One was General Arias Cárdenas, the governor of the state of Zulia. Another was Ali Rodríguez, a former guerrilla comandante of the 1960s who in 1999 became the minister of energy. Yet another was Aristóbulo Istúriz, the vice-president of the Constitutional Assembly. Pablo Medina became the secretary-general of the PPT, while Alberto Müller became Chávez's ambassador in Santiago de Chile. Only three of them remained loyal to the Chávez project into the twenty-first century.

19

CHÁVEZ'S ELECTION VICTORY, DECEMBER 1998

Once out of prison in March 1994, Chávez began to consider his political future. When I talked to him in January 2000 he told me that he had already determined then that he would become president of Venezuela. At his first press conference a journalist had asked him what he was planning to do, and Chávez said: 'I am going to get into power.'

He was uncertain initially about his own participation in future elections. The old system was too corrupt and too weighted against newcomers. So he concentrated at first on the two principal items on his political agenda: the need to dissolve and replace the existing National Congress, and the need to elect a Constitutional Assembly to draft a new constitution.

Chávez's rejection of the existing political system was so deeply rooted that he opposed the candidature of Francisco Arias Cárdenas, his then friend and colleague, as governor of Zulia in 1996. Arias was not supported by Chávez's Bolivarian Revolutionary Movement (MBR-200), as he might have expected to be, but by *La Causa R.*

Early in 1997, Chávez's outlook began to change. His popular support was growing, and his conversations with *La Causa R* and with the MAS were prospering. Looking forward to the presidential elections of 1998, he had just two years in which to channel this support into an organisation capable of mounting an election campaign – and winning it. By July 1998, six months before the election, he had secured 45 per cent in the polls.

First he began to build his Bolivarian Revolutionary Movement into a structured political organisation, with both military and civilian support, announcing in January 1997 that his Movement would be in power 'before the year 2000'. In April he formally declared his intention to stand for the presidency.

The Movement held its first congress that month, and the delegates decided that they would field candidates in all the elections scheduled for December 1998 – for president and Congress, and for state governors and local mayors. The fight for power in Venezuela, Chávez told the delegates, would be between two poles: the 'patriotic pole' led by the Bolivarian Revolutionary Movement, and the 'pole of national destruction' led by the old political parties.

For a number of reasons, the Bolivarian Revolutionary Movement – which included serving as well as retired officers – seemed an unsuitable vehicle for the preparation of a civilian electoral campaign. There was opposition within the Movement about the electoral strategy. Some members argued that it would lead to an eventual watering down of their radical programme, as had already happened with progressive movements like the MAS and *La Causa R*.

Chávez himself argued that they should not miss the opportunity to campaign when so many elected positions were at stake. But in view of this internal opposition, he decided to keep the Movement as it was, and to create a new political grouping that could be organised into a campaigning organisation. In July this new organisation came into being as the *Movimiento Quinta República* (MVR), the Fifth Republic Movement. Venezuela needed to create a new republic, Chávez explained, and the new movement's name was designed to indicate a complete break with the past.

Venezuela had had four republics since the declaration of independence from Spain in 1811. Two were formed during the wars of independence: the Confederation of the States of Venezuela in 1811, and the Second Republic of 1813; the Third Republic was created at the time of the formation of Gran Colombia in 1819. The Fourth Republic, founded in Valencia in 1830 by Bolívar's general, José Antonio Páez, was to last the longest. Built, said Chávez, by 'a class of oligarchs and bankers on the bones of Bolívar and Sucre', Venezuela's Fourth Republic had always been dominated by conservatives opposed to the ideals of Bolívar.

The Fifth Republic that Chávez now aimed at founding would be the first new start for the country for 140 years. His Movement, he said, would have 'a national and popular character'. It would seek to recover the ideals of the past, and would be founded on the ideas of Bolívar:

> Its mission is to secure the well-being of the national community, to satisfy the individual and collective aspirations of the Venezuelan people, and to guarantee a state of optimum prosperity for the fatherland.

While it is tempting to imagine that Chávez may have been seeking to make a parallel with the changes wrought in France by General Charles de Gaulle after the collapse of the French Fourth Republic in 1958, it may be that for many Venezuelans the idea of a Fifth Republic was not unconnected in their minds with the millenarian notion of the Fifth Monarchy. Certainly the bookstores of Caracas were groaning with New Age material in the last years of the twentieth century, one book even suggesting that Venezuelans were a nation of the elect, specially chosen for the accomplishment of God's purposes.

The Fifth Monarchy Men who were politically active in Britain in the seventeenth century believed that the four monarchies of Babylon, Persia, Greece and Rome would soon be followed by the rule of the Saints. The projected utopia of the Saints would be marked by the abolition of tithes, the reform of the laws, the humbling of the rich, and the exaltation of the poor. Chávez's millenarian notion of a new start after the evils and corruption of the past must have struck a chord with the thousands of voters familiar with the language of Protestant preachers and Seventh Day Adventists.

Chiliastic movements have been relatively common in the Third World, and Chávez's campaign was partly directed towards that huge underclass which, in Venezuela as elsewhere in Latin America in recent years, has embraced the Protestant evangelical church in all its different varieties with unusual fervour, and in growing numbers. Several Chávez campaign posters carried portraits of the comandante that were indistinguishable in style from the millenarian religious pictures distributed by evangelical sects. Since Chávez speaks with the rhetoric of an evangelical preacher, invoking pain and love and redemption, the chiliastic nature of his popular appeal should not be underestimated.

To start with, the new Fifth Republic Movement was quite small. An estimated 60 per cent of its initial membership came from the military participants in the Bolivarian Revolutionary Movement, while about 40 per cent were independent civilians of no fixed ideology.

Early in 1998, the election year, the bandwagon began to roll. Other parties offered their formal support to the Chávez campaign. First on board, in March, was *Patria Para Todos*, a wing of *La Causa R*. It was followed in May by the Movement to Socialism. Both groups were to split in the process. The MAS lost two of its 'historic' leaders, Teodoro Petkoff and Pompeyo Márquez, while the PPT lost Andrés Velásquez, their leader in Guayana.

The new *chavista* alliance, called the *Polo Patriótico*, effectively drew a line under the history of MAS and *La Causa R*, the two left-wing parties that had split from the Communist Party in the early 1970s and slowly built up their strength as independent forces. From now on their ideas would survive and prosper, to fill the ideological vacuum within Chávez's MVR, which had little concrete to offer beyond its ill-defined nationalism and its chiliastic enthusiasms. Yet at the same time they signed the death warrant of their organisations as independent operators. With Chávez firmly in the saddle, seducing more than half the country to accompany him on a journey towards an obviously positive though uncertain destiny, the need for separate political organisations was no longer self-evident. Their important contribution was to have infused the MVR with their particular and differing brands of leftist ideology. Much of this had already been outlined in the development plan, the Bolívarian Alternative Agenda, a significant text that Chávez had published in 1995.

In July 1998, the *Polo Patriótico* began to discuss the crucial question of a political alliance. How would the individuals within its component parts secure their election to the Congress or as state governors and mayors, in the elections now scheduled for November? Overwhelmed by the need for unity, they overcame their individual party loyalties, and it was agreed that the *Polo Patriótico* would support a single candidate in each state.

As the support for Chávez became firmer and more united, so the unpopularity of the old political parties became ever more manifest. Indeed the bosses of *Acción Democrática* and *Copei* were nervous about putting forward a presidential candidate of their own. Chávez clearly had a huge advantage as an independent who had come from nowhere, and *Copei* began to look for a popular outsider with a chance of defeating Chávez. Their obvious candidate was Irene Sáez, a former beauty queen who had been the successful and innovative mayor of the wealthy Caracas zone of Chacao. Six months before the elections, Irene was given an approval rate in the polls of about 22 per cent. Having no candidate of its own, *Copei* decided to support her.

It proved a poisoned chalice. A few months later her ratings had slipped to just 2 per cent. She herself was quite popular. Her collapse was entirely due to her mistaken alliance with *Copei*. Not wholly understanding how much it was disliked, *Copei* now rapidly abandoned the beauty queen and transferred its support, just weeks before the election, to Henrique Salas Römer, the candidate of the last remaining conservative grouping, called *Proyecto Venezuela*. At that stage, Salas Römer was registering an approval rating of over 40 per cent, just below Chávez.

Changing candidates in the middle of the campaign, far from reinforcing the prospects of the chosen figure, merely reduced his chance of victory. To receive the official blessing of *Copei* was tantamount to receiving a curse against which there was no appeal.

If *Copei* had behaved shabbily towards Irene Sáez, the perfidy of *Acción Democrática* was even more striking. Initially, in Luís Alfaro Ucero, they had a candidate of their own, an ancient party warhorse with considerable political skills honed over the years. Yet by November 1998, within a month of the election, the party bosses were getting worried. Alfaro's approval rating in the polls was hovering around the 6 per cent mark.

The leadership of *Acción Democrática* decided to jump ship. They expelled Alfaro from the party to which he had given a lifetime's service, and they too joined *Copei* on the liferaft provided by the unfortunate Salas Römer. With these two millstones – support from the two most unpopular and discredited parties in the country – on board, Salas Römer was lucky to come second on December 6 with 39 per cent. Irene Sáez came third with 4 per cent, and Alfaro Ucero came fourth, with a negligible showing. Hugo Chávez romped home first with over 56 per cent of the vote.

The personal vote for Chávez and the Fifth Republic Movement he had created was so large that it utterly overwhelmed the constituent parties of the *Polo Patriótico*. They might have provided him with a leg up, and they might yet give him ideas and the outlines of a political programme. But essentially they were no longer necesssary. Chávez could operate on his own.

Chávez received 3,673,685 votes at the December election, or 56.20 per cent. Their breakdown, according to the numbers for each of the component parts of his electoral alliance, was as follows:

Movimiento Quinta Republica:	2,625,839	40.17%
Movimiento al Socialismo:	588,643	9.00%
Patria Para Todos:	142,859	2.19%
Partido Comunista de Venezuela:	81,979	1.25%
Five other small parties:	234,365	3.59%

Chávez was now the dominant personality in Venezuela, the maker and breaker of individual politicians and of political parties. Within four years, he had come from prison to the gates of the presidential palace. The old political system lay in ruins all about him. An entirely new era was about to begin.

PART FIVE:
CHÁVEZ IN POWER: THE EARLY YEARS

20

THE CONSTITUTIONAL ASSEMBLY AND
THE NEW CONSTITUTION

At a formal ceremony in Caracas on February 2, 1999, nearly seven years to the day since his failed military 'intervention', Hugo Chávez assumed the presidential sash of Venezuela in the presence of a number of other Latin American presidents. The immediate aims of his government were made clear on the first day. He would rewrite the constitution of 1961, and he would integrate the armed forces into the economic and social life of the country through a programme he baptised 'Plan Bolívar 2000'. His other ambitions remained to be spelt out.

In his first speech as president, Chávez announced that he would immediately sign a decree for a national referendum: the people should decide whether elections should be held for a Constitutional Assembly that would draft a new constitution. As if to escape from the widespread belief that he was a military dictator in the making, President Chávez was anxious from the start to make his every move subject to the will of the people. This was to be a year with an unprecedented number of elections; Chávez campaigners did well in all of them.

In November 1998, there were elections for the Congress. In December 1998, there was the presidential election in which Chávez secured 56 per cent of the vote. In April 1999, the referendum was held on the desirability of elections to a putative Constitutional Assembly; the 'Yes' campaign received 88 per cent of the vote. In July 1999, elections were held for this assembly; Chávez supporters, standing as independents, received 119 out of 131 seats, and 91 per cent of the vote. Finally, in December 1999, a second referendum ratified the new constitution drafted by the Constitutional Assembly: 71 per cent voted Yes and 28 per cent voted No. If Venezuelans had ever felt deprived of democratic practice, they were now in receipt of it in abundance, and fresh elections were scheduled for May 2000 to re-legitimise every elected official in the country (including the president) under the terms of the new constitution. A failure of the automatic voting system, introduced from the United States, led to a postponement of these elections until July, when Chavez was re-elected president with an increased majority, 59 per cent of the vote. His Bolivarian Revolutionary Movement won a majority in the new National Assembly, and 15 out of 23 state governorships. (Though often referred to in US media as the Venezuelan Congress, the new legislature that arose under the terms of the constitution of 1999 was called the National Assembly.)

An integral part of Chávez's thinking since the 1980s had been the need to rewrite the country's old constitution, and to elect a fresh Constitutional Assembly to undertake this task. He and his supporters understood clearly that this was not a job to be left to the Congress elected in 1998. A clean break with the past was essential. While the proposal appeared to be a fresh idea, the possibility of revising the old constitution of 1961 had been under consideration for a long time. The crisis of the political system had been brewing for many years, and the successive governments that made efforts to address it had considered the possibility of constitutional changes. A Presidential Commission for the Reform of the State (Copre) had been established as long ago as December 1984, during the *Acción Democrática* government of President Jaime Lusinchi.

Copre had reported on the popular dissatisfaction with *Acción Democrática* and *Copei*, and recommended a series of reforms: a fresh approach to electoral funding; the development of internal party democracy; an overhaul of the electoral system; and a project of political decentralisation. Lusinche took no action, but President Pérez dusted down the proposals after 1989. The closed-block system of voting, which had enabled the two main parties to keep a tight control over who got elected, was replaced with a more open arrangement under which voters knew who they were actually voting for. State governors and mayors were to be elected by direct and secret vote under a simple plurality system.

The result of these changes was a number of victories, at a local level, for minority parties. In elections for state governors in 1989, *La Causa R* won Bolívar state, and MAS won Aragua. Both parties secured a handful of seats in Congress. In 1992, *La Causa R* won Caracas, and in the presidential elections of 1993, third parties made a major breakthrough. Yet although welcome in themselves, the reforms had not been able to address the wider problem of the country's generalised political disenchantment, signalled by the high abstention rate.

In the crisis atmosphere after the *Caracazo*, a fresh attempt was made in June 1989 to reform the state by tackling the constitution itself. The left-wing Patriotic Front, set up by Luís Miquilena and others, had been among the first to demand the holding of a Constitutional Assembly that would rewrite the constitution of 1961 and establish 'a new republic'. The Congress embraced the idea, and set up a Special Joint Chamber Commision for the Revision of the Constitution, presided over by former president Caldera. Although the proposal had come from the left, the commission was dominated, inevitably, by members of the old parties, *Acción Democrática* and *Copei*, who had a majority in the Congress.

The commission's original aim was to produce a number of quick reforms to the existing Constitution, but its meetings dragged on interminably. Then, in the wake of the Chávez 'intervention' of February 1992, when the depth of the political crisis was once again apparent, the discussions were speeded up. The issue of a new constitution came to the fore. To head off more extreme demands, the commission finally published a draft reform project at the end of March.

The debate in Congress over the draft took place over several months, yet it was so acrimonious that discussion was abandoned in August. Two years later, during his own presidential election campaign at the end of 1994, Caldera tried to revive the idea, but with no success. Eventually only Chávez was prepared to put the aim of a new constitution at the heart of his political project.

In his first year as president, the speed of events was breath-taking. The first referendum took place in April 1999, elections for the Constitutional Assembly were held in July, and it met for the first time, in the hemispherical chamber of the Senate, on August 3. Miquilena was elected president and Aristóbulo Istúriz vice-president.

On August 5, the members of the new Assembly listened to a lengthy speech from Chávez asking them to produce a constitution in the shortest possible time. To encourage them in their work, he provided a draft of his own. He then reminded them of Bolívar's words, addressed to the first Venezuelan Congress in Angostura in 1819:

> Our existing laws are disastrous relics derived from every despotic regime there has ever been, both ancient and modern; let us ensure that this monstruous edifice will collapse and crumble, so that we may construct a temple to justice away from its ruins, and dictate a new Venezuelan legal code under the influence of its sacred inspiration.

The plenary sessions of the Constitutional Assembly began on the following morning, with the skilled speakers of the opposition making most of the running: Alberto Franceschi, an old Trotskyist demagogue; Jorge Olavarría, a confused but brilliant journalist and editor who had oscillated across the political spectrum for decades; Allan Brewer Carias, the doyen of Venezuela's constitutional lawyers, an academic who once had had a spell in Cambridge and was reputed to have introduced the expensive and unreliable voting machines into Venezuela; and Claudio Fermín, known ubiquitously as '*el Negro*', the only serious politician of the four, who had been the unsuccessful presidential candidate for *Acción Democrática* in 1993. The majority of the assembly looked on, silent and confused, while the debate continued.

The plenary sessions were eventually abandoned and some twenty-one specialist commissions were created with the task of defining and rewording the separate articles of the constitution. One commission, chaired by Hermann Escarrá, was detailed to deal with requests and suggestions coming in from outside.

One issue remained to be decided – on the streets. What was the relationship between the new Constitutional Assembly, elected in July and the old Congress, with its senate and chamber of deputies, elected the previous November?

The Constitutional Assembly was now perceived by most jurists as the country's supreme authority, with all other governing institutions subordinate to it. Both President Chávez and Miquilena, as president of the Assembly, hoped for a period of peaceful coexistence between the old and the new before the ratification by referendum of the new constitution.

But an argument arose in August over the future of the judiciary. Chávez decreed a 'judicial emergency' on August 25, and a nine-member commission was appointed with powers to dismiss the Supreme Court. Eight of the fifteen members of the court supported the emergency decree, but their president, Cecilia Sosa, was bitterly opposed and resigned. She declared that the Supreme Court was now dead and that the country's democratic system was in danger.

The old political elite, still well represented in the Congress, now engineered a confrontation between the Congress and the Constitutional Assembly. They convened a meeting of the Congress on August 27, in emergency session, to consider the resignation of Cecilia Sosa. Their decision was considered provocative both by Chávez and by the Constitutional Assembly, but when the National Guard tried to prevent congressmen from entering the parliament building in the centre of Caracas, which was also used by the Assembly, violent protests broke out in the streets. The supporters of both sides came to blows.

After tempers cooled, there was a stand-off, and after discussions presided over by Church leaders, the Constitutional Assembly allowed the Congress to reconvene on September 9; members of the Congress opposed to the Chávez government (who formed a majority in the old Congress) agreed not to pass laws that would hinder the work of the Constitutional Assembly.

President Chávez, meanwhile, having wound up the constitutional clockwork, took himself on a long global tour to drum up political and economic support in Asia, visiting Japan, Malaysia and the People's Republic of China, and returning via Madrid and Paris.

Back in Caracas, he found that the Constitutional Assembly was on the verge of approving a number of articles with which he was not in agreement, some of which would cause him considerable political embarrassment. Two articles in particular, one referring to the freedom of the press and the other to 'the right to life' (but apparently giving the green light to abortion), seemed likely to bring down on his head the combined wrath of the international media and the Catholic Church – an unusual but powerful alliance. The Constitutional Assembly had also rejected his own pet project of renaming the country 'the Bolivarian Republic of Venezuela', a name change that appeared innocent enough on the surface, but encapsulated in coded form his ambitious plans for the future of Latin America.

One observer, Celina Romero, writing in late September, noted how 'international scrutiny' was beginning to play 'a significant role in the transition process'. Romero examined how 'the beleaguered opposition' was using 'its international ties and the media' to denounce what it perceived as 'the dismantling of the forty-one-year-old democratic system.' It was an augury of what was to come.

Chávez refused to accept this blackmail, and dealt firmly with the various international groups that descended on the city to complain about what was going on. He was in a difficult situation, since he realised that some of the clauses in the new draft constitution might be offensive to certain interest groups. On the other hand he did not want to interfere overtly in the affairs of the 'sovereign' Constitutional Assembly. The crisis passed, the clauses were toned down, and Chávez also secured the reinstatement of his desire to have the country renamed a 'Bolivarian' republic.

The draft constitution was ready in the middle of October. At one stage it appeared to have more than 1,000 articles, but these were gradually whittled down until there were first 450, and then finally 396. The Constitutional Assembly members were given just a month in which to meet in plenary session to debate further and revise the wording. Working every morning and afternoon, each day of the week, they finished on November 12. The document was submitted to a referendum on Wednesday December 15, 1999. As the votes were counted, the rain began to fall.

Hugo Chávez during his first election campaign at a meeting at La Guaira in November 1998.

Chávez on the election campaign trail, November 1998.

Chávez portrayed as Che Guevara during the election campaign of November 1998.

President Chávez in the Palacio Miraflores in Caracas beneath a portrait of Simón Bolívar, the Liberator, March 2003.

A Chávez meeting in March 2003 at the oil refinery at Punto Fijo with the workers who had seized the plant from the strikers in December 2002.

Chávez with his daughter María Gabriela at a meeting in Caracas in March 2003. His daughter had played a crucial role during the coup of April 2002 by telephoning Fidel Castro to tell the Cuban leader that her father had not resigned.

Chávez at the celebrations of International Women's Day at a school in Caracas in March 2003.

Mercal, a popular supermarket in Caracas, March 2003.

no hay Pueblo Vencido

(Left and opposite page) Political graffiti on the walls of the "23 de enero" housing project of the 1950s with a militant and well-organised population, March 2003.

Chávez greets the workers at the opening of a new hydro-electric dam on the Rio Caroní, February 2003.

The Plaza Bolívar, Caracas, March 2003: A Chávez supporter holds up her copy of the Bolivarian Constitution.

The Plaza Bolívar, Caracas, March 2003: Receiving a 'Bolivarian' haircut.

Chávez talking at a meeting to celebrate the first anniversary of his return to power, held on the Avenida Bolívar in Caracas in April 2003.

Everyone knew there would be a majority for the Yes campaign. The only question was the size of the turnout, which might just be affected by the bad weather. People had already been called out several times since Chávez's first election victory, and even in a country once assumed to be wedded to democratic practices, a referendum whose result was a foregone conclusion must have seemed an unnecessary chore. And it was raining.

Yet Chávez had called for a respectable vote, and people were happy to satisfy his request, with 71 per cent voting Yes and 28 per cent voting No. It was a good result for the president, setting the seal on a year of dynamic action and providing his government with the tools to take the country in a new direction. Then the heavens opened in earnest.

21

WHEN THE HEAVENS OPENED

The mountains of Venezuela rise up almost sheer from the shores of the Caribbean, with gashes of red earth below and vivid green forest above, and the peaks entirely lost in grey cloud. From the aeroplane window I like to imagine this as the land on which the local Indians stood when they first discovered Columbus on their beach in 1498, then as now steep and inhospitable, hot and damp – although he actually landed some 300 miles to the east, on the Peninsula de Paría, across the water from Trinidad.

The plane often flies along the shoreline before landing, past Naiguata, Macuto and La Guaira, and along to Maiquetía and Catia La Mar, a handful of small and rather grubby resorts with a handful of high-rise buildings and barely a couple of streets between the mountains and the polluted beaches. The airlines used to book the hotels there for their overnight passengers, since they lie closer than Caracas, and excellent fish can be eaten at the roadside open-air restaurants cantilevered over the beach.

When the plane eventually comes roaring in to land, it does so on a tiny ledge scraped out beneath the mountains, parallel to the shore, and you can sometimes catch a glimpse of the shanty towns climbing up the steep ravines. Coming here over the past thirty years or more, I have noticed how a handful of shacks, once crushed in between the hills and the shore, have crept up the mountainside to form an almost vertical urban panorama.

The rainy season is usually over by the end of November, so when heavy but intermittent storms struck this coastal area in the middle of December 1999, no one took much notice; they were assumed to be the last fling of a season that was finished. Tropical storms and wayward weather systems are common in the Caribbean and they often cause serious local damage, but it is rare for a provincial disaster to create a national emergency. On that particular day, December 15, 1999, the eyes of the country were concentrated elsewhere, fixed on the polling booths.

Fresh storms brought heavy rain on top of the accumulated waters of previous weeks, causing rivers to rise uncontrollably. In the early morning of December 16, the Avila mountain to the north of Caracas, towering above the coastal resorts by the airport, effectively exploded. Torrents of mud and water on its northern slopes created the land equivalent of a tidal wave. Walls of water swept down its steep gullies. All the way along the narrow coastal strip, from Macuto to Catia La Mar, past the airport at Maiquetía, the hills descended into the sea, carrying with them an uncountable cargo of people and houses. In Caracas too the floods brought death and destruction on an unprecedented scale.

Thousands of people were killed and hundreds of thousands lost their homes. The airport was closed for weeks, and the container port at La Guaira was smashed up completely, the containers tossed around like cardboard boxes. Some floated out to sea, others were looted, as were the local shops. Even in the midst of a generalised tragedy, people take advantage where they can.

Soon the mudslide was being described as Venezuela's worst natural disaster of the century. An intemperate Catholic bishop implied that it was a judgement of God on the government, but he was reprimanded by José Vicente Rangel, then the foreign minister, who said it would be a harsh God who took out his vengeance on the poorest section of the community. Others recalled that the formerly pro-Spanish Church had taken advantage of the Caracas earthquake of 1812, in the days of Simón Bolívar, to denounce the actions of the early independence leaders.

The Constitutional Assembly, largely filled with Chávez supporters and invigorated by the referendum result, provided the president with emergency powers. Putting on the camouflage uniform and red beret that he had worn eight years earlier when leading his military 'intervention' of 1992, Chávez took personal charge of the rescue operations. To have a former military officer running the country seemed a positive advantage.

Football grounds and stadiums were opened as makeshift accommodation for the homeless, and spare patches of land around army installations were filled with tents. Soldiers manned soup kitchens and started to build houses for refugees on army land. While room might have been found for the homeless on the spacious grounds of the Caracas Country Club, the spiritual retreat of the Venezuelan elite, Chávez was careful not to endanger the national unity created around the tragedy by making political demands on people who might not willingly have accepted them.

Initial casualty figures were alarmingly high, but a month after the tragedy they had narrowed down to somewhere between 15,000 and 20,000 deaths, with perhaps 100,000 people left homeless. The figures were inevitably vague since, as in most Third World countries, no adequate census has been taken in Venezuela and no proper land registry exists, and no one could count the victims washed out to sea or buried under layers of mud. The government acted with considerable competence and speed.

When the United States sent out two ships in mid-January, laden with soldiers and earth-moving equipment, the Venezuelans said they wouldn't mind a few bulldozers, but several hundred soldiers might be overdoing it. No one voiced what many people were thinking: how could a self-styled revolutionary government possibly allow imperialist soldiers to make a practice landing on beaches just half an hour from the capital?

I went to talk to Chávez a few weeks after the December tragedy. There was nothing new about it, he told me, only its size. 'A hundred people are killed every year when the rains come, and now we've got fifteen thousand. We've been warning people of this for years.'

The over-populated northern region of Venezuela, he explained, is not just 'a seismic zone of a quite worrying kind', but has also seen 'an immense accumulation of people – and children – into *ranchos*', the shanty towns on the hillsides. 'In Caracas there must have been thousands of victims over the last twenty or thirty years, yet no government thought of making an integrated development plan for the country.'

A proper development plan had been part of the Chávez project since the early 1990s, and he had given it much thought. 'We had been discussing it in prison, and even before. We had the basic idea of decentralising the country and dispersing people to embark on a reverse migration – and this is what we are now trying to put into practice. The idea is to strengthen 'lines of reverse migration', in a way that will serve to drive and motivate the decentralising strategy.

'Of course it's not easy. You can't just arrive at a *barrio* and tell the people there that they've got to decamp to the south, and then leave them to get on with it and survive as best they may. No, no, no, it's the task of the state to establish these 'lines of reverse migration', which are really the same as those that brought about the centralising migration in the first place.'

Warming to his theme, he called for a map to be brought, and stabbed vigorously at it with his pencil. 'We will simply put everything into reverse: education will be available, *over there*; health will be available, *over there*; sport will be available, *over there*; land will be made available – so that people can work – *over there*.'

Previous governments, Chávez told me, had made efforts in this direction, but their record had been pitiful: 'When I was an army captain in the south, in the days of President Jaime Lusinchi, south of the river Arauca on the frontier with Colombia, a settlement was established there that they called Pueblo Bolívar. Along with many others, I always said that this just wasn't going to work. They created a village on the banks of the Arauca, in the middle of summer, and brought people from somewhere quite else. They virtually forced them to come, paying them something to go and live there ...

'Yet it was a wholly artificial place: there was no economic activity of any kind. Look, if this is the town, and all the land around it is *latifundio*, where are these people going to work? In winter, the roads were covered with water; people had neither cattle nor land, and they were given no credit ... They built a school, but the teacher never turned up. Little by little, people began leaving, to look for a proper life somewhere else.'

The Chávez government had an alternative solution: to establish 'integrated centres' of development: 'We were looking for lands where we might put up houses and create *integral farms* – here a farm, here a house, here a warehouse or a micro-enterprise, here a place for people to work, and here a school for the children, with a hospital and doctors and medicine. We wanted somewhere where all these things could be put together, and where people could put down roots ...'

One of the early projects the Chávez government proposed was Proyecto País, *Poblaciones Agro-Industriales Sustentables* (PAIS), for the establishment of 'sustainable agro-industrial settlements'. Chávez explained that in its first year, the government had begun working on several test cases in various regions of the country, some quite close to Caracas. Now 'the catastrophe in December' had given them an opportunity to do something more ambitious. 'Last year, to be honest, few people wanted to leave the city, and I told them, "You are right to have your doubts, because you have been betrayed so often in the past."'

'Now we have at least a hundred thousand people who have been obliged to move by the forces of nature. This time they know that it's not just words; they realise that they really have been living at great risk; they have experienced death at first hand, and have had to bury members of their families ...'

The government had begun to accelerate its existing plans, and Chávez told me of the various projects that were under way: 'Yesterday we were in Cumaná, handing out houses. All the beaches there are very contaminated, filled with rubbish, and we are making a plan to recuperate them. We've put aside ten million dollars to clean up the coast. This is a much better zone for a large population than the coast near Caracas. There's much more room between the mountains and the sea. It's good for fishing, for tourism too, and for agriculture.'

One large site had been identified at the hydro-electric plant at Guri, south of the Orinoco. Houses had been left empty there by the workmen who had built the great dam on the Caroní river.

'I went to talk to the flood victims camped in the Caracas stadium, ten thousand of them, and I told them about Guri. First I had to explain to them where it was. Two of them – and they may have been drunk – immediately said "Yes, we'll go to Guri." Then, after two weeks of a promotional campaign, with photographs and videos, a group went to have a look. I told them to go and have a look and then to come back, and I said that they didn't have to stay if they didn't want to.' The visit was a success; people liked what they saw.

'We have established a community there of perhaps two thousand people. So many people wanted to go there that we had to apply the brakes. After living through their various personal tragedies, they are now repainting their houses, and remodelling the old apartments that once belonged to the workers that built the dam. They are working there, and even making their own furniture out of local wood, for this is a region of Venezuela with many resources. The children are studying at the secondary school that already existed there. Like almost all the schools in that region, it had many empty lecture halls.'

Workshops were being set up, and the government was looking for suitable land:

'Around these houses are ten thousand hectares suitable for agriculture and for fishing, for there's a huge lake created by the dam. Sporting tourism will be possible, indeed tourism of all types, for there are waterfalls nearby and the Gran Sabana, the great savannah. There's a lot of space here, and it's very healthy.'

These were emergency schemes, of course, yet they fitted in to the wider projects that Chávez was preparing for the country. It would be important to get it right, since Caracas remained a powder keg, still ready to explode were things to go wrong. Venezuela had been in a state of crisis for as long as anyone could remember. Showplace of a certain kind of democracy in Latin America for more than three decades and, thanks to its oil wells, notionally one of the continent's wealthiest countries, its unequal income distribution made it one of the most explosive. The gadarene rush from country to city in the 1970s, followed by the economic stagnation and unemployment of the 1980s, had led by the 1990s to social breakdown. Reversing that trend might seem utopian to some. To Chávez it seemed a necessary step.

His search for an alternative to the life of the shanty town is highly ambitious, for Venezuela is still a society replete with gangsters and looters – as the reports of the flood disaster made plain. In their unruly behaviour, the young in the shanty towns are only following the example of their elders and betters in the more rarefied spheres of the nation, who had grown accustomed to rob and loot the country's wealth on an unprecedented scale.

To turn these amoral people living on their wits into selfless pioneers going out to make the desert bloom will require a large dose of imagination and a huge leap of faith. The guinea pigs for his experiment, the people whose houses were swept away by the floods, did not find the choice an easy one. Would you rather live in a shanty town overlooking the Caribbean which falls into the sea every twenty years, or would you rather move to the distant shores of the Orinoco, teeming with unpleasant insects and diseases, that has never before in history supported a large population? Would you rather be in a Caracas slum, surrounded by friends and neighbours, with the possibility of selling oddments on the streets, or would you like to go somewhere in the country where a benevolent government might provide you with a home, and eventually with land and work? These are real and difficult choices.

22

PLANNING FOR AN 'ENDOGENOUS' AGRICULTURAL FUTURE

Travelling to the sandy shores of the Orinoco I hired a stretch limo. It had not been my intention to do anything of the kind. The car was parked outside the Caracas bus station, perceived as a dangerous part of town where you need to keep your wits about you – and to firmly clutch your wallet – and I couldn't resist it.

My initial destination was Cabruta, a forgotten village at the junction of the country's two great rivers, the Orinoco and the Apure, but buses only make the journey at night. The *llanos*, Venezuela's vast plains that provide grass for cattle in their millions, become unbearably hot during the day, so drivers familiar with the road make their journeys when it's cooler. I had no desire to sleep in a bus for eight hours in the dark; I wanted to see the great plains.

An offer by Gabriel, an overweight and jovial driver with the long black hair of the indigenous people, seemed the answer. The proud owner of a limo stretched along the side of the pavement, he said he would take me on the long drive to the Orinoco for $50. There was only one small snag. He had never been there before, and perhaps if he had known more about the nature of the road he might have had second thoughts.

The stretch limo was an old Ford in various shades of off-white, much dented and scratched, but certainly serviceable, and an object of uncommon interest in the Venezuelan countryside. Soldiers manning the small police posts along the road would stop us to embark on a short perfunctory search – and then to have a long discussion about the finer points of engine tuning. Gabriel was an enthusiastic Chávez supporter, and played tapes of folk singers such as Alí Primera and Cristóbal Jiménez who extolled the virtues of the president.

Every road trip in Latin America at some stage includes an involuntary stop to mend a puncture. Bus, lorry, van, car – all drivers use their tyres to the bitter end. Only when they are paper thin and go bang do their owners decide that a replacement is necessary. The bang came on a narrow busy stretch of road, and Gabriel carefully reversed the wounded limo onto a piece of hard ground. It was midday, over 100°F and without a trace of shade, but within twenty minutes we were back on the road again.

The road itself was a metalled highway, built in the days when Venezuela had more money than sense, with huge oil royalties and a government with a passion for infrastructure. The original smooth surface had disappeared years ago and no money had been made available to mend it. The cost of travel now fell on the individual driver, obliged to pay for the repair to his vehicle, shaken and shocked by the bumps. For Gabriel and his stretch limo, the problems were more dramatic, for often the front wheels might miss the potholes, but the back ones did not. When that happened, the entire chassis would scrape along the ground.

Eight hours after setting out, with ten minutes to spare before a violent orange sun disappeared beneath the rippled surface of the swiftly flowing Orinoco, we drove majestically into the bedraggled settlement of Cabruta, a mission station – one of half a dozen – established by the Jesuits at the junction of the Orinoco and the Apure in the early eighteenth century. When Alexander von Humboldt, the German scientist and traveller, came exploring here in 1800, the Jesuit missionaries had long gone, but the remains of the old settlements could still be seen: a handful of Indian families surviving by the shores of the Orinoco at Cabruta, La Encaramada, Urbana, Canichana, San Borja, and El Raudal.

Cabruta today has become the fulcrum of 'the Apure–Orinoco axis', one of President Chávez's projects to develop and settle the centre-south of Venezuela. Above Cabruta stands a large rocky headland, and from there you can see the Orinoco stretching down south towards Brazil and east towards the Atlantic. The Apure comes down from Colombia and the Andes far to the west. In these now empty lands President Chávez is hoping to develop agriculture in such a way that people currently living in the shanty towns of the great cities will be persuaded to move out to the countryside. This is underinhabited cattle land, but it could also be used for the industrial production of rice and palm, two products where the country has a strong competitive advantage.

'Look, here is the Apure–Orinoco axis', he exclaimed when we were poring over the map together at his residence at La Casona. His excitement was infectious. 'The land has been virtually abandoned; we won't have to build new towns here, we will simply strengthen the settlements that already exist.'

Chávez was also interested in another area, in the far west of the country, just to the north of the Apure–Orinoco axis. Here there would be a north–south axis, from Guasdualito close to the Colombian border to Lake Maracaibo. Chávez was showing me the settlement of La Fría on the map, an existing though abandoned farm project where the homeless survivors of the December floods might be resettled. Lying under the slopes of the Andes, close to the Colombian border, it was to be another pilot scheme for the ambitious long-term projects he had in mind.

'It's a place in the state of Táchira, to the north of the Apure–Orinoco axis, to the north of San Cristóbal. Here is the village, with about ten thousand inhabitants. It's a wonderfully rich region, at the foot of the mountains, just to the south of Lake Maracaibo. I once worked there in a military unit, and we used to go out on patrol.'

He pulls forward the map again. 'Look, here is the frontier with Colombia, here is the international airport, here is an abandoned industrial site. Here is the land, here are some houses, and here we will put in a school, a workshop, and a road.'

All this had been built ten years ago in the days of Carlos Andrés Pérez. 'They spent thousands and thousands of *bolívares*, and then Pérez himself abandoned it. They began to build a motorway to San Cristóbal, the capital, but it came to a stop because they never made the tunnels through the mountains. The road is still there, but without the tunnels.'

Chávez told me he had scheduled a visit to La Fría for the following week. 'Why don't you come with us?' So a couple of days later, with the sun barely over the hills that surround Caracas, I waited for him in the officers' lounge at the small airport of La Carlota in the centre of the capital, where the Venezuelan air force is based, while a secret service agent spent time crawling under the sofas to check for bombs. When Chávez arrived, wearing his camouflage uniform and his red beret, we set off in the presidential plane and headed for the Colombian border, an hour's flight away. Half the cabinet came too.

We landed at the deserted airport, the grass growing between the squares of the concrete runway. A military band greeted the president, and, after the usual military formalities, we climbed into four large helicopters to fly to a military farm nearby, at Guarumito. From the air, the settlement looked pitifully isolated, a huddle of tin roofs surrounded by the savannah stretching away into the distance. The indistinguishably similar territory of Colombia lay a couple of miles away.

On the ground, things looked marginally more encouraging. We landed on a piece of hard track beside a swamp where a small group of workers was busy repairing a dozen of the tin-roofed bungalows we had seen from the air. When Chávez emerged from his helicopter he was mobbed by a crowd that appeared from nowhere. He made his way slowly through to a large converted caravan that served as a mobile training workshop. This was the civilian component in this military–civilian operation, run by the government's national training institute, and containing carpentry benches and simple electric saws. Chávez interrogated the education supervisor, a nervous civilian, and fired off a stream of questions. How long have you been here? When will it all begin? When are the teachers coming?

'The teachers are being selected,' said the supervisor apologetically, 'but none have arrived yet.'

'Yes,' said Chávez, 'we know all about that. People get involved, and then they leave. A month later and everything's back to square one. You have to be really careful how you choose.'

He continued to badger the wretched superviser. 'You've got to be more productive. Why don't you put up some tents, build another building, bring more people in.' He discovered that the superviser was losing time by driving backwards and forwards every day from the town, a five minutes' journey in the helicopter, an hour each way by car. 'You can't do that all the time,' the president said, 'you'll get exhausted. Why don't you try staying here in a tent. Don't forget how important this job is. We are not teaching them so that they can go off somewhere else. We want people to stay here. We are colonising the country with our own people. How many times have we failed in the past? We can't fail this time.' The supervisor, in the tidy dark suit of a state official, nodded in agreement, but he looked appalled.

While waiting for Chávez, who was caught by another crowd, I talked to Jorge Giordani, the minister of development who once studied at the University of Sussex (see page 122). Gray-haired, looking older than his years, Giordani is the man behind the plan for 'endogenous' development, the economic stimulation of everything that is internal and indigenous. The professor had been working with his students on the formulation of a programme to revitalise the rural areas, and he told me how he used to visit Chávez in prison. The two men got on well together, and he became Chávez's economics tutor, supervising his university thesis. As planning minister, he brought in an influential team of university radicals to flesh out the president's plans, including a banking expert, Trino Alcides Diaz.

We moved to an assembly room in the barracks where Chávez began interrogating the commanding officer. He discovered that some of the land had been taken over by squatters who had been cutting down the trees and selling the wood.

'I want to know urgently who sold off the land. Anyone caught cutting down trees will go to prison. It's absolutely illegal. I want to know who owns the land round here in a fifty-kilometre radius. I know there are lots of people who own land here who actually live in Miami or in London. We shall expropriate it. The new constitution allows us to do so, but we shall pay for it of course.'

Then he began asking about what the land could produce. 'What used to be grown in this region? What did the Indians grow? Is milk production really the best idea, or would vegetables be better?' The audience started chipping in with their own ideas, and eventually everyone agreed that this would be good land for cattle. Chávez said sternly that he would return soon to see how they were getting on, and he warned them that he might fly in without warning.

We walked round to the bungalows that had already been refurbished and were about to be handed over to their new owners. They had been built in a circle, around a central plaza, and each had a patch of land out behind. Some makeshift awnings had been erected, but Chávez stood out in the centre in the burning midday sun for more than an hour. Most of the twenty-four families being provided with a house had come from the sites of the coastal tragedy in December 1999. One of the local men told me that his maize and yucca plantation was also carried away by the floods. 'We have no money, no capital, we need help,' he said. When I asked him to put his name in my notebook, he apologised for not being able to write.

The families came up in turn, and Chávez talked to each of them. Usually it was a young man and a young woman, with two or three small children, though sometimes there was an older, more careworn couple. They walked up in their family group and he handed them their title deed, asked them about their experiences and their skills, and offered words of warning and advice. They went away with a smile on their faces. The houses were not a gift to the settlers, who would live in them rent-free for only a year. After that, they would have to pay a regular quota to the cooperative that formally owned them.

When the formalities were finished, Chávez made a short speech, saying that he had been warned by his chief of staff that his trip was already running three hours behind schedule. 'Never mind, we are going to do these things properly.' He knew that it was important to provide some encouragement and some sense of ceremony as they took over their new homes.

'You are very daring to have come here,' he told them, 'and to found a new town. It is not easy for anyone to move from the sea coast to the inland savannah. Yet just think, we only started two weeks ago, and in a few months' time there will be a thousand homes here.'

Guarumito, he reminded them, is the name of the indigenous people who used to live here. 'I know this region, these are some of the best lands in Venezuela. I've been here on several occasions to patrol the frontier.' He told them not to be worried about being isolated. 'We are going to build a railway line that will pass near here, from the Apure river to Lake Maracaibo.'

He finished with a word of warning. 'Please don't call your roads or houses after me. I don't want to be remembered with anything like the Raúl Leoni motorway,' he said, recalling the extravagance of a previous president.

This was a heart-warming occasion, the new settlers standing up proudly, the children waving the blue and yellow flag of Venezuela, and everyone close to tears. Chávez played his role as the avuncular comforter, talking, asking questions, seeking answers, and spreading a sense of optimism and good will.

Our gaggle of ministers and hangers-on moved back to the helicopters, and we flew off to view another failed project of the *ancien régime*, an immense and abandoned industrial park, said to be the largest in South America. Chávez again plunged into the waiting crowd, to discover what it was they wanted. They had been living there for some years, and they only wanted one thing: work.

We clambered into a bus and drove slowly round the abandoned site. Chávez conducted an impromptu seminar with his ministers, as the man in charge explained what used to happen in each empty shed and warehouse. They discussed what would be taken over, and how investors might be encouraged to move here if provided with sufficient tax breaks. While the state can provide education and medical care, there will be no repeat of the failed state enterprises of the 1970s. The private investor would have to be encouraged to set up the large and small projects necessary to revive the failures of the earlier era. The minister of industry told me that if the military could assist with clearing up the site, it should be possible to establish fifty small enterprises, employing perhaps twenty people each, within the first year. Chávez wanted everything to be done more quickly.

When we returned to the military base at La Fría, many hours late for lunch, Chávez held an hour-long cabinet meeting to discuss what everyone had learnt, and what steps they should take next. We climbed back into the presidential jet, and the meeting continued. It was still going on at the airport terminal of La Carlota when I left to go home. Chávez stayed on talking, with no signs of exhaustion, and returned to La Casona for more meetings later that night; his civilian ministers looked completely worn out, as indeed was I.

The resettlement of flood victims at La Fría is just one in a long line of experiments made by Latin American governments over the years to try to reverse the rural migration that has been asphyxiating the cities. There have been more failures than successes. In the early 1970s the radical military government in Peru permitted legalised squatting in the *pueblos jóvenes* (new settlements) established around Lima, but the strategy merely brought fresh immigration from the rural Andes to the coastal city, and made the shanty towns even larger.

Chávez wants to be more original than that, by transferring the surplus urban population to new agro-industrial developments far from the delights of the city. This is not the strategy of Pol Pot in Cambodia, for there is no suggestion of coercion. The scale is small and the time scale long. Chávez told me that he was thinking of at least twenty years. Just conceivably, he might persuade a few thousand pioneers to take up the challenge, but it seems the real success of these projects will be to slow down the rate of rural–urban migration rather than to reverse it. That in itself would be worth the effort.

No president since the days of Pérez Jiménez in the early 1950s has done much for agriculture in Venezuela. Chávez would like to make the country capable of feeding itself. Venezuela imports more than half its food needs, 64 per cent in 1998. Where previous governments concentrated on oil, or on industrial development, or on trade and commerce, the Chávez government puts special emphasis on agriculture. Vast areas of Venezuela lie fallow or unused. Cattle roam over innumerable acres that could be more productively used.

More than fifty years ago, people talked of 'sowing the oil', using the income from the invested oil rent to improve agriculture. This never happened, and Chávez now plans that it will. In 1999, US$15 million was allocated to a pilot scheme that would assist peasant families to create new farming settlements in rural areas, a scheme devised to increase production of such staples as rice and maize, milk and sugar, and cooking oil.

You might think that rice would be the staple diet of Venezuela, a hot country with great rivers and swamps. Yet nowadays the Venezuelans eat more wheat than rice, since imported wheat from the United States, at subsidised prices, is cheaper than home-grown rice. According to Federico Cappellín, a columnist on *El Nacional*, Venezuelans eat only 12 kilos of rice a year, while in Colombia they eat 30 kilos, in Brazil 48 kilos, in Ecuador 58 kilos, and in Peru 32 kilos. Venezuelans make up for their failure to eat rice by consuming 65 kilos a year of wheat imported from the United States.

Rice is grown in Venezuela; indeed more is produced at present than is locally consumed. Wheat of course is not a suitable crop for a tropical country. So to change the country's priorities, Chávez will have to change the national diet, promoting rice and maize instead of wheat-based pasta. Cappellín suggests that rice should be made the national dish, and that the new constitution should have declared it to be the 'national cereal'. In doing so, he writes hopefully, 'we would change the mentality of the Venezuelans, who would eat mangos instead of apples, [maize] *arepas* instead of hamburgers, and rice instead of pasta'.

In one of the great shopping malls of Caracas, I made a list of the various places you could stop to eat. First came 'Wendy's Old-Fashioned Hamburgers', illustrated with a North American girl with short curls and two ribbons. Next came the 'American Deli', with the Statue of Liberty included on its logo. Then the 'Italian Coffee Company', with street signs for Canal Street and Manhattan. These were followed by 'Good Time Ice Cream', 'Happy Time Ice Cream', 'Chip-a-Cookie', 'Dunkin' Donuts', the 'St Möritz Chocolatier', and of course McDonald's. It is difficult to imagine that the cheerful young people who inhabit the shopping mall, with their North Americanised life-style, will want to eat *arepas* rather than hamburgers, or to exchange pasta for rice, yet this is the revolutionary change being required of them by the Chávez government as it seeks to reconstruct the country on more nationalist lines.

23

THE NEW POLITICS OF OIL

The teardrop shape of Lake Maracaibo is familiar to anyone who has ever studied a map of South America. A great expanse of water caught between the Andes and the Caribbean, it has become one of the man-made wonders of the world. A strangely romantic place, the lake is the legacy of the bold pioneering days of capitalism when taming and exploiting nature was done with simple technologies and the ingenuity and brute strength of workers. Today, it is an unmitigated ecological disaster. Filled with Christmas tree derricks, a forest of four-legged metal masts sticking up from the surface of the water, it evokes memories of early movies with an oil industry background, or the sepia photographs in old encyclopaedias.

The real thing far surpasses the folk memory, and there are surprises too. Lake Maracaibo is not a place for tourist pedaloes; beribboned captains drive brass-gleaming launches with pride and skill across the grey waters of this vast inland sea. This is a serious work environment, swarming with skilled men who know what they are about: divers, engineers, experts in rig construction.

The oil installations, thousands of them, are all the same but different: a small platform on four legs, festooned with pipes, accessible only by ladder; a construction with arms that move up and down remorselessly, like a Van Gogh sluice gate in the Camargue; a gigantic raft covered with metal masts lashed to six immense barrels; a concrete erection with taps and tanks, and a cornucopia of tube work. In the centre of the lake stands a great platform familiar from the North Sea, a giant among pygmies. Rooted on three legs, it pumps out oil from twenty thousand feet below the surface.

The practice of extracting oil from beneath the waters of a lake has gone on for nearly a century, and is now rendered commonplace by the elephantine technology that can secure it from the bottom of the sea. What still makes Lake Maracaibo rather special is that its surface stands far above the level of the surrounding countryside. So much oil has been taken from the Maracaibo basin since the 1920s that the surrounding land is steadily sinking into the huge hole that is left behind. The fields around the lake drop down a little lower every year.

Disaster might have struck had this not been an area developed originally by Royal Dutch Shell. The Dutch know a thing or two about low-lying land, and they are familiar with the construction of dikes. Years ago, with considerable ingenuity, Dutch engineers built a wall around the lake, and allowed the houses and the installations on the land side to gently subside behind this protecting stockade. The surrounding terrain is now some five metres below sea level, and it continues to collapse evenly at the rate of between 15 and 20 centimetres a year. It would probably descend further and faster if the engineers did not also pump in water to fill the oil-vacated spaces.

The sense that something is being permanently removed, the reality of physical diminishment, is one of the reasons why all Venezuelans have such a passionate attachment to their state oil company. For decades it seemed as though their national patrimony was being siphoned off by the great American and European oil companies, principally Shell and Mobil and Exxon. Generations of nationalist historians and politicians perceived this as a scandal, and the belief that the nation had been robbed remains deeply implanted in the national psyche.

Two events, one in 1943, the other in 1976, are celebrated as great and historic moments when the country stood up to the oil companies. In 1943, the government of General Isaías Medina Angarita took advantage of wartime scarcity to oblige the companies to comply with Venezuelan tax laws and to limit their concessions to a period of forty years. In 1976, after only thirty years, President Carlos Andrés Pérez secured the agreement of the fourteen principal foreign companies to a negotiated withdrawal from the country. On January 1, the state oil company, Petróleos de Venezuela SA (PdVSA), took over their assets, which included 11,000 oil wells, 11 oil refineries, and 14 oil tankers. The package also contained pipelines, port terminals, and innumerable office buildings.

Initially the three largest of the nationalised companies continued to maintain their individual status: Royal Dutch Shell became known as Maraven, Exxon's Creole Petroleum Company as Lagoven, and Mobil Oil as Llanoven. Maraven and Lagoven even kept their separate corporate identities, one very European and carefree, the other very American and authoritarian. Essentially they were still competitors. The complex of old Dutch buildings in Maraven's lakeside town of Lagunillas remained untouched, and in spite of the palm trees, it continued to look like an old-fashioned Dutch village, with wooden verandahs and high-pitched roofs. At the humming heart of a centre of late-twentieth-century technology, you half expected someone to come down the street in clogs.

Like oil companies elsewhere in the world, Venezuela's newly nationalised enterprises spent much time searching for fresh sources of oil. Once there was a panic that it would all disappear, yet soon it was popping up everywhere. At Lake Maracaibo, they simply began drilling deeper. The oil may be more difficult to extract, but there is plenty of it. Large reserves have been located further to the south, in the state of Barinas, on the slopes of the Andes.

Over the years, the state oil company has not been immune to the pressures of globalisation and privatisation. These began under the government of Carlos Andrés Pérez in 1989, and were continued with the so-called *Apertura*, or Opening [to the private sector], that was continued by the government of President Caldera. Foreign companies were allowed to engage in joint ventures with the state oil company, and Shell and BP proudly reopened their service stations in the capital to show that they were in business again. *Petróleos de Venezuela* had produced a draft investment plan in 1991, for US$65 billion, which envisaged a third of the capital coming from the private sector.

In 1997, the entire management of *Petróleos de Venezuela* was reorganised, and the individual companies within it, such as Maraven and Lagoven, the hangover from the previous era, were finally abolished. The state company was now divided up in another way, three new divisions being created, one for exploration and production, another for marketing and manufacturing, and a third for services. The management and employees of the company were only just beginning to adjust to these dramatic changes when the Chávez government arrived in 1999. One of the first changes made was to set up a fourth division to oversee the gas industry.

Venezuela's future was now dependent on the way that the Chávez government would reorganise the exploitation and commercialisation of oil, a subject of more than national interest, since Venezuela was accustomed to providing the bulk of the oil imports of the United States. The new man in charge, as minister of energy and mines, was Ali Rodríguez Araque, the former guerrilla commander in his sixties, who had been the oil expert of *La Causa R* and of *Patria Para Todos* (PPT). Born in Mérida in 1937, Rodríguez had studied law and economics at the Universidad Central in Caracas and the Universidad de los Andes in Mérida. He fought in the hills of Falcón state in the 1960s with Douglas Bravo, but after the collapse of the guerrilla war, and a period in the *Partido de la Revolución de Venezuela*, he parted company with Bravo. He joined up with Alfredo Maneiro's *La Causa R*, and worked as a labour lawyer in Ciudad Guayana.

In 1983, he was elected to Congress from the state of Bolívar, supported by *La Causa R*, and in November 1998 he was elected as a senator for *Patria Para Todos*. During the Caldera government, from 1994 to 1997, he had an influential position in Congress as the president of its Committee on Energy and Mines, and he had been closely involved in the congressional overseeing of contracts during the opening up of the oil industry to foreign markets. When the PPT joined the Chávez electoral alliance, he became Chávez's chief adviser on oil matters.

Rodríguez's first task in government was to reassert the primacy of his own ministry, Energy and Mines, over the state oil company, *Petróleos* de Venezuela. The company had been run for years as a corporatist enterprise, a state within the state, a vast conglomerate dispensing favours and bribes. With a rapid changeover of personnel, and even the replacement of Chávez's first choice to run the company, Rodríguez's initial objectives were achieved. But opposition within the company to the new regime remained powerful.

The second task was to alter radically Venezuela's policy towards OPEC, the Organisation of Petroleum Exporting Countries. Venezuela had had a low reputation within OPEC during the 1990s, when the policy of *Apertura* was in operation, as a member state that ignored all the guidelines. Successive Venezuelan governments had tried to go it alone. They had all but abandoned OPEC, disregarding the quotas set and trying to jack up production by bringing in foreign companies to develop new oilfields.

From the start the Chávez government had a different, and well-defined internationalist strategy. Rodríguez insisted on production cuts at *Petróleos de Venezuela*. He was determined to cooperate with OPEC, and to work towards securing a stable oil price. He journeyed round the OPEC countries, and also sought the cooperation of Latin American oil producers. Mexico, which is not a member of OPEC, and competes with Venezuela in the lucrative US market, was persuaded to curb its planned production increases.

Finally, after an OPEC meeting in March 1999, Venezuela cut back its output by 4 per cent, to 2.72 million barrels a day, and announced that it had plans to make further cutbacks both in production and in exploration. In May, celebrating his first 100 days in power, President Chávez proudly explained what had happened:

> The increase in the oil price has not been the result of a war or the full moon. No. It is the result of an agreed strategy, a change of 180 degrees in the policy of previous governments and of *Petróleos de Venezuela*. First, we decided to respect the cutbacks in production agreed with OPEC and with Mexico. Secondly, we decided to increase the level of cutbacks. Now the world knows that there is a serious government in Venezuela, and a new leadership in PdVSA ...

Later in the year, in September, a correspondent for the *Financial Times*, Robert Corzine, noted that the previous few months had proved to be 'one of the more successful periods in the history of OPEC's attempts to control the oil price'. Not only had its member countries stuck by the production cuts and avoided the previous practice of 'quota cheating', but non-OPEC members, like Britain and Norway, had been unable to take up the slack.

By the end of the year, Venezuela thought that the oil price was now high enough. Alí Rodríguez believed that OPEC should now agree on a broad band within which the price could be sustained by adding or cutting output. He proposed that a meeting of OPEC heads of state should be held in Caracas in the year 2000, and invitations were sent out to, among others, Saddam Hussein of Iraq, Muammar Gadafy of Libya, and Mohamad Khatami of Iran.

The other significant development was the modification of the economic stabilisation fund set up by the previous government. *The Fondo de Estabilización Macroeconómica* was a special fund designed to supplement the government's income in the event of a collapse in the international oil price. The idea was to even out the volatility in international prices. If the price of oil were to go above US$14 a barrel, the extra revenue would be channelled into the fund. Rodriguez decided to drop the benchmark to US$9 a barrel. This was a conservative figure, but not out of line with the low oil price of recent years. Venezuelan crude had sold at US$16.6 in 1997, and had dropped to US$10.75 in 1998.

In practice, the price went way above US$9 in the course of 1999, pouring large sums into the stabilisation fund. From US$11.95 in March 1999, before the OPEC meeting, it had gone above US$20 later in the year.

The new relationship with OPEC and the increase in the oil price, which was generally accepted with a good grace by the outside world, were among the major successes of Chávez's first year in government. But they left pending the conflictive question of the future of the state oil company.

Many influential citizens outside the government argued forcefully that individuals should have the right to a slice of the country's oil wealth. Alberto Quirós, once the head of Maraven, argued in newspaper articles that Venezuelan citizens should should have the right to buy shares in their national oil company. Under the clauses of the new constitution, this would not be allowed to happen. The state would continue to keep a tight rein on the company.

Quirós argued in favour of allowing the company to sell 10 per cent of its stock, so that the real worth of the company could be ascertained. He also thought that the company's financial resources, if suitably distributed, could help provide the basis for private pension funds.

For nationalists within the armed forces and within the Chávez government, these were dangerous proposals. Yet Rodriguez himself was not without some revolutionary ideas. Interviewed in May 1998 by Maria Cristina Iglesias, when still in charge of the oil policy of Patria Para Todos in Congress, he gave an outline of a strategy that would involve individual Venezuelan investors buying share in the state oil company:

> The idea was that during the period of exploration, which involves some risk, investment would only come from *Petróleos de Venezuela* and from international capital. Once suitable oilfields had been identified, some adjustments would be made: international capital would be allowed a maximum participation of 49 per cent, and *Petróleos de Venezuela* would also have a percentage share.
>
> The way would then be open for Venezuelan savers and investors to purchase share capital in the companies and consortia that would be set up to produce the oil. None of this, of course, would subtract from the legitimate remuneration due to foreign investors, who had taken the risks during the period of exploration. Such a programme would, without doubt, have attracted the solid backing of international capital.

This was just one of the possibilities still being discussed in Chavez's first year. In subsequent years, the politics of the oil industry came to the forefront of the political drama of the country, and an entirely new perspective began to open up.

24

DIVISIONS OVER THE ECONOMIC PROGRAMME

Venezuela may enjoy huge oil revenues, but these have traditionally been mopped up by a tiny percentage of the population. The great majority of the country is permanently poor and hungry. While the top 10 per cent of the population of 23 million receives half the national income, 40 per cent (according to an estimate of 1995) lives in 'critical poverty'. 80 per cent (according to the figures for 1996) earns the minimum wage or under. As if this was not bad enough, the situation has been growing dramatically worse. Real purchasing power declined by 35 per cent between 1989 and 1995.

These statistics were well known to Chávez and his government, and he would constantly tell foreign visitors how difficult it was to explain how such a rich country could at the same time be so desperately poor. He was also aware that he could wave no magic wand. Much of his time has been spent, with Christian rhetoric, in urging the poor to be patient, and the rich to acquire some sense of solidarity with the people with whom they are obliged to share the country.

Yet although disguised and not fully formulated in the early years, the government's economic policy has never been in doubt. In spite of the powerful rhetoric against neo-liberalism, Chávez has always been interested in securing foreign investment. He has sought to steer a difficult and almost impossible course, telling his nationalist country what it has wanted to hear, and making the right kind of reassuring noises that would not frighten the foreign investor. In this, of course, he has the warm support of Castro. According to Fausto Masó, a usually well-informed journalist, Castro had told Chávez that his own principal preoccupation was 'to secure the last US dollar for Cuba, because the only revolutionary way to secure development today is to open up the entire country to foreign investors'.

What is good enough for revolutionary Cuba would be fine for Venezuela, and Chávez sought to follow this implicit instruction. John Maisto, the US ambassador in Caracas in 1999, spent much time trying to get the Chávez government to sign the treaty on the promotion and protection of foreign investment that all other Latin American governments have been obliged to sign. Maisto tried to get the treaty signed before the first meeting of the Constitutional Assembly, knowing that the nationalist Assembly would be averse to its terms. He turned out to be knocking at an open door. Chávez's cabinet quietly agreed to sign, in October, and Chávez ensured that this was done when he was out of the country. 'He now goes round making speeches guaranteeing stability and investment,' one disillusioned economist told me.

Yet in Chávez's first year in office, his radical supporters made no objection to this strategy. Many of them were involved with another project, debating in the Constitutional Assembly the parameters of a future economic policy rather than contemplating the here-and-now. A strong element in their programme was the encouragement of local investors. This was always part of the economic policy of *La Causa R* and of *Patria Para Todos*: an attempt to befriend the small independent businessman and the entrepreneur against the large state barons and their commercial and banking friends.

Economic opinion abroad was divided in its initial attitude to the Chávez phenomenon. 'You're looking at a very, very ugly recession next year if oil prices don't recover,' said a pessimistic spokesman for Merrill Lynch in New York a week or two after the December 1998 election. He added gloomily that Chávez would 'have to be Superman to pull the economy out of trouble'. Other outsiders were equally glum at that time. 'We just think the risks are too high at the moment,' said an analyst at Deutsche Bank in New York.

The pessimism turned out to be ill-founded. Oil prices did recover, and never ceased to increase in subsequent years. Yet investors inside Venezuela had always been less alarmed. Most of them realised that things would certainly have been worse if Chávez had failed to win in 1998. The Caracas stock market went up after the election as these local investors, having moved out during the election in case of a freak result, came flooding back. 'When you see the flows,' said the man from Merrill Lynch cheerfully, 'it was really the locals bringing their money back.'

In spite of the rhetoric, Chávez in office turned out to be a pragmatic ruler. He believed, essentially, that the combination of honest men and honest government would provide good government. He was passionately hostile to 'corruption', of which there was no shortage in the past, and fiercely against the philosophy of 'savage neo-liberalism' imposed on the world by the United States. Yet he often found it difficult to describe just what it was that he intended to put in its place. His first speech as president in February 1999 gave few details about what lay ahead:

> Our project is neither statist nor neo-liberal; we are exploring the middle ground, where the invisible hand of the market joins up with the visible hand of the state: as much state as necessary, and as much market as possible.

The soundbite was admirable, but as directions for a minister in charge of the economy, it could only be read in one way: keep to the existing course.

'He's very radical everywhere else,' one academic economist told me, 'but he's conservative in the economic sphere. He's very positive and firm on foreign policy, but there is nothing remotely similar in the economic sphere. He concentrates his attacks on corrupt politicians, but he never mentions the bankers, and they were just as bad.'

Yet while Chávez personally has no great interest in the detail of economic strategy, his political supporters in the MAS and in *Patria Para Todos* have certainly evolved something approaching an economic programme over the years, though it might be more accurate to describe it as an attitude. During the course of 1999, the economic decisions and actions of the government received little publicity, but the economic debate in the Constitutional Assembly secured many headlines. Chávez supporters in the Assembly, both leftist civilians and retired military officers, were determined that the state should continue to play a significant role in the economy. This was the majority view in the Assembly, and certainly in the country as well.

Yet this controlling group had very disparate ambitions. Many from the MAS still hankered for the days when the state had an active developmental role; those from *Patria Para Todos*, reflecting the greener values of *La Causa R*, longed for a smaller state with fewer opportunities for corruption, and expressed their concern about the future of small enterprises, and about pollution and the environment.

Despite these differences, almost everyone in the Constitutional Assembly was united in their desire to see off the neo-liberal fundamentalists, whose nostrums played no part in the final formulation of the new constitution. Yet the victory was more apparent than real. Whilst only a small but influential handful were prepared to see *Petróleos de Venezuela* sold off to private interests, almost everyone agreed that it would be reasonable to make deals with foreign oil companies. In practice, it appeared that significant parts of the economic policy developed during the 1990s – which had opened up the oil industry to foreign participation and begun a process of privatisation – would be continued.

This appearance of continuity was reinforced by the presence in the cabinet as economics minister of Maritza Izaguirre, who had been inherited from the Caldera administration. She resigned in June 1999 to be replaced by her deputy José Rojas, who had also worked in the ministry under Caldera. 'Poor Maritza really didn't know what was happening,' I was told, 'and José Rojas is now finding the same, although he's a supporter of the *Quinta República*.'

The change making the ministers nervous was the introduction of military personnel into the senior reaches of the public administration. 'The military are everywhere,' one senior economic adviser explained to me. 'It sometimes seems as though there is a secret project that you don't quite know about. There really is a military party. In some of the ministries, it's a case of dual power.' Senior military officers had in fact been placed in all the principal ministries, including *Petróleos de Venezuela*.

'Many come from the lower classes,' my academic economist told me, 'and will tell you "my dad was a worker".' Yet they have studied at the university, and their intellectual preparation is pretty good; when I was teaching at the university there were three officers out of a class of twenty. But their mentality is rather different, and they are certainly autocratic. Some are on the left, but I have met some *Pinochetista* officers.'

Most of the officers introduced into government were at a level just below the top. They were watching and waiting, and keeping their eyes open. But one central figure was running his own show, and he certainly wasn't a *Pinochetista*. Colonel William Fariñas was appointed president of the *Fondo Unico Social* (FUS, the Social Fund), a new and potentially powerful creation that linked together a number of earlier government organisations that used to deal with health and social welfare.

The *Fondo Unico Social*, together with the *Banco del Pueblo*, or People's Bank, was one of a raft of new organisations designed to carry through the social policies that were aimed at improving the health and welfare of the poor majority of the population. The political impact of such institutions has echoed down the years: Eva Perón used to run the ministry of social welfare in Argentina in the 1940s, and it served as her power base when trying to improve the conditions of the poor. The Velasco government in Peru in the 1970s had a somewhat similar institution set up by the military, the *Sistema Nacional de Apoyo a la Movilización Social* (Sinamos, the National System to Support Social Mobilisation). Sinamos sounded brilliant on paper, but was a disastrous failure in practice.

Colonel Fariñas, like other senior officers in the Chávez government, had done time at the university. He was a professor of strategic planning and social policy at the Universidad Central in Caracas, and he also had a doctorate in organisational training. As a retired air force colonel, he has many heroes: Bolívar, of course; the Sacred Heart of Jesus, the Virgin Mary Auxiliadora; the Archangel Michael – and Che Guevara.

> Che is the one single figure who represents commitment and altruism, and complete dedication to the cause of the people – everywhere in the world. He is an icon for all revolutionaries, as he is for me ... he has been always, ever since I was a student and began to hold revolutionary convictions. The revolutionary spirit that animates the military and other citizens taking part in this process has been nourished on the thoughts and ideals of Che, and of what once were the events of May in France ...

This sixties' revolutionary was in charge of an organisation with huge political potential and a large budget. The budget derived partly from the ordinary budget of the earlier organisations that it had gobbled up, and partly from the *Fondo de Estabilización Macroeconómica* (FEM) that channels oil money to government projects. Indeed the FUS will receive 40 per cent of the FEM's budget.

The FUS helped to fund schools, hospitals, and even churches, but its most ambitious new funding project was the *Plan Bolívar 2000*, one of Chávez's most original ideas. The details were announced on February 27, 1999, within weeks of his inauguration. The idea was to mobilise the spare capacity of the armed forces, to link it up with local community groups, and to make an impact on Venezuela's increasingly derelict social infrastructure. Soldiers would make available to local communities their barracks, their sports grounds, and their canteens. They would go out into the community and help rebuild roads and schools.

The *Plan Bolívar* was designed to be implemented in three stages. Stage one, called *Pro-País*, would involve the armed forces in the provision of social service. Stage two, *Pro-Pátria*, would involve the military in helping local communities to seek local solutions to their problems; and stage three, *Pro-Nación*, would launch the country on the road towards economic self-sufficiency and endogenous (sustainable) development.

In the *Pro-País* phase, the country was divided into 25 action zones, and some 40,000 soldiers and volunteers began work on the reconstruction of roads, health centres and schools, working with the local authorities. President Chávez told reporters that 'mobile field hospitals' would be dispatched to remote villages and slums 'as if to a war zone'. In December 1999, after the terrible mud slides in the coastal state of Vargas, the war zone metaphor proved uncomfortably apt.

25

REFORMING THE JUDICIARY

At the heart of the crisis of the old Venezuelan state lay the corruption of the judiciary. Many people hoped that the election of Chávez would remedy this glaring problem, and the government itself was pledged to reform. One of the tasks of the Constitutional Assembly was to draft the legal clauses of the new constitution, and it established a Judicial Emergency Commission to examine the state of the existing provisions, and to evaluate the work of the judges and the members of the Supreme Court.

The commission was presided over by Manuel Quijada, a lawyer and a Chávez supporter who had been a member of the Patriotic Front set up in 1989 in the aftermath of the *Caracazo*. Long an advocate of an alliance between soldiers and civilians, Quijada was a veteran of the attempted military coups of 1962.

In September 1999, his commission revealed that at least half the country's 1,200 judges were guilty of corruption or incompetence, and suggested that they should be sacked. Checking through the files of the National Judges Council (the organisation responsible for investigating complaints against the judiciary), the commission discovered that 4,000 complaints had been made in the past ten years against judges and prosecutors.

The corruption and incompetence of the judicial system have been known about for years, and many of the complaints about it concerned its failure to mount trials to bring corrupt politicians and bankers to justice. One member of the commission, Carlos Tablante, denounced 'the judicial power in Venezuela' as 'a refuge of illegality, vagrancy and corruption', and he recalled a particular instance when a group of corrupt judges had heard charges against two dozen bankers accused of causing a scandalous banking crash in 1994 that had 'nearly bankrupted the financial system'. In spite of public outrage, the charges against the bankers had been dropped.

What now made the situation so serious and explosive was the fact that most of those held in prison – some 23,000 people – had never been brought to trial. The appalling state of Venezuela's prisons – even by the standards of Latin America – had been well known for years, and the dreadful conditions had frequently sparked off large-scale riots. More than 500 prisoners were killed in 1998. Chávez was pledged to make things better. Judicial reform had been high on his list of priorities; now prison reform would have to be tackled as well.

Chávez issued a new penal code by decree in July, as he was entitled to do while waiting for the exact wording of the new constitution. The decree was designed to modernise the judicial system, and to give suspects the presumption of innocence and the guarantee of a swift trial.

The publication of the decree inevitably encouraged prisoners to think that something might soon be done, and in September riots broke out at a number of prisons throughout the country. A dozen prisoners were killed. At one prison outside Caracas, the National Guard were sent in with tanks to restore order.

In the first week of October, the Constitutional Assembly declared a 'prisons emergency' that proved to be an impressive example of government on the hoof. Chávez announced on his Sunday morning radio programme on October 3 that teams of judges and prosecutors, together with human rights activists and priests, had gone into four of the country's most dangerous prisons to try to speed up prosecution and sentencing. He said he wanted to accelerate justice for prisoners awaiting trial, and to speed up the implementation of the new penal code. He thought many people could be released immediately because of the length of time they had already served, while the prison teams hoped to clear 6,000 cases of prisoners awaiting trial by the end of the year.

A day-release scheme was promoted to enable prisoners to work outside the prison during the day.

Chávez said he also hoped that the prisons would be able to begin to segregate prisoners awaiting trial according to the crimes they were accused of committing. In many prisons, people accused of being pick-pockets shared cells with murder suspects. He told his radio audience that the National Guard had spent the weekend searching the prisons for weapons. He said it was the usual custom for prison guards to confiscate them – and then sell them back to the prisoners.

The crisis in the prisons refocused attention on the reform of the judiciary. Judges in Venezuela had traditionally been appointed by the majority party in Congress, as were the members of the Supreme Court. While a quarter of the Supreme Court members held permanent positions, the rest lacked any independence and could be dismissed at will. These members were at their most vulnerable when they tried to take action against politicians or their business partners, or moved against the presidents of powerful commercial concerns. Corruption charges against President Lusinchi had been held up by the Supreme Court for years. Recommendations by an investigating magistrate that he should be put on trial were simply ignored. One Supreme Court justice had resigned in protest in 1992, and a group of intellectuals had urged other members of the court to do the same, but nothing ever happened, and the Lusinchi case faded away.

Quijada's Judicial Emergency Commission drafted several legal clauses for the new constitution and suggested new procedures for the selection and training of judges. The new ways of supervising their activity that it recommended were similar to those of the United States. One suggestion was for candidates for the Supreme Court to face public hearings. While some hostile critics argued that these reforms would take years to take effect, most people agreed that the advances made would eventually prove beneficial. Yet it was not until 2004, with the enlargement of the Supreme Court, that the government was finally able to make the necessary changes.

26

DEVELOPING A 'BOLIVARIAN' FOREIGN POLICY

Chávez set out with high ambitions in the field of foreign affairs. His aim was nothing less than the 'Bolivarian' dream of the union of the peoples of Latin America. Others have paid lip service to this notion during the past half century, most notably Fidel Castro and Che Guevara. Castro, in his early days in power in Cuba, invoked the tradition of 'Our America', in the 'First Declaration of Havana' in 1960. With his wonderful sense of history, he eulogised 'the America that Bolívar, Hidalgo, Juárez, San Martín, O'Higgins, Sucre and Martí wished to see free'.

Che Guevara, in his guerrilla camp in Bolivia at Nancahuazú in December 1966, invoked the spirit of the continental revolution, drinking a toast to the new '*grito de Murillo*' that his guerrilla group was making, invoking the cry of the lawyer in La Paz in 1809 that had been designed to spark off the liberation of Latin America.

The fascination of Chávez with the story of Bolívar and the 'Bolivarian' project of emancipation continues this tradition of radical American leadership, and as a Venezuelan he can draw on his own country's rather special relationship with the Liberator. In an interview with Agustín Blanco Muñoz in 1995, Chávez argued that 'the geopolitical concept of Bolívar, envisaging the union of the continent, still has tremendous contemporary force'.

None of his generals at the time of independence, at least none of his Venezuelan generals, had this vision, this notion of uniting all these balkanised territories of Latin America in order to confront the imperial power of the north. Now everyone is searching and struggling towards this goal, not just the Venezuelans but all of Latin America.

An emphasis on Latin American economic integration is of course nothing new; this has been the established rhetoric of every government over many decades. The emphasis that Chávez has placed on politics is by contrast fresh and interesting. One of his ambitions has been to follow in the steps of Bolívar, and to convene a *congreso anfictiónico* in Caracas of all the Bolivarian states of the continent, just as Bolívar did in Panama in 1826.

> The twentieth century was a lost century. Our peoples lived better in the previous century than in this one, much better. So this can only be the union envisaged by Bolívar. *La patria* for all of us is America; and union is fundamental. Everyone has shared this aim: Martí, O'Higgins and Artígas – and Sandino and Perón said so too. The union of all our peoples.

His strategy, he says, 'is directed towards the creation of an alliance, a great Latin American and Caribbean union'. What he seeks is 'a community of nations and states'.

This, he implies, must be politically driven, but he does not forget the economics. 'We have defined as a priority in the definition of our foreign policy the integration of the three entities that surround Venezuela' – the Caribbean (the Cuenca del Caribe), the Amazon (Mercosur and Brazil), and the Andes (the Comunidad Andino).

In May 1999, Chávez explained to Heinz Dieterich, an Argentine journalist, that he hoped Venezuela would soon be able to 'press the accelerator' on the integration of the Andean Community, Mercosur, and the Cuenca del Caribe, 'including of course Central America up to Mexico, Cuba, and Santo Domino, and all the islands of the Caribbean'.

'Why', he asked rhetorically, 'don't we think in terms of a currency, not the dollar, but a Latin American currency, just like the euro of the European Community ...'

Chávez has extended this idea of integration to the military field. In November 1999, he addressed a party of time-servers from the Andean Parliament, a harmless talking-shop whose members are chosen from the national parliaments of the Andean republics. Chávez woke them from their slumbers to suggest that they should consider developing a Latin American Nato, a project for a continental military alliance that could hardly have been further from their minds.

Nato, of course, is an institution organised by the United States, which operates largely for its benefit. Chávez, by a sleight of hand, was suggesting something rather different – a Latin American Nato without the United States. For many years, of course, a Latin American Nato of sorts has been in existence, called the *Junta Interamericana de Defensa*. Its headquarters is in Washington, and although some US generals like to speak in Spanish, its meetings are conducted in English. Several Latin American armies, in return for political support, receive extensive economic assistance from Washington, and almost all of them have a privileged entrance into the US second-hand arms market.

Yet not every Latin American officer has been happy about this arrangement. Many remember the Falklands/Malvinas war in 1992 when their United States ally sided with the British against Argentina. Others recall the military interventions of the United States in the past decade – in Panama and in Haiti (and in Grenada in the 1980s). Everyone recognises that the threat of intervention in Colombia is high.

There is another military concern. The United States occupied Panama and then abolished the Panamanian army. Many officers in Venezuela fear, and Chávez has given voice to this fear, that this is now the US programme for the continent. Abolish the armed forces!

In the first year of the Chávez government its foreign policy was in the competent and emollient hands of José Vicente Rangel, a man well known for his sentimental attachment to the Cuban Revolution and for his hostility towards the policies of the United States on Latin America. Three times presidential candidate of the left, and for decades one of Venezuela's most outspoken journalists – with a weekly programme on radio and televison and a Sunday column in *El Universal* –

Rangel was charged with implementing Chávez's 'Bolivarian' foreign policy. Later he became vice-president.

On the walls of his office, beside the statutory portrait of Bolívar, only one other picture hangs, a photograph of José Ignácio Arcaya, the foreign minister in the early 1960s who – uniquely – refused to endorse the United States demand that the Latin American countries should boycott Castro's Cuba. Arcaya is remembered as the 'minister of dignity'. In a bleak decade he did the right thing. His son was Chávez's first minister of the interior. Rangel's son was a Chávez supporter in the Constitutional Assembly. The photograph is well chosen.

Broad-shouldered, white-haired, and with a military moustache, Rangel conjures up the image of a genial Colonel Blimp or, perhaps, of an insurance salesman, which of course he once was. Exiled to Spain in the 1950s during the dictatorship of Pérez Jiménez, he took the first job he was offered.

Born in 1929, in the days of the old dictator Juan Vicente Gómez, Rangel is a product of the radical euphoria of the era after 1945. Educated at the conservative Catholic Liceo La Salle in Barquisimento, he studied law at the university of Mérida, and then moved on to the Universidad Central in Caracas, ever a hotbed of radical politics. He had originally joined Jovito Villalba's *Unión Republicano Democrático* (URD), and was a member of the party's national leadership for many years, from 1950 to 1963.

Much of his political life has been influenced by his deep distrust of *Acción Democrática*, and particularly of its first leader, Rómulo Betancourt, who adopted a bitterly anti-communist and pro-United States position. This enduring hostility to *Acción Democrática* is shared by Chávez, and is one of the characteristics of all the senior figures in his government. Rangel finally left the URD in 1964, when Villalba allied himself with the hated party. In the 1970s, Rangel moved towards the Movement to Socialism of Teodoro Petkoff, which had split from the Communist Party; he was their presidential candidate on several occasions.

So why had this once fiery leftist teamed up with Comandante Chávez? By happenstance, he told me, he had been aware of the existence of Chávez before the failed coup of February 1992 brought him to national attention. Rangel's son, José Vicente junior, had studied at the military academy in Caracas in the 1980s. His commanding officer (and indeed his tutor) had been Hugo Chávez. At weekends, the (rather famous) former presidential candidate of the left and the (wholly unknown) future coup leader would meet. Later, Rangel was to visit Chávez in Yare prison.

Paradoxically, Rangel junior was obliged to leave the academy. It was thought that this son of a well-known leftist must be trying to infiltrate the military for the purpose of promoting a coup. No one realised at the time that the commanding officer rather than the raw recruit was behind the plotting.

One of José Vicente Rangel's tasks as foreign minister was to try to improve the image of the president abroad. Throughout the presidential campaign of 1998, the conservative opposition painted Chávez in the most sombre hues: at best Nasser and Atatürk, at worst Hitler and Mussolini. John Maisto, the US ambassador, refused to grant Chávez a visa to visit the United States when he was a candidate, and greeted his election with considerable alarm. An unambitious career diplomat who did not intend to go down in history as the man who had 'lost' Venezuela, Maisto believed Chávez to be a dangerous and anti-democratic *golpista*. 'I don't know anyone in Venezuela who thinks that Chávez is a democrat,' he is alleged to have said. Richard Wilkinson, the British ambassador, and the other European ambassadors took a more measured view. Chávez was invited to Britain in 1998 and made an excellent impression on everyone he met.

After his election as president, Chávez set out on a round of visits to the countries of Latin America, notably to Mexico, Brazil, and Argentina. He was politely received everywhere, although most of the other presidents clearly hoped that his Bolivarian dream of continental integration would remain just attractive rhetoric. He went to Rome to see the Pope and to Spain to see the king. He needed to shake off the negative image that had been constructed for him.

After some months as president, he repeated the exercise. In September 1999, he spoke at the United Nations in New York, and pressed the flesh in Washington. The United States had remained hostile during the early months of the Chávez government, and in August 1999, after the arguments between the old Congress and the new Constitutional Assembly had spread to the streets of Caracas, Washington expressed its anxieties openly.

The situation in Venezuela is a matter of 'growing concern', said James Foley, a State Department spokesman, on August 30, and he earnestly expressed the hope that all parties would 'come to agreement about how to exercise power' and how 'to assure the establishment of a constitution that preserves Venezuela's long-standing commitment to democracy'.

Yet with Chávez actually present in Washington, the atmosphere began to change. He won over the editors of the *Washington Post* at a breakfast meeting. 'He spoke in colorful and dramatic images', according to Nora Boustany's report, 'about the pain he felt from Venezuelans as he roamed the countryside on horseback and on foot after he finished a jail term five years ago for trying to stage a coup in 1992.' She noted that he had 'vowed to be inventive in tackling the country's problems, but promised no miracles or overnight solutions'.

'Serious leadership is needed,' he told the *Washington Post*, 'not irresponsible populism.'

Later in the year, Chávez set out to other parts of the world, including China, Japan, South Korea, Hong Kong, Malaysia, Singapore and the Philippines. Ever since the first presidency of Carlos Andrés Pérez in the 1970s, Venezuela had been counted among the nations of the Third World. Previous presidents, notably Pérez himself, had made a habit of visiting distant continents. Indeed, during his second presidency in the 1990s, Pérez was accused of spending too much time playing the role of international statesman. Yet Venezuela's position as a founder member of OPEC obviously made it a world player, and Chávez, although inevitably busy at home, was well aware that he needed to secure as much international support as he could get.

In this context, his visit to China in October was of considerable importance, both politically and economically. Venezuela's potential need for rice and cheap consumer goods, and China's need for oil, made them complementary partners. But Chávez also liked the Chinese political position on world affairs. His enthusiasm for the 'third way' of the British prime minister, Tony Blair, had waned after the Kosovo war, when he understood that the British position of abject support for the United States was in direct opposition to his own view of how world affairs should be conducted.

Chávez told the Chinese leaders in Beijing that he was in favour of 'an open and multipolar world' that would respect the sovereignty of peoples: 'In Venezuela, far away in America, we have already raised the banner of popular sovereignty, and in that we are wholly in agreement with the people of China and their revolutionary government.'

Paying a visit to the tomb of Mao Tse-tung on October 12, he wrote a eulogy to the 'great strategist, great soldier, great statesman, and great revolutionary'. And when he met the Chinese minister Zhu Rongji, he said simply that Venezuela was beginning to 'stand up', just as China had 'stood up' fifty years earlier, 'under the leadership of its great helmsman'.

Chávez told the Chinese he did not believe in 'the neo-liberalism that had been such a disaster in the Third World and had tried to impose economic models from the centres of world power in the West; it had resulted in millions of people leading lives of poverty, and had led to unemployment, misery, and death'.

> Soviet power has collapsed, but that does not mean that neo-liberal capitalism has to be the model followed by the peoples of the West. If only for that reason, we invite China to keep its flag flying, because this world cannot be run by a universal police force that seeks to control everything.

After travelling through Asia, Chávez returned home through Europe. He told the German prime minister, Gerhard Schröder, that he was hoping 'to create a different economic model', and that his advisers were 'looking with close attention at the German and European model'. He said that the new constitution in Venezuela would give 'greater stability and security to national and foreign investment'.

But he also reverted to his emphasis on multipolarity. The world should understand that 'a people had the right to reorganise its arrangements as it sees fit. There is a fundamental principle: the self-determination of peoples. There cannot be an international politics that watches what other people are doing, and then imposes its own model.'

The enthusiasm of Chávez for a 'multipolar' world still seems unusual in a Latin American context, although in the years since the end of the Cold War, the Europeans have frequently referred to its desirability. 'We cannot accept a politically unipolar world, nor the unilateralism of a single hyper-power,' announced the French foreign minister, Hubert Védrine, in a speech in Paris on November 3, 1999. Yet in Latin America in the 1990s, the leading countries, notably Mexico and Argentina, and to a lesser extent Chile, have perceived themselves as members of 'the West', as potential members of the so-called First World. In their view, Latin America forms part of the American pole – an attitude not altogether different from that of Tony Blair in England. Yet even in the European debate, few people have indicated where potential poles other than the United States and Europe might be found.

Hugo Chávez has taken an entirely different and innovative stand, lining up with Védrine in favour of multipolarity, and making a specific bid for the formation of a Latin American pole. In this ambition he had the warm but tacit support of Brazil where President Fernándo Henríque Cardoso, while happy to accept the US neo-liberal economic model, shared the traditional belief of successive Brazilian governments in the geo-political importance of a continent-size country like Brazil.

Chávez is optimistic about what he sees as a global renaissance of nationalism.

I think we are living through a period in which nationalism is being reborn. You can see this in the conflict in Chechnya against the Russians. It's like the return of history, just as the old nations came back after the First World War ...

Before, there was a dual globalism, two imperial powers that wanted to gobble up the world, and then one of them collapsed and the other said, 'Now it's my turn, I am the owner of the new world order, the single-power world.' Then that idea collapsed, and quite rapidly.

What we have now is world disorder. There is no order, and there is not a single superpower. The future will have many centres, and we shall see the formation of alliances and blocs.

Chávez's problem is that there is no sign as yet of the countries of Latin America organising themselves into a bloc capable of negotiating with the world outside the continent. It will take time for his message to percolate through. Many Latin American presidents will be reluctant to listen to it, for none of them has ever perceived Venezuela as a natural political leader in the continent.

In Venezuela, Chávez talks over the heads of his immediate listeners to the wider audience beyond. The same technique has been paying dividends in Latin America, where he has been gaining an increasingly large audience.

27

COLOMBIA: THE VIOLENT NEIGHBOUR

For the armed forces of Venezuela, and therefore for Chávez, the most stretching external problem facing the country – today, yesterday, and tomorrow – is its relationship with Colombia. Venezuela has hundreds of miles of unguarded borders with Colombia, a country involved for many decades in the kind of prolonged and vicious civil war that characterised Venezuela in the nineteenth century.

That war often spills over the frontier. On occasion Venezuelan landowners in the states of Zulia and Táchira have been kidnapped, and lorry drivers taking goods in and out of Colombia have been attacked. Both sides in the war, the 'guerrillas' on the left and the 'paramilitaries' on the right, have been involved in these frontier incidents.

Yet the Colombian problem is far more significant and central to Venezuela than the relatively simple issue of border incidents. Colombia is a country in a state of profound crisis, and the future of the Chávez government will inevitably be affected by what happens next door. The existing Colombian state is on the verge of collapse; indeed in much of the country it has already collapsed, undermined by the drugs economy that is now much larger than the traditional national economy.

More significant, the new emerging forces in Colombia, associated with the Revolutionary Armed Forces of Colombia (the FARC) and the National Liberation Army (the ELN), express similar Bolivarian views to those of Hugo Chávez. Venezuela's public desire is to assist in peace negotiations between the warring factions. In private, Chávez leans towards the FARC. Chávez hopes that it will be so successful in the peace negotiations that its incorporation into the government will entirely change the political complexion of Colombia. Were that to happen, Chávez's dream of re-creating Gran Colombia – the old nineteenth-century alliance of Venezuela, Colombia, and Ecuador, devised by Bolívar – would come true. The Bolivarian project that lies at the heart of his hopes for the continent would be well on its way.

The crisis in Colombia has been so prolonged, and has run through so many different phases, that anyone without a detailed knowledge of the country and its past finds it difficult to follow, let alone understand, what is going on. For most of its history Colombia has endured cycles of violence of extreme intensity. Much of this violence has been generated by peasant wars and struggles over land rights. The situation of civil war and local anarchy is so pronounced that the collapse of the central state has often been prophesied. Large swathes of this vast, continent-sized country have never come under the control of the central government. In the past decade or so, the situation has altered significantly, partly because of the end of the Cold War and partly because of the changing nature of the drugs trade.

Manuel Marulanda, the FARC leader, is effectively the ruler of a third of the country. The ELN is not so large as the FARC, but it too has the capacity to mobilise and motivate a substantial slice of the population. Marulanda has been running great chunks of Colombia for nearly forty years, and his guerrilla forces can pop up at any moment in almost any region. For most of that time, he was a peasant leader allied to the Colombian Communist Party. He took his orders from Jacobo Arenas, one of the most sophisticated Communist Party theorists in Latin America. The peasant movement, for better or worse, was run by the party – encouraged at some moments, switched off at others, according to the perceived political needs of the time.

Sometimes there were successes, as when the Communist Party and the guerrillas of the FARC survived the 1964 attack on their base at Marquetalia, an attack launched by the Colombian army with United States assistance. Sometimes there were disasters, as occurred in the late 1980s when the Party recommended the acceptance of peace offers and the establishment of a civilian front organisation, the Patriotic Union, that would participate in conventional politics. Many guerrilla leaders, from the FARC and other groups, descended from the hills to take part in the political campaigns of the Patriotic Union. The leaders, and thousands of their supporters, were promptly slaughtered by right-wing paramilitary groups. Plainly the policy had been an error. The experience had such an impact on Marulanda that to this day he is concerned that a peace agreement might lead to a repeat of the earlier catastrophe.

Although the FARC is at war with the Colombian army, their more formidable opponents are the paramilitary organisations. These are separate from the armed forces, though they often operate with their tacit support. Funded by the drug traffickers, they are immensely rich and powerful, and ruthless in war. The FARC also secures its financial support from the drug economy, though chiefly from the cultivators and the producers rather than the sellers and traffickers. This may be a fine distinction, and there is at least one documented case of a FARC chieftain who funded his independent operation from the trade itself.

Since the destruction of the Patriotic Union, the situation is considerably changed. The FARC is in a more dominant position, which has obliged the government to come to the negotiating table. The FARC is not the same political animal as it was in earlier decades. With the collapse of the Soviet Union and the end of the Cold War there is no longer a powerful Communist Party capable of manipulating the peasant war. Jacobo Arenas, the *éminence grise* of the old, Soviet-style FARC, has died and Marulanda has returned to his previous incarnation as a traditional peasant leader operating on his own, conducting his war with peasant cunning and with forty years' accumulated experience behind him.

At the same time, the nature of the countryside, and of work in the countryside, has been changed out of all recognition, partly by the disruption and devastation of the war itself, and partly by the transformations in the drugs trade. Twenty years ago Colombia was a large producer of marijuana, the third in the Americas after the United States and Mexico, but it grew no poppies (mostly cultivated in Mexico and Guatemala) and very little coca. Colombia merely processed the coca – grown in Peru and Bolivia – into cocaine, and exported it. Coca processing was not very labour-intensive.

Today the picture is rather different. The land area devoted to growing cannabis, coca and poppies has grown fivefold. Colombia is now the second-largest producer of coca in the Americas, and the largest exporter of heroin. The sums of money generated by this economic activity are so gigantic as to defy belief. According to one recent account, the drug traffickers had amassed a total of more than US$75 billion in 1997, more than Colombia's gross national product. Yet more significant, from the point of view of the peasant war, is the impact on rural employment. Thousands more people work on plant production for drug use than twenty years ago, and they are seriously affected by indiscriminate drug eradication programmes.

As a result, the armed forces at the disposal of Marulanda are no longer small peasants fighting for their land, they are rural labourers fighting for their work. Marulanda has mobilised this rural proletariat that works the coca and marijuana plantations, and has defended them with great success against the efforts made to destroy their livelihood – by the government, the army, and the United States. Part of the reasons for the FARC's success is that Marulanda, too, has money to spend.

These developments were not just of interest to those concerned with the history of Colombia; they also had an impact on Venezuela. For part of Marulanda's 're-branding' of the FARC involved a recovery of past history comparable to that undertaken by Chávez. The Colombian left, having escaped from the Marxist dislike for Bolívar espoused by the Communist Party, began to restore the figure of the Liberator to their pantheon of heroes. The FARC described some of its guerrilla units as 'Bolivarian militias'. (Colombia, it should be said in passing, had traditionally had some difficulty with the figure of Bolívar, since their very own hero of Bolívar's time, Francisco de Paula Santander, was responsible for the break-up of the Bolivarian project of Gran Colombia.)

Nor has the FARC been the sole player within the Colombian left. Floating somewhere in the background have been the former supporters of General Gustavo Rojas Pinilla, the dictator of the 1950s who oversaw the conclusion to the civil war of that time, the *Violencia*, and who has subsequently begun to enjoy a recovered reputation not unlike that of Medina Angarita in Venezuela. When Rojas Pinilla attempted a come-back in the 1970s, he had considerable support from socialist nationalists of the kind who today give support to Chávez.

The Chávez government in its early years was content to follow in the footsteps of its predecessors in the 1990s in its dealings with Colombia. It held discussions about the border problem both with the government in Bogotá and with the guerrilla organisations. The minister for frontiers in the Caldera government had been Pompeyo Márquez, an influential member of the Petkoff wing of the Movement to Socialism. A former Communist leader with a long-established relationship with Marulanda, he had used his contacts to secure a promise from the FARC that they would not operate in Venezuelan territory. Other contacts with the FARC in the 1990s were made by Arias Cárdenas when governor of the frontier state of Zulia. He made public his belief that the right-wing paramilitaries were run by the Colombian army.

When the Colombian government began to contemplate peace negotiations with the FARC in the late 1990s, Colombia and Venezuela agreed that Venezuela should have a role. Caldera met Colombia's president, Ernesto Samper, at the border town of Guasdualito in August 1997, to formalise this agreement. Venezuela subsequently suggested that Colombia might follow the Central American example and allow a 'group of friends' of the 'peace process' to be formed, which Mexico, Costa Rica, and Spain might join.

The peace process was given fresh impetus in 1999 with the arrival of a new Colombian president, Andrés Pastrana, who made a dramatic visit to Marulanda in the jungle in May that year. A cease-fire was agreed, and the FARC, in effect, was left in de facto control of large, if remote, areas of the country. The peace agreement was frequently broken, but lasted for three years.

Chávez made clear that he was anxious to continue the policy of support for the process begun by Caldera. Several members of his government had informal contacts with the guerrilla movements, and meetings between guerrilla representatives and Venezuelan government officials took place both in Caracas and in Havana. While Chávez broadly followed the policy laid down by Caldera, Chávez himself as well as Arias Cárdenas and Rangel were clearly not unsympathetic to the aims of the FARC.

In September 1999, President Pastrana began to express his concerns about Venezuela's intentions, as he explained to the *Washington Post*: 'I'm asking Chávez, please stay in your yard and we'll manage our own problems. We don't want to talk about the internal problems of Venezuela, because we don't want them to intervene in domestic issues in Colombia. If Chávez contacts the guerrillas, we want him to tell us first.'

Hovering over these occasional differences between Caracas and Bogotá was the government in Washington. This had become a major player in Colombia in 1999 after the start of Plan Colombia, a multi-faceted US aid package designed to help curb the drugs trade. The United States pledged itself to prop up the government in Bogotá regardless of the cost, promising US$1.5 billion in the first year. The figure had grown to US$3.9 billion by 2005, making Colombia the fifth largest recipient of US aid (and the embassy in Bogotá the largest US embassy in the world).

The peace process finally broke down in February 2002, and the new right-wing government led by President Alvaro Uribe Vélez was elected in May that year, with a programme to eliminate the guerrillas by military means. The FARC which had previously been perceived as an honourable negotiating partner was now branded by the government in Bogotá as a 'terrorist organisation'. The result of the fresh military conflict was growing trouble on the Venezuelan border, with guerrillas and paramilitaries – and growing numbers of refugees – crossing and re-crossing the long and ill-guarded frontier almost at will.

In this new situation, Chávez tried to sustain reasonably cordial relations with the Uribe government while also keeping up Venezuela's long-established contacts with the FARC. This delicate balancing act almost collapsed in December 2004 when Colombians kidnapped

Rodrigo Granada, one of FARC's political leaders, while he was visiting Caracas. A threatened break-down of diplomatic and trading relations was averted only by the timely intervention, in Caracas and Bogotá, of Fidel Castro.

Venezuela had grown increasingly concerned by US military activity in the area, involving not just Plan Colombia but the fresh US deployments as a result of the implementation of the Panama Canal treaty. The immense US military bases in the Panama Canal Zone were finally handed over to Panama in December 1999, and US land, sea, and air forces were reallocated to other places, some in the United States itself and some in the Caribbean.

Since the United States now had access to airports in the Dutch Antilles, offshore from Venezuela, the Americans put pressure on the Chávez government to allow them the right to overfly Venezuelan territory withour prior permission while engaged in their campaign against the Colombian drugs trade.

Chávez, to the irritation of the Americans, refused to allow them to do so. Yet since this refusal was supported not just by the left but by the high command of the Venezuelan armed forces, the United States had to recognise that this was an argument they could not easily win. Venezuela's reluctance to cooperate in military exercises became yet another cause of fricton between the two countries during the early Chávez years.

28

NEW RIGHTS FOR INDIGENOUS PEOPLES

Venezuela produces more beautiful women than any other country in the world, according to the definitions of beauty created by the organisations that have devised the competitions for Miss World and Miss Universe, yet none of the winners ever comes from the indigenous peoples or the community of blacks.

If there is one single individual responsible for this state of affairs it must be Osmel Sousa, a former advertising designer who is the boss of the Miss Venezuela Organisation. He works from a small pink-washed villa in the centre of Caracas that serves both as an office and as a finishing school for aspiring beauties. It is painted rose pink inside as well as out, and its lush interior might well be the setting for a Hollywood brothel. Here twenty-six young women come for five months every year to learn the finer points of deportment, style and presentation.

Señor Sousa sits behind a huge desk in a small room, framed by a huge and ornate full-length mirror. In the middle of the room is a tiny round pink-carpeted stage, where his potential pupils can display their attractions.

Sousa holds the franchise to operate the Miss Venezuela Organisation and he organises an annual competition on Venezuelan television which presents the young women from his school. 'This programme has the largest rating of the entire year,' he says with some pride, 'so it's the most expensive. The sponsors have to pay a lot of money – and this finances our organisation and our school.' His school has won the Miss

Universe and Miss World competitions many times. How does he spot the winners for his finishing school?

'I go to modelling schools and to fiestas as a kind of talent scout. We do a casting of forty girls from which we choose ten. And then we go on until we've got twenty-six. They then come here to the school and prepare for the competition. They come for five months. We show them how to prepare themselves, we teach them some phrases in English if they don't know it already. They learn how to do their hair and their make-up as though they were professionals, and they learn how to walk the catwalk. And of course they go to the gym, take exercise, and learn how to look after their bodies.'

In practice, the girls who come to the school are on a scholarship. 'They pay nothing. We only insist that they dedicate themselves to this full-time. They can't study or do anything else.'

Every year, there are fifty judges. 'They come from all strata of society,' Sousa claims, 'and they change every year. They are singers, actresses, politicians, hairdressers, designers, ex-beauty queens, diplomats. We have even had the British ambassador.' This is the organisation that defines the nature of Venezuelan loveliness. How does he do it?

'Venezuelan beauty doesn't exist, for here there is a great mixture of races. If I was to choose a beautiful Venezuelan native, she would be an Indian, with a round face and rather short; so our philosophy is not to choose a Venezuelan beauty, but to select a young woman who was born in Venezuela. She could have a Hungarian father, a Spanish mother, anything, as long as she was born in Venezuela.'

What about blacks? Venezuela is a Caribbean country which once had a large slave population, and blacks still form a large minority in the coastal provinces.

'Yes, we have blacks,' says Sousa, and he leafs through a publicity brochure with the faces and figures of the previous years. 'Look, we always have a black. Here's one,' and he points to a picture of the pouting Miss Delta, one off-white face among a dozen full-blooded Aryans. 'She looks like Naomi Campbell, doesn't she?'

Yet there is a terrible truth to which he feels obliged to admit. 'Miss Venezuela has never been black.' And why should that be? 'Because the

Venezuelan people would not perceive themselves to be well represented by a black.'

So as long as the advertising industry goes on portraying white women in their advertisements, and so long as institutions like the Miss Venezuela Organisation go on providing examples of white European beauty, this will almost certainly continue to be true.

What happens to Venezuela's former beauty queens, the ones that don't turn into presidential hopefuls like Irene Sáez? Sousa looks at his book of photographs. 'This one married a multi-millionaire. This one married a petrol magnate. This one was our third Miss World, she's an actress in America. This one works for a telephone company in the United States and earns lots of dollars. This one's a model in Italy.'

He leans back in his chair and reflects on the success of his charges. 'All of them come from the middle class and all of them marry very rich men. All of them have done very well, and we're very pleased. Rich girls in Venezuela have no desire to compete in beauty competitions. The rich have too much money.'

So just who are the Venezuelans? A million Europeans have come to settle in Venezuela in the years since 1945. Are they Venezuelans?

The Caribbean shores of the country throb to the rhythms of the progeny of former slaves from Africa. Are they Venezuelans?

More than 300,000 indigenous peoples live in the country's frontier provinces; in the forgotten areas of the states of Zulia and Táchira in the west, and in Amazonas and Bolívar to the south, live innumerable tribes and nations. Are they Venezuelans?

These are questions that 'the Venezuelans' rarely seem to ask themselves. For decades they have mouthed nationalist slogans and bowed down silently before the image of Columbus and Simón Bolívar, yet they do not ask themselves who they are or where they came from.

This is the challenge being addressed to the government of Chávez, and he does not shrink from it: 'History is not a single epic tale,' he told Agustín Blanco Muñoz, 'it is the history of culture, how the country was created, why we are the colour we are, why the country is called Venezuela, what was the process that brought us to where we are now.' In 1999, during the meetings of the new Constitutional Assembly, some of these questions about national identity began to be asked. The most heated discussions concerned the rights to be granted in the new constitution to the country's indigenous peoples.

Out of Venezuela's population of 23 million, some 316,000 are identified as indigenous peoples, about 1.4 per cent, although the number is almost certainly much larger. The most numerous group, the Wayúu, also known as the Guajíra, are probably about 197,000, and live chiefly in the state of Zulia, between Lake Maracaibo and the Colombian border.

In the half-empty areas of the east and the south live another 100,000: 44,000 in Amazonas, 35,000 in Bolivar, and 21,000 in Delta Amacuro. To the north of the Orinoco, 7,000 live in Anzoátegui, and 6,000 live in Apure.

Some 26 different ethnic groups are believed to live in Venezuela, and they deserve to be named in the names that they give themselves: Wayúu, Warao, Pemón, Añú, Yanomani, Jivi, Piaroa, Kariña, Pumé, Yecuana, Yukpa, Eñepá, Kurripakao, Barí, Piapoko, Baré, Baniva, Puinave, Yeral, Jodi, Kariná, Warekena, Yarabana, Sapé, Wanai, Uruak.

The Chávez government took a fresh interest in the future of the indigenous peoples from the start. Atala Uriana, a Wayúu leader from Zulia and a supporter of the *Polo Patriótico*, was appointed as the first minister of the environment, though he later resigned to become a member of the Constitutional Assembly.

In the run-up to the elections to that assembly special arrangements were made to ensure the election of at least three representatives of the indigenous peoples. Conive, the National Council of Indigenous Peoples, held a conference in March 1999 to choose their delegates: Nohelí Pocaterra, a Wayúu and a social worker and the President of the World Council of Indigenous Peoples; José Luís González, a Pemón and a sociologist, who was a prominent member of Conive and the founder of the *Asociación Indígena* in Bolívar state; and Guillermo Guevara, a Jivi and the director of the *Organización Regional de los Pueblos Indígenos* of Amazonas state. All three had long experience of promoting the rights of indigenous peoples.

The history of white settlement and indigenous resistance in Venezuela is long, complicated, and under-researched, though what has long been clear is that independence in the early nineteenth century made matters worse for the indigenous peoples. For two centuries the Spaniards had permitted the Capuchins, the Jesuits and the Franciscans to organise mission stations, and the Indians in the areas of missionary influence enjoyed some measure of protection. But the Jesuits withdrew in the 1760s, and a more violent fate awaited the Capuchins half a century later. Their extensive missions along the Caroní river had been planted close to the Orinoco delta for strategic reasons, for they helped to guard the country against the English and the Dutch. In 1817 they were affected by the arrival of the forces of Bolívar, who realised that whoever controlled the rich Capuchin missions would win the war. The missionaries, like most of the Catholic Church, had sided with the Spanish, and on May 7, 1817, they suffered for their decision. Twenty missionaries, aged between thirty-two and seventy, were slaughtered. The troops of the Liberator seized the missions, stole their grain and cattle, and enrolled the mission Indians into their regiments.

Throughout the nineteenth century, successive governments had no policy for the indigenous peoples other than a vain hope that the old missions might be restored. The Indians were driven relentlessly out from the centre towards the frontiers of the state.

Further to the south, in the middle of the eighteenth century the Spanish had begun pushing up into the waters of the Upper Orinoco. The Yecuana, then known as the Makiritare, did not care for the new arrivals, and between 1765 and 1775 they organised a serious resistance campaign. On a single night at the end of 1775, they captured and burnt down nineteen Spanish forts and camps along the road constructed from Angostura, or Ciudad Bolívar, to La Esmeralda on the Upper Orinoco.

More than a hundred years later, in May 1913, during the rubber boom, the whites hit back. Colonel Tomás Fúnes seized control of San Fernándo de Atabapo with a small force of rubber workers, and the town's governor, Roberto Pulido, was killed, as were his wife and brothers and 130 settlers. It was but a preliminary to the slaughter of the Makiritare Indians. Colonel Fúnes controlled the town for nine years, far beyond the control of the central state, and killed Indians on a massive scale. The book *Los Hijos de la Luna* describes how 'dozens and dozens of Makiritares villages were destroyed and their inhabitants killed. At a rough calculation, two thousand Indians were slaughtered during those tragic years …'

Colonel Fúnes surrendered in 1921 to the forces of General Emilio Arévalo Cedeño, a famous anti-Gómez guerrilla leader allied with Maisanta, the great grandfather of President Chávez. Fúnes foolishly believed that he had surrendered in return for his life, but he was shot anyway. The indigenous peoples of Venezuela remember the stories of their oppression with greater detail than do the heirs to the white settlers, and even today their complaints are often ignored or rejected.

In October 1999, Pemón Indians living in the south-east corner of Venezuela drew attention to their presence by destroying a number of electricity pylons. The construction of the pylons across their territory, to conduct a high-voltage line from the Guri dam to Brazil, had begun during the Caldera government. The Pemón disliked the pylons, and claimed that the easy availability of cheap electricity would serve to encourage further development by mining companies. The gold deposits in the region had already attracted an army of labourers with scant respect for the rights of the Pemón.

The government's official position was that the pylons would inflict little environmental damage; development of the region was needed in order to create jobs. The electricity project, costing US$110 million, could not be stopped, since contracts had already been signed with towns in northern Brazil. The completed line was inaugurated by Chávez in August 2001, in the presence of Fidel Castro and Fernando Henrique Cardoso of Brazil. Chávez claimed that he had done what he could to avoid disturbing the virgin forest.

In December 1999, one of the great indigenous leaders of Latin America, Rigoberta Menchú, arrived in Caracas to give her blessing to the changes relating to indigenous rights in the new constitution. Rigoberta, from Guatemala, had won the Nobel Peace Prize in 1992, and been a tireless protagonist in the continental campaign to secure rights for indigenous peoples:

In many countries they have been discussing these questions during the last fifteen or twenty years, and they have imagined that to give rights to indigenous people might be a bad thing, or might affect adversely the rest of the citizenry. But we have shown that we are patriots; that's where we stand, even if we have been affected by racism and exclusion ... It's important that people should abandon these fantasies, for they are a shackle on the development of peaceful coexistence between different groups.

White settler attitudes towards indigenous peoples have been changing in recent years all over the Americas. In some countries, the indigenous people are the majority of the population and have begun to glimpse the power that is their due. Elsewhere the *mestizos*, those of mixed race, are beginning, like the blacks, to wonder how to define themselves in new and changing situations.

These ethnic issues have already become important subjects for debate and action in the twenty-first century, notably in the countries of the Andes. Venezuela under Chávez is one of the vanguard countries where these issues are being brought out into the open, where the white racist opposition – typical of the white settler countries of the Americas – has been most vocal, and where the government has come down most decidedly on the side of the blacks and the indigenous peoples.

29

THE CHANGING CHARACTER
OF THE OPPOSITION

Every afternoon in Caracas during Chávez's first year in power, concerned and politically aware citizens would make a special effort to go out to buy *El Mundo*, the evening newspaper published by the Capriles group and edited with great flair and brilliance by Teodoro Petkoff, the veteran erstwhile leftist now fighting a rearguard action. *El Mundo* at that time was the intelligent face of the opposition to Hugo Chávez: accurate, informed, and intensely irritating, it spoke its mind with considerable vitality.

Teodoro Petkoff, like so many participants in the Venezuelan drama, was a guerrilla fighter of yesteryear. Born in 1931, the son of immigrants from Bulgaria who had settled near Maracaibo, he joined the youth movement of the Communist Party in 1949, at the start of the Pérez Jiménez era. Although he studied to be a doctor like his mother, he was soon drawn to political activism and to journalism. In the central committee of the Communist Party in 1961, he was a keen advocate of armed revolt against the government of Rómulo Betancourt, and in 1962 he followed Douglas Bravo into the hills. Twice detained, he was held in the San Carlos prison in Caracas for three years, from 1964 to 1967, from where he took part with others in a spectacular escape.

Petkoff became a permanent dissident, increasingly unhappy with the strategy of the Communist Party. He was an early critic of the Soviet Union's invasion of Czechoslovakia in 1968, an event supported by both the Communist Party and Fidel Castro. In 1969 he accepted the offer made to the guerrillas by President Caldera to come down from the hills, or to return from exile, and in 1970 he helped to set up the Movement to Socialism, the party founded by Americo Martín that split off from the Communist Party.

During the subsequent thirty years, Petkoff was a major figure of the ever-squabbling Venezuelan left. A eurocommunist *avant la lettre*, he was the presidential candidate of the left on several occasions. In the 1990s, as the crisis of Venezuelan society became ever more grave, he put his name and his credibility, and his immense energy and talent, at the service of President Caldera, the octogenarian Kerensky of the *ancien régime*. As Caldera's minister of development, Petkoff gave this last-gasp government the capacity to survive. It was a typically courageous gesture.

Then, in the middle of 1998, when the leaders of the MAS decided to harness the party to the presidential campaign of Hugo Chávez, Petkoff jumped off the political vehicle he had once helped to create. His resignation from the MAS was a defining moment for many of Venezuela's old leftists. Some remained with the Chávez project, while others became columnists on *El Mundo*, the paper Petkoff took over in order to propagate his own political position hostile to the new president.

For most of the first year of the Chávez government, the columnists of *El Mundo* and the other newspapers, particularly *El Universal*, sniped away at the new politics. Surprisingly for a revolutionary project with so many journalists within its ranks, the Chávez government proved notably poor at public relations, and found it difficult to rebut the attacks of the overwhelmingly hostile press.

The hostile pack of columnists, drawn up and orchestrated by Petkoff, made a formidable noise; yet they were voices crying in the wilderness, quite without political backing. The overwhelming defeat of the traditional parties in the elections at the end of 1998, and their notable lack of support or affection in the hearts and minds of the great mass of the people, had meant the collapse of any organised political opposition to Chávez. Such was the discredit into which yesterday's politicians had fallen that many of them simply crept away, or stayed at home to write their memoirs.

The only serious opposition in the first year, apart from the newspaper columnists, came from the leaders of the once powerful economic groups, traditionally accustomed to sounding off and being listened to: men like Vicente Brito, the president of Fedecámaras; Antonio Herrera Vaillant, the vice-president of the all-embracing Venamcham, the Venezuelan–American chamber of commerce that groups together a thousand foreign and national businesses; and Luís Eduardo Paul, the president of the Cámara Petrolera. Notably, during the debates about the new constitution, these individuals and their groups took it upon themselves, through interviews and press conferences, to outline their opposition to the economic clauses that might adversely affect their interests. Yet they, like the communists, were without significant political backing.

Occasionally, a voice from the former era could be heard. Many old conservatives feared what they called the 'neo-populism' of Chávez. Eduardo Fernández, once a presidential hopeful of *Copei*, denounced 'the messianism, the paternalism, the centralism, and the rentier vision of the economy' that he believed to be sweeping Venezuela and Latin America, with 'pathetic and depoliticised masses' rising above the old parties and ideologies.

Towards the end of 1999, during the referendum campaign for the new constitution, this opposition became increasingly shrill, clothing itself in the traditional garments of the Latin American right. Fears were expressed that democracy was in the process of being destroyed by democratic means. Chávez was attacked as a long-term 'conspirator' and criticised for his use of violent language, 'the language of civil war'. The opposition complained that the customary civilities of debate were being abandoned, with 'the country split in two halves that do not speak to each other'.

Much of the overblown rhetoric of this embryonic opposition was designed to summon potential opponents to Chávez to join a new political crusade against him. Chávez, it was claimed, was against the political parties, against the business community, against the media, and hostile to the Catholic Church. If these sectors of society would only wake up to the menace that he posed, then a new political movement of opposition might be organised. Some critics even began to hint that sections of the military were unhappy with the Chávez project, and might be willing to listen to subversive talk of a new coup.

Critics could also be found in Chávez's old Bolivarian Revolutionary Movement, people unhappy about the way things were going in government. Such people wanted Chávez to be more revolutionary, not less. They wanted action against the rich and privileged, and a firmer defence of Venezuelan interests against those of the United States. Yet as is obvious from the details in this book, the planning of a military coup is not an everyday event that any disgruntled officer can organise. Even when planned by men of competence and vision, with popular support, it can very easily fail.

Many of the old politicians hoped that their discredited parties would arise once again. This is what had happened in General Velasco's Peru and General Perón's Argentina, where the old parties eventually sprang back into action. Yet Venezuela was going through a more profound upheaval that was likely to leave the political landscape changed for ever. If a serious and democratic political opposition were eventually to emerge, it would more probably come from within the ranks of the *chavistas* than from the opposition. Yet as Chávez became more firmly rooted in power, after the successful referendum in support of the constitution at the end of 1999, the opposition took on a more ominous role. The paper tigers represented by Petkoff and his ilk became increasingly irrelevant, while the real forces behind the scenes – in the business community, within the state oil company, and in the US embassy – came to the fore. Power shifted from the newspaper columnists to the newspaper owners.

30

THE OLD TRADE UNIONS OPPOSE
THE REVOLUTION, OCTOBER 2001

The Chávez government has been sustained neither by a significant political party nor by an important trade union. Indeed what remained of the
country's traditional parties and unions after 1998 have been prominent
in their support for the right-wing opposition, the 'yellow' unions joining
hands with the employers' organisation to oppose the government.

Chávez has preferred it that way. So anxious was he to sweep away
the *ancien régime* that had misgoverned the country for so long that he
had no wish to re-establish the institutions that sustained it. His aim
was to establish a revolutionary government in Latin America that
would be genuinely 'original', as commanded by his nineteenth-century
philosophical guru, Simón Rodríguez, to whom he owes more than to
Marx or Castro. Rodríguez's political advice to the newly independent
countries of the 1820s was crystal clear:

> Spanish America is an original construct. Its institutions and its govern-
> ment must be original as well, and so too must be the methods used to
> construct them both. Either we shall invent, or we shall wander around
> and make mistakes.

Chavez was determined 'to invent' from the start, and that meant
dispensing with old political models. This neglect of institutions such
as a political party or a trade union was a curious and unusual phenomenon to anyone on the left. Leftist rhetoric for more than a century had

concentrated on 'building the party' and creating the institutions of the working class. Even in the Third World conditions of Latin America, where the organised working class has often been in a small minority, leftists have usually regarded a party and a trade union movement as an essential part of their political project. Castro's Cuba, Allende's Chile, and the Nicaragua of the Sandinistas all considered these institutions to be important. How should the people, newly emancipated, be organised if not through these traditional political organisations?

Chávez was recognisably a leftist in the Latin American tradition, with a strong anti-imperialist rhetoric and a genuine desire to secure benefits for the poorest sections of the population, and his ambitions were laid out in the constitution of 1999. A dozen articles in the constitution are directly concerned with labour and the rights of workers, and among these (articles 95 and 96) are solid confirmation of the right to form unions and the right to strike.

Yet Chávez did not put his shoulder behind moves made by others to create a new union movement. He started from the firm belief that parties and unions had been discredited in Venezuela by the actions of previous governments over half a century. When elected president in 1998, he arrived on the scene as someone wholly unconnected with what had gone before. His victory was achieved over the ashes of the previous system, which had effectively imploded. Why then would he want to re-create a political structure that had failed so dismally?

Support for Chávez had come precisely from that large (majority) section of society that was hitherto disorganised, effectively out of reach of traditional politics. He mobilised his supporters by appealing to them as the poor and the disenfranchised, and as peasants and shanty town inhabitants. He made no appeal to them in their condition as workers – and still less as the privileged workers that made up the bulk of the politicised unions of the previous era. When he sought to mobilise workers in the early years of his presidency, he turned first to the disorganised informal sector, hitherto untouched – indeed ignored and rejected – by formal unionism.

The traditional organisation of the country's working class over several decades had been the Confederation of Venezuelan Workers (the CTV). This was a politically powerful and influential institution, founded in 1936, which had participated in all the progressive struggles of the past half century. Yet it had never embraced more than about 12 per cent of the workforce. Organically linked to *Acción Democrática*, the principal party of government since 1958, the CTV had begun to suffer from this connection in the 1990s, when neo-liberal governments introduced reforms that adversely affected workers' interests. The CTV became widely discredited as a bosses' union, with attendant thugs, and its decline was attended by the growth of several independent unions associated with *La Causa R*, notably in the industrial complex in Ciudad Guayana. These new movements paved the way for the defeat of the old political parties and their attendant unions, but did not lead to their own success. Chávez, rather than the politicians thrown up by the independent unions, took advantage of the new situation, and started his presidency with a *tabula rasa*.

After Chávez's victory, the CTV was perceived as an important part of the discredited *ancien régime*. Losing members, and without the political funding that had formerly come its way, the CTV now embarked on an internal reform process to try to regain strength and credibility. With the financial support of its principal external ally, the American Center for International Labor Solidarity (ACILS), the international arm of the US AFL-CIO, it modernised its internal structure, ousted some of the old guard, and held elections for a new leadership. (The ACILS is funded by the US National Endowment for Democracy, an organ of the US Congress.)

Battle was soon drawn between the CTV, which wished to capitalise on its existing strength within organised labour, and the Chávez trade unionists who were more interested in mobilising the hitherto unorganised informal sector – where half the country's workforce was to be found. The CTV successfully kept out the informal sector from membership of their union.

Leadership elections for the CTV were held in October 2001 in which the union organisations favourable to Chávez attempted to secure representation. But the *Acción Democrática* slate remained firmly in control. Their candidate, Carlos Ortega, won 57 per cent of the vote, while Aristóbulo Isturiz, the Chávez candidate (once a leader of *La Causa R*), secured only 16 per cent. The government quickly claimed the elections were fraudulent.

Chávez's supporters went on to organise a rival trade union, the National Union of Workers (the UNT), which held its first congress in 2003. But without powerful support from Chávez himself, it was more of a radical talking-shop than a significant new institution capable of organising both the formal and the informal sectors. Chávez began to rely on *ad hoc*, semi-military mobilisations – 'Bolivarian circles', electoral 'patrols', educational 'missions' – to organise the hitherto disorganised sectors of society. Chávez was the master of 'invention', but in the struggle for 'originality' the role of organised labour had still to be mapped out.

The CTV leadership remained passionately hostile to Chávez since he threatened their powerful position built up over decades, and in the autumn of 2001 Carlos Ortega joined those who had begun plotting to overthrow the president. Yet although Ortega's union had considerable industrial muscle, it lacked countrywide support. He was obliged to join with other disgruntled elements in society, notably the employers' organisation, *Fedecámeras*, to try to bring down the government. The CTV was to participate in the preparations for the military coup of April 2002, and it helped in the work stoppage of December 2002 that briefly closed down the petroleum industry. It was an unusual kind of trade union that cooperated with the bosses to try to bring down an elected government.

PART SIX:
THE THREE OPPOSITION ATTEMPTS TO OVERTHROW THE BOLIVARIAN REVOLUTION

31

THE REVOLUTIONARY DECREES OF NOVEMBER 2001, THE RESIGNATION OF LUÍS MIQUILENA, AND THE MOBILISATION OF THE OPPOSITION

The great city of Caracas spreads over innumerable mountainous hills, and in the rainy season the peaks poke up through the clouds that hover in the valleys below. Several million people live on these steep slopes in distinctive *ranchos*, a word usually translated into English as 'shanty towns' that does little justice to the reality. For these are not just settlements of corrugated iron and wattle-and-daub, though these materials are not wholly absent, but well-established homes of cheap bricks and breeze blocks set in concrete frames. Their defining characteristic is close proximity, each tiny habitation piled high above another, fighting for space.

A vast mass of humanity passes by in perpetual movement. Some people are white or of mixed race, but the great majority are dark-skinned, either black or of indigenous origin. Venezuela is poised geographically between Brazil and the islands of the Caribbean, and the children of slaves and Indians far outnumber those of the European settlers. The people are both cheerful and motivated, but in one of the richest countries in Latin America they live in permanent and absolute poverty. Education and health care are in short supply. So is work. Many people scratch a living as hawkers in the valleys below.

The air is clear, and the views are breath-taking. The atmosphere is that of a hill town in medieval Europe, although the facilities are more modern. Water and electricity are notionally available, but rubbish removal is poorly organised and waste often piles up on the steep stone staircases and along the narrow terraces that criss-cross these immense urban conglomerations. These are unplanned pedestrian precincts, for no bus or car could negotiate the hills on which they are constructed. Security is the principal concern, with iron grilles and locked doors being the most important and expensive element in house construction.

From their hillside eyries the poor look down on the self-satisfied settlements of the rich, the 'other' Venezuela that has run the country since the Conquest, with the comfortable homes of the elite, the business class, and the foreign diplomats and journalists.

This tiny minority of Venezuelans, mostly white, live in sprawling condominiums with maids and swimming pools; they shop in supermarkets; and they travel to work in air-conditioned cars along spreading motorways. The image of South Africa comes to mind, the black township of Soweto contrasted with the white suburbs of Johannesburg. There is no legal apartheid in Latin America, but the phenomenon of racial division and injustice exists all the same. White settlers have ruled the continent since the time of the conquistadors, and in countries like Venezuela a steady stream of European immigrants in the nineteenth and twentieth centuries reinforced the white elite. Its ingrained and often unrecognised racism continues to dominate the country's politics.

The abiding fear of the white population of Caracas over the years has been that the dark and impoverished citizens in the hills above would one day descend on their happy playground and wreak vengeance. The *Caracazo* of 1989 had left a raw memory of what could happen when the inherited systems of social control collapsed. Something similar, though without violence, was to happen in April 2002, when the shanty town dwellers silently and spontaneously filtered down from their hilltops to block the streets and motorways, and to restore their president to power – after he had been briefly overthrown in an operetta *coup d'état*.

A new era had began in Venezuela in 1999, after a decade of economic and social crisis and the collapse of the old and corrupted political parties. Hugo Chávez appealed to the poor in the shanty towns to help organise a revolution, and they had already begun to respond at the moment of his (temporary) overthrow in April 2002. Yet his style of government during his first years in power had created many enemies, and had increasingly irritated the country's white elite. They disliked his radical proposals for land reform, and they hated his plan to halt the programme of oil industry privatisation devised by previous governments. Most of all, they feared his mobilisation of the poor. Senior generals, conservative businessmen, oil executives and media moguls began to conspire against him – to seek his overthrow. By the end of 2001 this burgeoning opposition had formulated plans to stage a *coup d'état* on the Pinochet model.

The country had experienced a growing sense of crisis throughout the year. An ever-increasing number of large protest marches were staged in Caracas by the opposition, with the support of an unusual alliance between Fedecámeras, the employers' federation, and the Venezuelan Workers' Federation (CTV), the trade union movement associated with *Acción Democrática*.

These opposition protests were given a fresh focus at the end of the year after a government decree of November 2001 that introduced a series of 49 radical laws. This comprehensive raft of legislation was designed to revolutionise the country's economic infrastructure, and to build on the changes already outlined in the new constitution of 1999. Some three years after Chávez had come to power, the 'Bolivarian' revolutionary process was beginning to change gear.

The *Ley Habilitante*, or Enabling Law, that permitted the enactment of the new measures was published in November with little prior warning. (The government had suddenly woken up to the fact that the original authorisation, granted by the National Assembly in November 2000, had only been made for one year.) Chávez announced the details while speaking on television from the Miraflores palace, and to emphasise the significance of the new legislation he was flanked by his Council of Ministers.

The 49 laws were designed to regulate (among many other things) the tenure of land, the production and taxation of oil, and the operations of the fishing industry. One of the laws reversed the plans of the Caldera government to privatise the country's social security system. The details of the new legislation had been prepared over several months by a committee chaired by the vice-president, Adina Bastinas, an economist previously at the Inter-American Development Bank.

The law on land reform, always a subject of contention in Latin America, prohibited individual landholdings of more than 5,000 hectares, and gave the government powers to take over and redistribute landholdings that were idle or unproductive. Venezuela's landowners had dwindled in number during the years of the oil boom, for they had mostly moved over into industry and commerce. Yet the government's threat to their large, and often underutilised and unprofitable acreage in the *llanos* affected their sense of *amour propre*. The land reform became a symbol of the Bolivarian Revolution, indicating its intention to make a dramatic change. Land reform was also extended to the urban areas. In a decree of February 2002, local committees were encouraged to survey urban land and to provide title deeds to long-term residents.

Ultimately more significant was the Hydrocarbons Law, which envisaged the collection of higher oil royalties, and insisted that the state oil company, *Petróleos de Venezuela*, should have a 51 per cent stake in all joint ventures with foreign companies. Drafted by Alvaro Silva Calderón, who had been appointed minister of energy and mines after Alí Rodríguez became the secretary-general of OPEC, it established a minimum royalty rate of 30 per cent, to be paid by private oil companies to the government. The eventual aim of the radicals was to oblige the state oil company to spend less on overseas investment and to provide more money for social projects at home. The new law marked an end to the hopes of the old guard of oil executives at *Petróleos de Venezuela* that they would be able to privatise the company – and to open it up for sale to investors at home and abroad.

This fresh twist in the revolutionary screw – the first real indication after the drafting of the new constitution that Chávez had a genuinely radical agenda – was a serious threat to the interests of the white elite and to the rulers of the oil company, and it led immediately to opposition protests – and the organisation of fresh street demonstrations. Opposition spokesmen declared that they had not been consulted about the new measures, and they objected to what they saw as a threat to private property. Chávez insisted that hundreds of experts and interested parties had been consulted, but he admitted that there had not been time 'to sit down with everyone'.

The first senior figure to protest publicly was General Guaicaipuro Lameda, the boss of *Petróleos de Venezuela*. General Lameda had been appointed by Chávez, but he had joined the ranks of those within the company who thought it should be privatised. He attacked the new Hydrocarbons Law for requiring an increase in oil royalties. Chávez sacked him at once, and replaced him with Gastón Parra, an old-fashioned radical from the university. General Lameda transferred seamlessly to the opposition camp, and joined the plot to secure the overthrow of the president.

The organisation of immense demonstrations and political strikes now became the opposition's hallmark. Coupled with adverse opinion polls, which appeared to suggest that support for Chávez was slipping, the demonstrations gave credence to the widespread notion that the government was unpopular and under threat.

There was also a serious weakening within the ranks of government. General Lameda had been a personal appointment by Chávez, and soon Luís Miquilena, the most important civilian adviser of Chávez since his days in the Yare prison, had also decided to abandon ship. In the early years of the Chávez government, he had been responsible for vetting all *chavista* candidates for the National Assembly and the Supreme Court. Chávez had relied on him to navigate through the waters of civilian politics, with which the president had been wholly unfamiliar, and in the autumn of 2001 he held the important post of Minister of the Interior. Miquilena now felt the time had come to call a halt to the revolution's forward march. In early December he asked for a meeting with Chávez and told him bluntly that it would be necessary to abandon the new laws. 'They have been the cause of these protests and we should withdraw them,' he said.

Chávez replied that this was not the moment to slow down, but rather the time to move ahead with their project to transform the country. Miquilena disagreed, and set out his arguments. Chávez refused to accept them, and Miquilena was forced to resign – and he followed General Lameda into the opposition camp.

Miquilena's departure was a considerable blow to Chávez: not just because he had been an important ally but also because he had a considerable personal following, both within the judiciary and in the National Assembly. Since many members of both institutions had been chosen by Miquilena for the Chávez list, the withdrawal of his support had a seriously negative effect. At the end of 2001 the government was on the verge of losing its majority in the Assembly, and its position within the judiciary was weakened.

Miquilena represented the quite considerable group of Chávez supporters of the first instance who had themselves been disenchanted with the *ancien régime* and who had hoped that Chávez might have been harnessed to their own rather modestly reformist agenda. Such people had begun to understand by the end of 2001 that Chávez was his own man, and could not be used by others. Opposition groups, encouraged by these important defections, now came to believe, wrongly as it turned out, that they were in the majority, and could force the president to resign. They went on the offensive, effectively using street demonstrations to mobilise their supporters, and to give colour and credibility to their anti-government protest. In December they organised a general strike, the first of many.

Chávez now sought to put fresh popular energy into his own ranks, and launched a new initiative: the Bolivarian Circles. His supporters were called upon to organise themselves into small groups of a dozen or more, who would undertake to campaign in their localities and neighbourhoods, helping people to understand how they could take advantage of government programmes. People were encouraged to organise themselves locally, to secure micro-credits from the government bank, and to form their small businesses into cooperatives. The principal purpose of the Circles was to create a political organisation from those who had long remained outside society – and outside the formal structure of the existing political parties.

The battle between government and opposition was now joined, taking the public form of rival street demonstrations, each side seeking to prove that it had the majority. In private, the government sought to shore up its political position, while the opposition rehearsed its plans for a *coup d'état*, seeking support within the armed forces – and in Washington. By the beginning of 2002 the scene was set for a trial of strength.

32

THE FIRST OPPOSITION THREAT: THE COUP AND COUNTER-COUP OF APRIL 2002

The atmosphere in Caracas in the early months of 2002 was explosive and conflictive. A sense of impending disaster spread over the city. Demonstrations and counter-demonstrations took place each week, as the country mobilised behind rival banners. Groups of retired officers, politicians from the old political parties, union leaders, and spokesmen for the Catholic hierarchy united to denounce the government and to claim that they had support within the armed forces for a possible coup; newspapers and the private television channels kept up an endless litany of stories hostile to Chávez; and officials in Washington began to make critical comments about what was widely seen as a deteriorating situation.

For experienced observers of Latin America, Caracas in April 2002 was growing to resemble Santiago de Chile in September 1973. No one had any doubt that a *coup d'état* was in the making. Among those who knew more than most was the US Central Intelligence Agency. A US intelligence brief of April 6, entitled 'Conditions Ripening for Coup Attempt', described what was happening in Caracas:

> Dissident military factions, including some disgruntled senior officers and a group of radical junior officers, are stepping up efforts to organise a coup against President Chávez, possibly as early as this month …[deleted] The level of detail in the reported plans …[deleted] targets Chávez and 10 other senior officers for arrest.

The April brief went on to explain how the planned coup would unfold: 'To provoke military action, the plotters may try to exploit unrest stemming from opposition demonstrations slated for later this month.' All the evidence indicates that the plot in Caracas was known to the US government, yet no effort was made to inform the Venezuelan government of what was going on. Quite the reverse. The Americans had no desire to spike the plans of the plotters, since opposition leaders had visited Washington on several occasions in the early months of 2002 – and secured the go-ahead for their schemes.

Washington made no secret of its dislike of the radical direction taken by the Bolivarian Revolution. The conspiracy against Chávez had been carefully planned by the country's principal industrialists and business-men, the leaders of the principal trade union movement, the owners of the main newspapers and television channels, the bishops of the Catholic Church, and conservative officers in the armed forces. Washington gave its go-ahead to their plans.

The conspirators focused their attacks in the early months of 2002 on the structural reform of *Petróleos de Venezuela* proposed by the government in the November 2001 laws, and so vehemently opposed by General Lameda. In April 2002, a two-day strike was called to protest against these planned reforms, but its real purpose was to secure the downfall of Chávez. Pedro Carmona Estanga, the president of the busi-nessmen's federation, *Fedecámeras*, and Carlos Ortega, the leader of the Venezuelan Workers' Confederation (CTV), had made a deal to work together. Their joint call for a strike on April 11 and 12 was made with the explicit assumption that it would only be lifted after the resignation of the president. The strike turned rapidly into an insurrection.

Thursday April 11, 2002

Early on Thursday morning, a large crowd began marching from Parque del Este, in the east of Caracas, to the main offices of the oil company in the city centre. There they were addressed by Ortega who called on them to continue their march to the Miraflores palace, urging them 'to expel the man who has betrayed the Venezuelan people'. Nothing loth, some 150,000 demonstrators marched on towards Miraflores. On the way, they were met by a comparable, though smaller crowd of Chávez supporters, hastily assembled that morning from the shanty towns. The forces of law and order took up positions between the two groups: the National Guard loyal to the president, and the Metropolitan Police controlled by Alfredo Peña, the mayor of Caracas, another former Chávez supporter who had joined the opposition.

The march concluded with a violent clash in the environs of the Miraflores palace, and several people were killed. Firing had apparently come from both sides, and the question of who bore the responsibility for these deaths became a matter of immediate and lasting controversy, but the majority of those killed were Chávez supporters.

Several senior military figures, including General Néstor González González, the former commander of army schools, then appeared on television to demand the president's resignation, a request designed to appear to be the culmination of a spontaneous crisis, caused in the heat of the moment by a popular explosion in which the government had lost control of the street. In practice, the march and the shootings had been carefully orchestrated.

Already aware at midday of the dangers inherent in the situation, Chávez – in Miraflores – decided to unroll the so-called Plan Avila, an existing military plan designed to mobilise an emergency force to protect the palace and to resist an impending coup. One of the most senior and loyal officers in the palace, General Jorge García Carneiro, was given orders to set the plan in motion, but on contacting army headquarters at the immense military base of Fuerte Tiuna to give the necessary commands, he was told that a group of generals there had plans to arrest the president. García Carneiro was also told that all exits from the base had been blocked. Military units wishing to leave to come to the aid of the National Guard units outside Miraflores would not be able to do so.

Worse was to come. The palace soon discovered that a number of National Guard officers had joined the conspiracy, as well as a group of air force generals gathered at the Francisco de Miranda air force base in the heart of the city.

Chávez now sought to regain the initiative, making a speech on television on the national chain, which all private television stations were obliged to broadcast. The impact of his speech was neutered by the four principal private stations, who split the screen to show violent scenes in the streets outside the Miraflores palace while the president was seen to be talking as though nothing much was going on. Chávez ordered the private stations off the air, but the order was not obeyed. Canal Ocho, the only channel at the government's command, was conveniently sabotaged, apparently by electronic means, and unable to broadcast.

Chávez called the military high command to come to Miraflores from Fuerte Tiuna for discussions, but the request was refused. Two of the most high-ranking officers, General Efraín Vázquez Velasco, the commander of the army, and General Manuel Rosendo, the head of the joint chiefs of staff (CUFAN – *the Comando Unificado de la Fuerza Armada Nacional*), were busy plotting his downfall.

José Vicente Rangel, minister of defence at the time, noted later that most of the officers with command of troops, many of them loyal to Chávez, were assembled at the defence ministry building inside Fuerte Tiuna. This was a grievous error. 'Instead of being at the head of their troops, they were all stuck in an office.'

Many of these officers in Fuerte Tiuna, according to Chávez's own subsequent account (in an interview with the journalist Eleazar Díaz Rangel), were confused by the images they were seeing on television, their immediate and principal source of information. The television channels had repeatedly shown pictures of Chávez supporters apparently firing on the opposition crowd of demonstrators, and a succession of retired officers had appeared on the screen to call for the president's resignation. The odds seemed stacked against him.

One channel played a dramatic video, repeated throughout Thursday evening, showing a naval officer, Vice-Admiral Hector Ramírez Pérez, denouncing the government: 'The President of the Republic has betrayed the trust of the people, he is massacring innocent people with snipers. Just now six people were killed and dozens wounded in Caracas.' Only later was it revealed that the video had been recorded earlier in the day, in the presence of several journalists.

Chávez might have believed that some of the officers at the Fuerte Tiuna base were confused and ill-informed, but he had no contact with them. At Miraflores he had little alternative except to prepare for armed resistance to the coup plotters – defended only by the Honour Guard at the palace, a few tanks, and a handful of the National Guard. He dressed in his military combat jacket and his signature red beret, and he took up a pistol and rifle. He also made a number of telephone calls.

One was to his most important neighbour, Fernando Henrique Cardoso, the president of Brazil, to tell him what was up. Others were made to the various regional military commands, to see if they had remained loyal. He received encouraging news from General Raúl Baduel, the commander in Maracay, and from the tank commander in Maracaibo. All was by no means lost.

Within the palace the assembled ministers and loyal officers began to discuss their options. Would it be possible to fight? Would it be possible to get to Maracay and establish the government there? Some urged resistance, others were more cautious. The possibility of a negotiated settlement eventually came up for discussion. At about midnight, Fidel Castro called from Havana to ask what was happening. Recalling the fate of Salvador Allende in 1973, he told Chávez that he was on no account to sacrifice himself in a useless battle of resistance – '*no te vayas a inmolar*'.

'Save your people and save yourself. Do what you have to do. Negotiate with dignity. Do not sacrifice yourself, Chávez, because this is not going to end here. You must not sacrifice yourself.'

Chávez was too important a figure for the future of Latin America, Castro argued, for him to allow himself to be killed off in a coup. The advice was wise and timely.

Chávez outlined to his closest advisers a scenario for a possible negotiated settlement. He would be prepared to resign, but only on four conditions: his resignation would be presented to the National Assembly; the constitution would be respected; the physical safety of those present in the Miraflores palace would be secured; and passage out of the country would be guaranteed for all.

General Rosendo and General Hurtado were told by Chávez to take this offer to the coup organisers in Fuerte Tiuna, and he telephoned the Cardinal, Bishop Báltazar Porras, and asked him to go there. Chávez also phoned a number of ambassadors – those of France, China, Mexico, and Cuba – to keep them abreast of developments.

Meanwhile, in Fuerte Tiuna, the coup leaders gathered together at around midnight on the fifth floor of the main defence ministry building: Pedro Carmona was there; so too were two officers from the US military mission in Caracas, Colonel James Rodgers and Colonel Ronald McCammon. They had a suite of offices in the building, and, although the US ambassador had been asked to close them some months earlier, this had not been done. Also present was General Enrique Medina Gómez, the military attaché at the Venezuelan embassy in Washington, who had flown into Caracas earlier in the day.

General Rosendo called the Miraflores palace from Fuerte Tiuna to announce that the coupmakers had accepted the conditions that Chávez had proposed. Then, almost immediately, he rang again to say that they had been rejected. Chávez would have to resign unconditionally. Such an ultimatum was clearly unacceptable to the president.

Friday April 12, 2002

At this stage, and in these circumstances, in the small hours of Friday morning, Chávez withdrew his conditional resignation. He would sign no document, and he would offer no resistance at the Miraflores palace. He feared that even if he were to hold out overnight, there would be fighting and loss of life in the morning. More people would inevitably be killed. So he declared that the coup leaders would have to detain him, and General Rosendo and General Hurtado were ordered to return to Fuerte Tiuna to make clear his decision. The officers assembled at the military base were still, according to all accounts, vacillating and uncertain how to proceed. The coup was not proceeding according to plan.

Under threat that tanks and planes would attack the Miraflores palace at dawn, Chávez agreed to go to Fuerte Tiuna, knowing that he would be detained on arrival. He was taken there at 4 a.m. on Friday morning, to find a number of generals from the army and the National Guard awaiting him. The majority treated him with respect, according to his own account. The bishop had also arrived. 'I also found there the two *monseñores*, Porras and Azuaje, and I went to sit beside them, and saluted them, and for a while we sat in silence.'

Chávez had a sixth sense that once back in the military environment of Fuerte Tiuna he might be able to reverse – or at least ameliorate – the difficult situation he was now in. He noticed the differences of opinion amongst many of the officers and generals present. He understood that Pedro Carmona, the civilian picked to take over as president, was somewhere in the building, but he did not see him:

'General Fuenmayor León was the first to speak; he made an analysis of the situation and said he was asking for my resignation, in the name of all those present, in view of what they regarded as a situation of ungovernability.

'I told them, with a serene voice that was a little louder than usual so that all could hear, that they should think long and hard about what they were doing, and what they planned to do – the responsibility that they were assuming with regard to Venezuela and the outside world – and I told them that I was not going to resign. They already had a piece of paper for me to sign, and I said that I was not going to so much as look at it.'

Chávez then reiterated that he would only sign a letter of resignation if they agreed to the four conditions that he had already put forward. The generals made no reply.

'I told them that I was not sure that they would be able to control the military, and that I had talked to various commanders who had assured me that they would not accept a *coup d'état* ... I could see that I was catching their attention, since, clearly, some of them had been manipulated. Others began to take notice.'

Chávez was interrupted by General Nestor González González, who perceived the dangers inherent in this line of discussion. 'We have not come here to discuss anything,' he told the assembled gathering. 'We know what we have to do; and I ask you to move into the room next door.' The officers got up to leave, and stayed in the next-door room for an hour, while Chávez remained behind with the bishops.

When the officers came back, it was the turn of Vice-Admiral Ramírez Pérez to speak. One of the principal coup leaders, he said the officers were not prepared to accept Chávez's four conditions, and they certainly would not allow him to leave the country: he would have 'to answer to the people for the crimes he had committed'.

Chávez replied that he would sign no statement of resignation, and that they would have to arrest him. 'They should not forget that they were taking prisoner the president of the Republic, and they should do whatever they felt necessary.'

At this stage, General Lucas Rincón Romero, the chief of the armed forces and the most senior officer present, joined with the commanders of the other services to announce – in a declaration on television – that they had requested the resignation of Chávez, that he had agreed to resign, and that they would themselves now resign.

Chávez was taken to a small room and allowed to change into shirt and jeans, and brought some breakfast. By then, it was 8 a.m., and he had had no sleep for two nights. Fortunately for him, he was able to make two requests to the friendly soldiers who were guarding him: for a television set and a telephone. His requests were granted. On watching the television news programme, he saw immediately that the news of the coup was being falsely interpreted. The newsreaders repeated continuously that Chávez had resigned, and that the coup was supported unanimously by the armed forces. At the bottom of the screen appeared a permanent motif: 'Chávez resigned; democracy restored'.

With the gift of a telephone, Chávez managed with some difficulty to contact his wife Marisabel and his elder daughter, Maria Gabriela. As president, he was not accustomed to making his own telephone calls, and he had to phone the Miraflores palace first to get their numbers. He told his wife and daughter to try to get the correct news out to the outside world: he had not resigned; he was being held prisoner by the army; and he was in serious danger of being murdered.

Marisabel managed to contact CNN, the American television channel, while Maria Gabriela was able to talk to Castro in Havana. Both CNN and Radio Havana were soon broadcasting the news abroad that Friday morning that Chávez had not resigned, but it took another day before the news was broadcast in Caracas.

After making these vital telephone calls, Chávez was at last able to sleep for a few hours. When he awoke he was interviewed by two women from the military legal department. He reiterated to them that he had not resigned, and that he was therefore still the president of the Republic. Again he had a stroke of good fortune. The two legal officers prepared a statement about his health, and then, when the security guards had left the room, one of them added a few words at the bottom: 'He said that he had not resigned.'

The document was subsequently photocopied, and the message was passed by fax to Isaias Rodríguez, the government's chief legal officer. He, in turn, was able to appear briefly on television to declare that the president had not resigned. The word was beginning to get out.

At midday on Friday, from his guarded room, Chávez was able to watch on television the swearing-in ceremony in the Miraflores palace of Pedro Carmona as the new president. This was an extraordinary scene, in which the new regime proclaimed its attachment to democracy while ordering the close-down of the National Assembly and the Supreme Court, the dismissal of the elected mayors and state governors, and the abolition of the constitution. The word 'Bolivarian' was to be struck from the title of the Republic of Venezuela. The ceremony was controlled and managed by Daniel Romero, a former political secretary of Carlos Andrés Pérez. Armed squads were sent out to harass families of prominent Chávez supporters in their homes, and to surround the Cuban embassy.

Carmona announced the formation of a new government, which included General Lameda as the head of *Petróleos de Venezuela*. Luís Miquilena appeared at a press conference to give his support to the new government. Carlos Ortega, the union leader and one of the principal figures of the conspiracy, was left off the cabinet list – a serious political mistake. Another mistake was to order a complete restructuring of the high command of the armed forces, effectively dismissing many senior generals, including General Vázquez Velasco, the existing commander of the army and one of the leading supporters within the armed forces of the overthrow of Chávez. The representatives of organised labour and several senior generals were left looking rather foolish.

The radical right-wing programme of the new regime was not popular with many officers who had been prepared to countenance the coup, and they called on General Vázquez Velasco to preside over a meeting to discuss events, scheduled for 1 p.m. on Saturday, the following day. In the course of Friday afternoon, the tide was already beginning to turn against the coup plotters.

Chávez claims that he later heard noises outside Fuerte Tiuna that seemed to indicate that people were mobilising there in his support, but he could find no one to confirm this news. People had in fact already begun to congregate outside the military base, shouting, '*Yo quiero ver a Chávez*, we want to see Chávez.' But soon Chávez was no longer there.

After dark, he was told he was to be moved from Caracas. He was taken out to a helicopter and flown westward along the coast to the naval base at Turiamo, outside Puerto Cabello. He did not know if he was to be deported – or killed. According to his own account, given to an audience in Porto Alegre, Brazil, nearly a year later, he thought his time had come:

> Do you know who I remembered at that moment? I remembered Che. I remembered him because I had read somewhere that, a few years later, one of the eyewitnesses of his killing wrote that Ernesto Guevara was sitting in pain, wounded in the legs, when his killer came in holding a pistol. Then Che said, 'Hold on a second, don't shoot yet.' Laboriously he got to his feet, while leaning against the wall, and said, 'You can shoot now and you will see how a man dies'.

Meanwhile, the plotters had been in close contact with foreign governments, notably those of the United States and Spain. The right-wing Spanish government of José María Aznar had long been at the forefront of European efforts to oppose the Castro government in Cuba, and it had extended its support to the opposition to Chávez. On Friday morning, when the first news of the Caracas coup was flashed to the outside world, Spain and the United States were ready with a joint statement. The two governments requested that 'the exceptional situation' in Venezuela should lead in the shortest possible time to 'democratic normalisation' to achieve 'a national consensus and the guarantee of fundamental liberties'. The Spanish minister for Ibero-American cooperation, Miguel Angel Cortés, later explained that the text of the statement had been prepared after 'five or six telephone calls' with Otto Reich at the US State Department. Reich, a former US ambassador to Caracas, had been in close touch with the coup plotters. He called the Latin American ambassadors in Washington into his office that morning to secure their support for the US–Spanish statement, but the great majority of the governments in the Organisation of American States came out in support of Chávez – to Washington's surprise and irritation.

The British government was not directly involved in the plot, but a junior British minister, Denis McShane, writing an article for the *Times* newspaper published on Saturday April 13, shed no tears at the departure of Chávez, and described him as a 'ranting, populist demagogue'. McShane told how he had met Chávez a few days earlier when he had been 'dressed in a red paratrooper's beret and rugby shirt and waved his arms up and down like Mussolini – an odd, disturbing spectacle'. By the time McShane's offensive diatribe was published, Chávez was already on his way back to power.

Saturday April 13, 2002

When Chávez awoke at the base at Turiamo on the morning of Saturday April 13, a young soldier brought breakfast and asked him why he had resigned. 'No, I didn't resign,' said Chávez. A young lieutenant came in and asked him the same question, and received the same answer. 'Then,' said the officer, 'you are still the president, and these people have violated the constitution. They are deceiving us.'

The lieutenant brought news that Baduel, commander of the parachute regiment at Maracay, inland from Puerto Cabello, had refused to take orders from the new government of Pedro Carmona.

'General Baduel has said that he will not recognise any government that is not yours. He has taken Maracay.'

Chávez asked the lieutenant how he knew of this development. 'My wife is there, and I've just talked to her on the telephone, and the people of Maracay are out in the streets.'

What about other military units, asked Chávez. 'I don't know,' replied the lieutenant, 'but those of us here are with you,' and he led Chávez to understand that there was a plan to take him to Maracay, some two hours away by road.

The coup plotters, anxious to avoid such a possibility, decided to move Chávez away from Turiamo, and he was taken off that day by helicopter to the small offshore island of La Orchila.

In Caracas, meanwhile, isolated in the Miraflores palace, President Carmona had summoned the media owners and editors to a meeting at midday. He needed to reinforce his support. Gustavo Cisneros of Venevisión arrived at his office, followed by Alberto Ravell of Globovisión, Marcel Granier of Radio Caracas TV, and Omar Camero of Televen. Also present were Miguel Henrique Otero of *El Universal*, and Andrés Mata of *El Nacional*. Cisneros suggested smoothly that the communications strategy of the new government should be left in their hands, a suggestion to which Carmona agreed.

This should have been a moment of triumph for the media moguls, since this was the outcome they had so strenuously worked for. Yet as they arrived at Miraflores for the meeting, the palace was already surrounded by a huge crowd of Chávez supporters, and soon they heard news of General Baduel's insurrection in Maracay. The safety of the moguls, and the continuing future of the new government, was by no means clear.

Soon Colonel Jesús Morao Cardona, the commander of the president's Honour Guard, located in a large building across the road from the palace, decided that the moment had come for him to act. He had watched the events of the previous twenty-four hours in silence, but now the palace and the surrounding streets, and even the motorway down to the port at La Guaira, were occupied by the population of the hilltop shanty towns. They had surged down into the city to create an immense sea of people demanding the return of their president. Colonel Morao ordered his men to seize the palace.

Carmona and his advisers had imagined that his coup had bought the loyalty of the staff of the palace – and of the soldiers who guarded it. This was not so. The staff did their duty, and served coffee when requested, but their hearts were with Chávez. When Colonel Morao's troops emerged from the basement tunnel that joined his headquarters with the palace, they seized as many of Carmona's suppporters as they could. Others leapt into their cars and disappeared into the crowds. The humiliating scenes were captured on camera. Carmona himself fled to join the military plotters at Fuerte Tiuna.

There, the meeting of senior officers with General Vázquez Velasco, scheduled for 1 p.m. that Saturday, was already under way. Here, too, the building was surrounded by thousands of people supporting Chávez and demanding his return. The meeting was hectic and confused, but several loyal officers complained that they had been lied to by the coup plotters. Where was the evidence that Chávez had resigned? 'I never saw the resignation statement,' said one commander. 'I was deceived. No one told me that they were going to eliminate the existing order.'

Generals who had initially supported the coup began to draft a second declaration. They would recognise Carmona as head of state but provide guarantees to the population that the social conquests of the Chávez government would be maintained. When handed the draft, General García Carneiro, one of the loyal officers, crossed out the name of Carmona and gave it to General Vázquez Velasco to read out on television. The private television channels that day, on instructions from their owners, had refused to show coverage of the shanty town dwellers seizing the city, and had entirely abandoned their morning news coverage. Only cartoons and old movies were on show. The general was forced to read his declaration over the phone to the CNN channel.

General García Carneiro then went to speak to the crowds assembled outside the base. Climbing on a tank and grabbing a microphone, he announced that the armed forces had refused to recognise the government of the coup plotters, that they would not accept Carmona as commander-in-chief, and that they would do everything possible to ensure that Chávez returned to power.

Carmona, meanwhile, had arrived at Fuerte Tiuna and was conferring with the coup plotters. Around 7 p.m., he was arrested, together with the officers who had supported him. When he asked what crime he had committed, he was told that he had 'violated the Constitution of the Republic'.

Outside, the loyal officers acted as DJs before the enormous crowd, interspersing recordings of the protest songs of Alí Primera, the folk singer from the *llanos*, with short announcements that yet another provincial garrison had come out in support of the legitimate government.

Sunday April 14, 2002

Finally, at 2 a.m. on Sunday morning, news came through that Chávez was leaving La Orchila by helicopter and would be brought to the Miraflores palace. Three helicopters had been sent from Maracay to pick him up. He arrived back at Miraflores at 3.45 that morning. Greeted by loyal troops and ministers who had evacuated the palace just forty-eight hours earlier, he made an emotional speech to celebrate his return.

Outside the Miraflores palace, the crowds sang their new chant, developed from the sporting field and destined to become the iconic signature of the Bolivarian Revolution: '*Ou, ah, Chávez no se va!*' an untranslatable appeal meaning 'Chávez, Please Don't Go'.

The coup had collapsed within less than two days, destroyed by just the alliance between soldiers and the people that Chávez had been so painstakingly constructing over the previous three years. The ill-fated Carmona became known as *Pedro El Breve*.

Later that Sunday morning Chávez flew to Maracay to speak to Baduel's paratroop battalion, rallying the troops with a stirring attack on the 'oligarchs' who had tried to bring down his revolutionary government.

Monday April 15, 2002

On Monday, Chávez had second thoughts about criticising the oligarchy. Seeking reconciliation in the country, and uncertain of his own strength and of the possibility of moving forward on a radical track, he called for a 'national dialogue' with the opposition. He acknowledged that there were 'a large number of Venezuelans in disagreement with the government', and he agreed that the current polarisation was not 'positive' for the country. There needed to be communication among the different sectors of society.

He now replaced his economic team with a group of less radical ministers, and he also found a more emollient alternative for Gaston Parra and the other more nationalistic (or 'patriotic') directors of *Petróleos de Venezuela*. Yet far from welcoming these conciliatory gestures, the opposition perceived them as signs of weakness, and were soon again on the attack. The Supreme Court, where the opposition had a majority, issued a ruling declaring that the April coup had been 'a power vacuum' rather than 'a *coup d'état*', and the detained coup plotters – both military and civilian – were set free. They continued to plan the overthrow of Chávez as though nothing had happened.

33

THE ATMOSPHERE
AFTER THE APRIL COUP

To take the popular pulse in Venezuela after the April coup, I spent a fews days in the hills of Caracas, first visiting one of the more organised *ranchos* to the south of the city. A single road winds steeply upward through a bleak landscape of shacks and burnt-out cars, eventually arriving at a high plateau with panoramic views over the valley below. Half a million people live hereabouts, some in breeze-block huts, some in concrete residential blocks, some in tin shanties. Stopping at one of the schools, where 15 teachers cope with 1,500 students, I asked a local organiser what had happened during the days of the April coup.

'We have a cooperative radio here,' he said, 'and on the first day [Thursday] we called people to go down to the Miraflores palace. Some went in buses and lorries, others just walked.' On the second day, 'the fascist police came here to intimidate us – the repressive forces of the state [the local police controlled by Alfredo Peña, the anti-Chávez mayor of greater Caracas] – but they soon left.' In the evening, the local population had been called out again to descend to the city, to the military base at Fuerte Tiuna. 'The fascist police were still around, but many people went down. Some of the mothers stayed behind to look after other people's children, while others organised food.

'We are not *chavistas* here,' my informant was keen to tell me. 'We are revolutionaries.

'We have to defend this government, but we are more libertarian than they are. We defend Chávez because he's better than any president there has ever been. We think he's the product of our struggle. People recognise him as an equal. Obviously he is Indian and black, and maybe a little white!

'People went to rescue the president who had never done anything like that before. Now they have become very politicised, and are trying to organise themselves – more than ever before.'

Not everyone in these hills supports the Bolivarian Revolution. In one small hut in a *rancho* in Catia, on the other side of the city, I found a self-employed plumber who expressed his disillusion with the government. 'I voted for Chávez,' he told me, 'but now I regret having done so. I was completely deceived. I've seen no improvement. I don't want conflict between rich and poor, because if that happens where will I get work?' The plumber depended for his livelihood on his clients in the upper-class section of the city.

Echoing the views of the opposition, he argued that no coup had taken place in April. 'There was a power vacuum, a coup by the government against civil society. The military were protecting the civilians. I might be mistaken, but Chávez should resign. This government has not given the results that were expected.'

The shanty towns of Caracas had mobilised themselves to defend the president, but much of the population was still confused and divided. The April coup had been a defining moment for the revolution, but there was clearly much work still to be done.

When I came down from the hills, I went to see the *Comandante*, as they often call him, in his second-floor private apartment in the Miraflores palace. Chávez was sitting alone with some papers at the table of a sparsely furnished dining room looking out onto a roof garden. Dressed in slacks and an open-necked brown shirt, he looked relaxed and considerably fitter than when I had seen him six months earlier in Paris. I am a privileged visitor: we have met several times, and he greets me as an old acquaintance, with a friendly hug.

A president used to glad-handing his way through pressing crowds of supplicants, an activity that he both enjoys and finds politically rewarding, he had been cooped up in the palace since the April coup, while his bodyguards – fiercesome figures in black suits carrying sinister briefcases that turn into bullet-proof shields – practised new drills. He was now perceived to be seriously under threat of a *magnicidio*, the word Spaniards use to describe the assassination of an important person. (An *asesinato*, the more usual word, is so common in the *ranchos* and *barrios* of Latin America – at least two dozen every weekend in cities like Caracas or São Paulo – that it has come to be synonymous with mere homicide.)

Chávez himself was reasonably upbeat. 'Almost anything is possible here, Richard,' he told me, when I asked him to outline what he was now doing to combat the various strategies the opposition still had up their sleeve. 'I'm sure they're still thinking about a *magnicidio*, and for some of the most desperate ones, this must seem to be the only way out.' Chávez had been warned of the seriousness of the threat by Castro a couple of years earlier, but he had only recently begun to take adequate preventative action.

He was keen to emphasise that the people had given solid support to those elements within the military who had stood firmly in favour of the constitution:

'There was a rapid response to the coup, from both the military and the civilians. Hundreds of thousands of people all over the country came out against the coup. And where was it that they went to? They assembled at the army barracks, and they did so because of the existing understanding that had been built up between officers and civilians through the *Plan Bolívar*. It was because of the contacts that had been made between the military and the poorest sectors of society that the people supported the army.'

The revolutionary project on which Chávez had originally embarked had involved a close alliance between the armed forces and the civilian population, and I asked him if this basic strategy had been affected by the coup, since senior members of the armed forces had clearly been found wanting.

'We cannot ignore the possibility of another coup,' he told me, but all was not lost. Although the Supreme Court had refused to take action against the coup plotters, Chávez himself had been able to move fast within his own very special area of responsibility. No civil justice had been available, but he had been able to promote his own form of military justice. Some sixty admirals and generals had been forced into retirement.

Chávez claimed that there would be no change in the overall strategy, but he admitted that there would have to be a revision in the speed and rhythm of military involvement in the country's development programme. The strategy had derived from the experience of the early nineteenth century, when Simón Bolívar had created an alliance between the army and the people, and had made independence possible. Today the strategy was still viable, even if a handful of counter-revolutionaries had remained within the officer corps.

I told Chávez that I had been struck by the fact that the television channels, in the weeks after the coup, had devoted air-time to the dramatic proceedings in the National Assembly, where a procession of generals and admirals implicated in the coup had appeared before a parliamentary sub-committee. It would be difficult to recall a time in Latin America when senior officers had been obliged to go through such a humiliating procedure, yet everyone was exquisitely polite during the interrogations. The generals were arrogantly self-righteous in their justification of their actions, since, although they had been placed on the retired list, they still imagined that they might make a comeback.

One distinguished-looking officer in his fifties, with close-cropped hair and dressed in a grey uniform covered with decorations, argued that he had acted during the coup out of duty to the nation and the armed forces. He echoed the traditional arguments of the opposition, complaining that the military had been dragged into politics, and that this had been a humiliation for the officers and their families. He recalled how people had clinked their glasses when an officer came into a restaurant, not as applause but as a gesture of contempt. This offensive behaviour towards senior officers had happened, he said, to himself and his wife.

Talking to Chávez, I recalled the case of General Prats, Allende's commander-in-chief in Chile in August 1973. His family home in a comfortable Santiago suburb had been surrounded by middle-class women banging saucepans and calling for him to resign. Prats had felt obliged to go, paving the way for the promotion of General Pinochet.

General Prats and his wife were assassinated by a car bomb the following year, when in exile in Buenos Aires. Was there not a danger in Venezuela of this pattern being repeated?

Chávez was well aware of the problem: 'An important number of senior officers have acquired a standard of living that is comparable to that of the upper middle class. They have been subjected to these pressures and attacks, in the places that they go to and within their family circle, and this certainly helped to undermine the unity and strength of this sector of the military leadership.'

The pressure on the military had been substantial, said Chávez, yet many officers had been strong enough to hold out. 'A considerable number of senior officers did not give in to these class pressures. They refused to allow themselves to be neutralised. At some personal risk to their lives, and their military careers, they stood up at the most critical moment and expressed their view in support of the constitution.'

Chávez admitted that the possibility of another coup still remained. The failure of the April coup was a serious setback to the country's traditional political class. It still had no popular mandate, but it would clearly continue searching for ways to overthrow him. One possibility was a 'legal coup', a demand that could theoretically have been made by the National Assembly to secure his resignation. Such a device had been much canvassed in the press. It had been used in Ecuador in the 1990s, and also in Venezuela in 1993, when Carlos Andrés Pérez was removed from office by the Assembly on charges of corruption.

'Well, you've seen the pressure from the newspapers and within the National Assembly,' said Chávez, 'but I think it's going to be very difficult for the opposition. I talked to our group of revolutionary parliamentarians the other day, and, after what happened during the coup, when many of them were pursued and threatened in their homes, they have drawn closer together. There used to be eighty-six, now there are ninety.' The April coup had concentrated the minds of wavering deputies, and Chávez now had a clear majority in the National Assembly.

'The opposition talk of Chávez Lite,' he said with a smile, 'or of *Chavismo* without Chávez, although I think that's a myth. But they continue to insist on my resignation.'

What about the possibilities of an economic coup, I asked, recalling Henry Kissinger's threat 'to make the economy scream' when he was planning the overthrow of Allende in the 1970s.

'It's quite possible they will try to generate economic trouble,' said Chávez. 'They may try to make the country ungovernable according to their definition, as was done in Chile. I am sure that is one of the ways out that they are looking for.'

Chávez made it clear that he was preparing for this possibility. On his side was the fact that he still retained a rock-solid majority – as he had throughout his early years in power – based on class and race. For the first time in Venezuelan history, the country's hidden majority – black, indigenous, and mestizo – had a president with whom they could identify. Things might not have gone too well for them in the early years, maybe even sections of the poor had got poorer, but faced with the overt racism of the country's traditional elite, Chávez was a president in whom they still had faith, and who they were still prepared to defend.

Opposition leaders could point to their unusual capacity to mobilise large sections of the middle and upper classes in anti-government demonstrations on the streets of Caracas, but nobody knew what their real electoral strength might actually be. They were divided into a dozen individual parties, and could in no way be viewed as a solid electoral force. No obvious opposition leader had emerged, and no agreed programme was promoted.

The April coup had thrown up a particularly hopeless businessman, Pedro Carmona, without a political bone in his body. His only programme was to abolish the National Assembly and the new constitution, which had been long debated by a popularly elected assembly and ratified by referendum. The general outlines of what an opposition government might have done were well known. They would have reintroduced a neo-liberal programme, with attendant privatisations of state enterprises, of the kind applied almost universally in Latin America.

They would have privatised the oil industry, withdrawn from OPEC, ceased cheap oil sales to Cuba, and increased oil production.

The opposition's mistake was to believe its own propaganda, a belief reinforced by battalions of newspaper columnists. Because the protest marches against the government had been unusually large, and because the opinion polls at the beginning of the year had appeared to indicate a decline in support for Chávez, a euphoric feeling arose in the upper middle class, and among its spokesmen and columnists, that one more push would bring about the president's downfall.

Yet in practice opinion polls in Third World countries provide no guarantee of accuracy, since the pollsters rarely reach the areas where the great majority of the people live. Protest marches, too, are an unreliable guide. They can be very large, yet this does not necessarily mean that this symptom of discontent can be translated into votes. Journalists and commentators in Caracas were unaccustomed to getting out and about, to making their own, old-fashioned, informed guesses about the state of public opinion. Their failure, and that of the media generally, became an important item on the national agenda in the months ahead.

34

'THE FOUR HORSEMEN OF THE APOCALYPSE': THE MEDIA WAR

Few institutions in Venezuela were so closely scrutinised in the aftermath of the April coup as the media. The owners and editors of the newspapers and the private television channels had clearly played a significant role both in fomenting the coup and in influencing events while it was going on, as much by their absence as by their presence. The 'mediatic' coup was denounced by the government, and it soon became a case of how the media should not behave, celebrated and discussed internationally.

The established Caracas dailies, notably *El Universal* and *El Nacional*, are traditional conservative newspapers of the kind that exist in most Latin American countries. They reflect the generally backward-looking ideas of the commercial and financial elite, and express warm sympathy and support for the political and cultural world of the United States. Although their owners had recognised in the 1990s that the *ancien régime* was coming to an end, and thought that Colonel Chávez might possibly be a convenient vehicle who would help to introduce a new era not too different from the old, they had rapidly distanced themselves from his government during the early months of his rule, as the unfolding debate about the constitution revealed the emergence of a new and more radical Venezuela. They understood correctly that Chávez intended to break the mould.

Since no powerful political party had survived to oppose Chávez, during the year leading up to the April coup the Caracas dailies had effectively moved into the vacuum, taking up a significant political role themselves. In earlier years, their owners and editors had been closely involved, through family and financial links, with *Acción Democrática*. With the collapse of their favoured political vehicle, and going beyond all internationally accepted norms of fairness and objectivity, they campaigned relentlessly against the elected president.

Unfamiliar with the techniques of reportage, these newspapers rarely, if ever, sent reporters out into the shanty towns or the countryside to cover what was actually going on. Their tone was set by a stable of regular columnists whose social and political attitudes smacked of the library and harked back to the nineteenth century. Undoubtedly their commentaries reflected the ill-informed views of much of the country's middle and upper classes, yet they were also the leaders of elite opinion, helping to create a climate in which a Pinochet-style coup was both recommended and then welcomed.

Among the more pernicious outcomes of this steady drip of venom from the local newspapers was its impact on the international press. Since foreign journalists in Caracas invariably lived in the bourgeois quarters of the city, and absorbed the views and attitudes of their neighbours and the papers that they read, much of the reactionary agenda of the white elite crept into foreign reports about Venezuela, and particularly about Chávez, referred to in agency reports as 'a firebrand colonel'. Thus the image of the Bolivarian Revolution that reached the outside world was seriously distorted by the writings of a handful of foreign journalists, notably those writing for *Le Monde* and *Libération* in France, the *Economist* and the *Financial Times* in Britain, *El País* and *El Mundo* in Spain, as well, of course, as the *Washington Post* and the *New York Times*. Rarely have political developments in an important country – one of the great oil producers of the Western world – been so inadequately reported and analysed by the foreign media.

Particularly important in the distortion of reality was the use of dubious opinion polls by both the local and the foreign press, creating a climate in which it was regularly assumed that Chávez's support had dwindled to well below 40 per cent, and that therefore the large street demonstrations of the opposition represented a hostile majority that could not be ignored. The fact that the opinion polls could not and did not reflect the views of the population in the shanty towns, or in the rural areas, was never explained to readers. Nor was it clear whether the 60 per cent allegedly hostile to Chávez were actually supporters of the opposition.

If the newspapers were hostile, the private television channels were openly subversive. Their owners were involved with the plotters of the April coup, and much of the action over the two days of the coup was reflected (or not) in the distorting mirror of the television output. On the first day, the channels gave priority to the opposition march, to the apparent news that it had been fired on by Chávez supporters, and to the continuous publication of the untruth that Chávez had resigned. On the second day, the media owners visited the Miraflores palace to express their solidarity with President Carmona, and then, as the coup crumbled, their television channels abandoned all attempts at objectivity. They refused to film the crowds coming down from the hills to call for the return of their president, and contented themselves with showing cartoons and old movies.

Chávez, once returned to power, described the four privately owned television channels as 'the four horsemen of the Apocalypse' – with some justification. Their owners were among the wealthiest individuals in the country, and they wielded their power with an awesome lack of social responsibility. Venevisión, the station with the highest ratings, was owned by Gustavo Cisneros, sometimes described as 'king of the joint ventures'. An immensely rich man, intimately linked to political and commercial groups in the United States, Cisneros had built his empire through alliances with US-based multinationals, starting with Coca-Cola and Pizza Hut and ending up with AOL Warner.

Radio Caracas Television (RCTV), a station famous for its soap operas, was run by Marcel Granier, a multimillionaire with a penchant for collecting Ferrari cars. A third channel, Globovisión, was run by Alberto Federico Ravell and Ricardo Zuluaga, both once prominent supporters of *Acción Democrática*. Globovisión's 24-hour news channel was unrelentingly hostile to the government, while its ordinary channel carried a series of discussion programmes similar to the commentary-propaganda of the newspapers. A fourth private channel, Televen, was owned by Omar Camero.

The two principal Caracas newspapers were also run by people formerly associated with *Acción Democrática*. Andrés Mata was the editor of *El Universal*, and Miguel Henrique Otero was the editor of *El Nacional*. The Caracas dailies are a special case. Elsewhere in the country, the newspapers often adopt a more neutral tone. Unknown to most foreign observers, *Panorama*, a paper published in the oil town of Maracaibo, in the west of the country, takes a remarkably independent line. *Panorama* is a wealthy, well-established, family-owned daily, with the second-largest circulation in the country. In the weeks after the coup I flew to Maracaibo to talk to Estéban Piñeda Belloso, the only newspaper owner in Venezuela who had refused to join in the general media demand for Chávez to resign.

It is easy to see why *Panorama* has been such successful paper. On the day of the counter-coup, when the Caracas papers closed down for a day in a state of shock at the defeat of the coup they had promoted, *Panorama* kept going, producing no less than four separate editions to report each successive stage of Chávez's return to power.

Piñeda is one of the most prominent, and successful, entrepreneurs in Maracaibo, and he told me how other newspaper magnates had tried to drag him into their conspiracy to overthrow the president. He had refused to join in, and after the April coup he had withdrawn from the *Bloque de Prensa*, the national newspaper publishers' association, in protest against its overt enthusiasm for the coup.

Although his paper, which is widely read in the armed forces, does not campaign for Chávez, Piñeda was of the firm opinion that the president was anxious to do something for the 80 per cent of the population that is poor. He was one of the few people I met that year who was optimistic about the future. He thought that an 'economic coup' was bound to hurt the businessmen involved more than Chávez, and he felt that the opposition's efforts to get rid of the president by constitutional means were bound to fail. He was right.

35

THE SECOND OPPOSITION THREAT: THE 'ECONOMIC COUP' OF DECEMBER 2002

In the months after the April coup attempt of 2002, in their wealthy neighbourhoods, large sectors of the upper and middle classes continued their noisy protests against the government. In response, the poor came down from their shanty towns at regular intervals to demonstrate their loyalty to 'their' president. The uncertain mood in the country, demonstrated in 2001, continued throughout 2002. The opposition, unchastened by its failure in April, again adopted the strategy of a general strike – called for December 2.

This time, aware that they had little support in the large, unorganised and mainly self-employed sectors of the community, the opposition's efforts were devoted to creating havoc in the strategic oil industry. They planned to bring *Petróleos de Venezuela* to a complete halt. The strike, more correctly a 'lockout' since it was called by Fedecámeras, and affected management more than the workers, was designed to cause the economy to collapse – and Chávez to resign. 'Christmas without Chávez' was the opposition slogan. This was the 'economic coup' that had been gestating since April.

But the opposition soon discovered that the situation was no longer so favourable to their ambitions. The armed forces were now more solidly behind the president than before, since the conservative generals implicated in the coup had been sent into retirement. Now they could only grumble from the sidelines.

The international situation was also different. The United States had welcomed the April coup, but by December it was faced with more important problems elsewhere: the planned invasion of Iraq was only months away. Washington was obliged to be more circumspect, and publicly threw its weight behind the formal negotiations between government and opposition that were sponsored by the Organisation of American States. These began in November 2002, and were conducted by Cesar Gavíria, the former president of Colombia and leader of the Organisation of American States, and blessed by the former US president, Jimmy Carter. A negotiated solution to Venezuela's political and social crisis was devoutly wished for by the outside world – though less welcome within.

More significant than the changing attitude of the military and of the US was the increased mobilisation of the poor. The poor had voted repeatedly for Chávez since 1998, yet his revolutionary programme had been largely directed from above, without much popular participation. After the April coup, many of the less privileged realised they had a government that they needed to defend. The repeated protest marches of the opposition had an unexpected effect. They conjured up a phenomenon that most of the middle and upper classes would have preferred to leave sleeping – awakening the political consciousness of the poor, and the spectre of a class and race war.

Opposition spokesmen complained that Chávez was an incompetent leftist leading the country to economic chaos. Yet underlying the fierce hatred aroused within the traditional ruling class was the terror of this white elite when faced with the mobilised mass of Venezuela's majority population – black, Indian and mestizo. Although class played a role, it was racism that explained the degree of hatred turned against the Bolivarian Revolution in the course of 2002. Venezuela's racism was both old and new. At one level it dated back over five centuries, directed by the European settlers towards their African slaves and the country's indigenous inhabitants. At another it came from the new generations of white settlers from Europe who arrived in the twentieth century, attracted by the economic promise of the oil industry. Such people were but loosely attached to their country of choice, and often ignorant of its human reality. Chávez – who made no secret of his aim to be the president of the poor – became the focus of their racist rage. Yet the rich were few and the poor were many. If the poor could be fully mobilised, the rich were outnumbered.

Unequal in numbers, the opposition believed that they possessed a trump card in *Petróleos de Venezuela*. Nationalised more than twenty-five years earlier, the state-owned company had been run over the years for the exclusive benefit of its employees and managers – its profits being invested anywhere except Venezuela. Prior to the arrival of Chávez, the company had been made ready for privatisation, to the satisfaction of most of its engineers and directors – the potential beneficiaries of such a development. Chávez had put a stop to this possibility, for the new constitution of 1999 put a permanent block on privatisation. The company's now desperate elite were happy to enlist as the shock troops of the opposition. When the general strike was called in December, the oil company's directors did their level best to bring their entire industry to a halt. Like the rest of the opposition, they wanted to provoke a regime change.

They were in for a shock. Chávez had prepared the ground well. On December 6, at the end of the first week of the insurrectionary strike, he celebrated the fourth anniversary of his electoral victory of December 1998. In April he had already displayed a Houdini-like capacity to escape from a tight situation. This time, he told his listeners, he was not going to allow himself to be surprised. The government knew what was going to happen, and it had made its plans.

These worked well and, as December passed, the opposition grew increasingly frustrated by the failure of their strike action to have a political impact. The mass of the population bore the food shortages with equanimity. They tolerated the electricity blackouts, the oil scarcity, and the transport failures. By the end of December, Chávez was fighting back with vigour, leaving a divided and leaderless opposition – who had never expected their strike to last beyond Christmas – with an uncertain future.

In two areas of the oil company's activity the government had failed to anticipate the extent of the strike action: the strike affected the company's tanker fleet and its computer technology. Many tanker captains joined the strike, and it took time to seize their ships and put in skeleton crews. Securing the computers and preventing sabotage were even greater problems. Chávez explained the extent of the sabotage in a speech at the beginning of January 2003:

> You know that all these systems – all the industry – are computerised and systematised … The sabotage consisted in changing the adjustment points in the control systems. A variable had been introduced into the computers of the control systems so that the temperature in the boilers does not rise above 600 degrees, which is the temperature ceiling. Above 600 degrees, the plant reaches a dangerous level.
>
> Well, these gentlemen not only abandoned their posts but changed the adjustment points before leaving. That is, they raised the ceiling from 600 degrees to 800 degrees centigrade. What would have happened if our patriotic and well-trained technicians had not checked these control systems and adjustment points well? What would have happened if they had started the systems and valves and all the operating system? When the temperature had gone above 600 degrees and reached 800, there would have been a disaster – an explosion.

Sabotage, like the strike itself, had the opposite impact to what was expected. Chávez was well aware that the opposition's attempt to cripple the oil industry – the icon of the country's nationalists – was not popular with the armed forces. At the start of January 2003 he was given *carte blanche* by senior officers to crush the strike. The army was brought in to guard the installations, the ports and the pipelines.

With the strike defeated, the essential task was to bring the oil company back under government control. The corporation's existing directors were sacked, and its entire structure was reorganised. It was split into two regional entities, and its centralised operations in Caracas were closed down entirely. An upbeat oil minister claimed that oil production would be nearly back to normal within a month. Chávez outlined the changes ahead for the oil company and its management in a speech in Caracas on January 5, 2003:

> We have reached the far-reaching decision to begin a thorough restruc-
> turing of our company, *Petróleos de Venezuela*, to make it stronger and
> more efficient, and more responsive to the interests of the nation – and
> not to those of a small group of privileged people who would like to
> keep their sinecures indefinitely.

These executives, said Chávez, had been fired. They would now be
legally accountable 'for their wrongdoings and excesses'. The conservative management was replaced by the radical executives forced out in
earlier internal struggles. Senior management were not the only ones
to lose their jobs. Initially 1,000 strikers in the oil industry were sacked,
then 2,000, and finally 18,000 lost their jobs – nearly half the workforce of 40,000.

Ali Rodríguez outlined the scale of the problem in an interview in
July 2004 with the American writer Greg Wilpert:

> Almost 19,000 people left *Petróleos de Venezuela*, and among these were
> a majority of those who managed all of the operations of the corpora-
> tion: exploration, production, transport, refining, commerce, supply,
> and finances. This obviously implied a problem in the reconstruction
> of all these systems.

Petróleos de Venezuela had been seriously overmanned, but slimming
down the business would have been politically impossible had the
managers not gone on strike. Since they had 'abandoned their employment obligations for 62 consecutive days', they were legally sacked,
according to the terms of article 102 of the organic labour law. Ali
Rodríguez explained how they had been replaced:

> Despite the loss of all these employees, among whom were highly
> specialised people with long experience in the corporation, workers of
> the company were able to substitute for them … We also counted on
> the reincorporation of retired employees. A characteristic of the oil
> industry has been that in many cases people retire in their prime and
> go to work for other companies, within and outside the country, often
> as consultants …

A newly confident Chávez continued a vigorous campaign against strikers elsewhere in a series of speeches in January 2003. He announced that troops would be sent in to stop the hoarding of food, and to keep schools and banks open. He also threatened to revoke the licences of the four private television channels that had been actively campaigning for his overthrow. The period of dialogue and conciliation embarked on after the unsuccessful coup attempt the previous April was over. The damage to the economy had been devastating, and the government was now obliged to impose capital and price controls in an attempt to stop capital flight.

This change of mood in Venezuela was a reflection of a radical change sweeping over other countries in Latin America, coupled with an atmosphere of uncertainty in Washington. The election of left-wing presidents in Brazil and Ecuador provided a beacon of hope for Chávez, if not necessarily a lifeline. Luiz Inacio Lula da Silva had been inaugurated in Brasilia on New Year's Day 2003, and Lucio Gutiérrez (another progressive former colonel) took office in Quito a few days later. Indeed the gathering of Latin American presidents in Ecuador for the ceremony saw the formation of a group of 'friends of Venezuela' designed, through the good offices of the Organisation of American States, to find a peaceful solution to the Venezuelan crisis.

Meanwhile the trumpet in Washington continued to sound with an uncertain tone. Otto Reich had failed to secure the support of Congress for his appointment as the government's chief Latin American operative, and his departure was a blow to the neo-conservatives in the US government. So too was the resignation of Mexico's pro-US foreign minister, Jorge Castañeda. Democrats in the US Congress were now beginning to make themselves heard, and a group of them came out with a message of support for Chávez.

To the dismay of the opposition, Chávez now embarked upon a radicalisation of what he had always perceived as a 'revolution'. The country's poor were now mobilised behind him in a way that would have been unimaginable a year earlier. When several schools joined the strike, parents and pupils organised themselves in the poorer shanty towns to keep them open. Banks, newspapers, and television channels began for the first time to be seriously preoccupied by the perceived threat of expropriation.

Caught on the back foot, the opposition remained a formidable force – a bizarre assortment of discredited politicians and trade unionists from the *ancien régime*, of oil executives from the nationalised oil company, of important business interests, of media magnates, and of large swathes of a middle class with their feet in Venezuela and their hearts in the suburban culture of the United States. Yet the failure of the December stoppage had left them disheartened. Chávez had been able to defeat them once again by conjuring up the country's forgotten underclass, unleashing forces that would be difficult for him, or for any alternative government, to put back into the bottle. Venezuela was visibly changing.

36

PROVIDING FOOD AND EDUCATION TO THE PEOPLE: THE DEVELOPMENT OF THE 'MISSIONS', 2003-2004

The defeat of the oil strike and the establishment of government control over *Petróleos de Venezuela* introduced an entirely new and yet more radical phase in the development of the Bolivarian Revolution. For the first time, the government was able, as it were, to seize the nation's oil pipelines and to point them directly into the shanty towns and the rural areas. In the course of 2003, huge sums of oil money were redirected into imaginative new social programmes, known as 'missions', that were gradually established throughout the country.

The missions fought against illiteracy, provided further education for school dropouts, promoted employment, supplied cheap food, and extended a free medical service to the poor areas of the cities and the countryside, with the help of thousands of doctors from Cuba. The oil company buildings in central Caracas, emptied of their bureaucrats, were commandeered to serve as the headquarters of a new 'Bolivarian' university for the poor, and oil money was diverted to set up Vive, an innovative cultural television channel that began to break the traditional US mould of the Latin American media.

The missions were established to bypass the lethargic bureaucracy of the state, which had remained largely in the hands of the opposition. Thus the various educational missions were not run initially by the ministry of education, nor was the health mission in the hands of the ministry of health. These were the singular products of the Bolivarian Revolution, developed outside the institutions of the *ancien régime.* The sense of purpose and enthusiasm they engendered recalled the atmosphere of the early years of the Cuban Revolution in the 1960s.

The most immediately important mission was *Misión Barrio Adentro,* an extraordinary medical programme, staffed by Cuban doctors in the poorer neighbourhoods of Caracas and other cities, and stretching out into forgotten areas of the countryside. Cuba had been exporting health practitioners throughout the Third World over many years, and by the 1990s more than 40,000 were working in many countries in Africa and Latin America. Venezuela had benefited from this programme since 1999, when a couple of hundred Cubans had arrived to set up a few health centres.

A new and enlarged programme was started early in 2003 under the auspices of Freddy Bernal, the dynamic mayor of Libertador, the largest municipal administration in greater Caracas. More than 8,000 doctors came from Cuba, and working in pairs they set up shop in the shanty towns, squatting initially in people's houses, and working in community centres. A year later many were operating from freshly constructed accommodation. During this second year, the number of Cuban doctors increased to more than 13,000, working along 5,000 Venezuelan health assistants. At the same time, Venezuelan patients were sent by the plane-load to Cuba for advanced medical treatment, while hundreds of young Venezuelans were sent to Cuba to study.

The political impact of these programmes was immediate, and wholly beneficial to the Chávez government. Previous governments, notably in the 1970s, had tried to do something similar, but the *ambulatorios* of that era were only a memory by the end of the century. The scale of *Barrio Adentro* (Into the Heart of the shanty town) was something entirely new. I visited several of these Cuban-run health centres in 2003 and 2004, in both town and country, and the enthusiasm and commitment of the Cubans and their warm reception by local people were clear indications of the forward march of the revolution. Many of the Cubans had already had experience of working in Third World countries – in Haiti and Honduras, in the Gambia and Angola – and this was their first chance to see a Latin American society so dramatically divided between rich and poor. They provided a local health service twenty-four hours a day, week in week out, and had soon become a familiar institution in the localities.

Their makeshift dwellings in the first year were replaced in 2004 by custom-built, two-storey hexagonal brick buildings housing a clinic on the ground floor and with living quarters above. The doctors were paid US$250 a month for their local expenses, while the medicines were provided free by Cuba. The doctors put particular emphasis on preventative medicine, and in the second year they were able to offer dental treatment and eye care.

A second programme, *Misión Robinson*, was a literacy campaign. Although run by Venezuelans, it took its cue from one of the early triumphs of the Cuban Revolution in 1961. This was an alphabetisation programme, designed in the first instance to teach 1 million people to read and write, and to use basic arithmetic. *Misión Robinson* took advantage of recent Cuban experience in this field in other countries of the Third World. Where once Cuban students had gone out with pencils and notebooks, the Venezuelans were provided (by Cuba) with television sets, video recorders, and reading glasses, and the printed manuals (some translated into indigenous languages) necessary for a mass literacy campaign in the twenty-first century. The project was named after Samuel Robinson, the *nom de plume* that Simón Rodríguez gave himself to honour Robinson Crusoe.

An additional literacy programme, *Misión Ribas*, was designed to provide a service to young adults who had fallen out of school – a serious problem in most Third World countries – and wished to continue their secondary education. In 2004, some 600,000 students were enrolled in this night school programme, and paid a small stipend. They were taught grammar, mathematics, geography, and a second language. The course was scheduled to last for two years.

Misión Ribas was named after another distinguished figure of the early nineteenth century. José Felix Ribas, a participant in the wars of independence, was born in 1775, and married to Josefa Palacios, the aunt of Bolívar. He fought in the battle of La Victoria in 1814, declaring famously that 'we cannot choose between victory or death, we have to be victorious'. The following year he was betrayed by a slave and captured by Spanish forces. His severed head, boiled in oil, was displayed in Caracas in a cage.

Another project, *Misión Sucre*, called after the conqueror of Bolivia, was directed towards those with a high school diploma (or a diploma from *Misión Ribas*) who needed additional preparation before entering a university. Some 70,000 students were enrolled in this programme during its first year of operation.

Yet another programme, *Misión Vuelvan Caras*, was designed to help the unemployed. Students who had passed through *Misión Ribas* and *Misión Sucre* were provided with assistance to find work, the aim being, in the first year, to reduce unemployment by 5 per cent.

A number of other missions with a specific remit were developed in the course of 2004. *Misión Identidad* was a voter registration drive, designed to ensure that the entire population was registered on the electoral roll. As well as locating those without papers, it arranged for hundreds of thousands of foreigners who had lived in Venezuela for many years to be formally naturalised and given voting rights. The majority of those without papers came from Colombia and Ecuador, but many were Europeans who had never troubled to register before.

Three other missions dealt with groups in the rural areas: *Misión Zamora* was a programme to look after peasants; *Misión Piar* was devoted to the problems of mining communities; and *Misión Guaicaipuro* dealt with indigenous groups. And finally *Misión Mercal* was established to build and operate supermarkets, to provide cheap food for the urban population.

The opposition bitterly opposed the new projects during the first year, and dismissed them as 'populist', a term customarily used with pejorative intent by social scientists in Latin America. Yet faced with the tragedy of extreme poverty and neglect in a country with oil revenues to rival those of Saudi Arabia, it was difficult to see why a democratically elected government should not have been allowed to embark on crash programmes to help the most disadvantaged. So successful were they that even opposition supporters – during the election campaigns of 2004 – were obliged to admit that they would maintain spending on most of these projects were they to be elected.

37

THE THIRD OPPOSITION THREAT: THE RECALL REFERENDUM OF AUGUST 2004

Ever since the radical programme of the Bolivarian Revolution had been spelt out in the '49 laws' of November 2002, the opposition to Chávez had sought his overthrow. They had organised a coup in April 2002, and a strike at the oil company in December. Both had been unsuccessful, and they were now left without a strategy. What else could they do?

One fresh possibility that emerged in 2003 was a campaign for a referendum, permitted under the constitution, to revoke the president's mandate. If the opposition could secure the signatures of 20 per cent of the registered electorate, this could trigger a referendum that would ask whether Chávez should continue or cut short his presidency. The opposition, now united in an umbrella organisation called the *Coordinadora Democrática*, were confident that they would win such a contest.

They turned for help to the former US president Jimmy Carter. His Carter Center in Atlanta had made a speciality of checking election campaigns in distant countries, and in verifying their results. Carter himself had taken an active interest in the continuing political crisis in Venezuela during the course of the oil stoppage, and – in tandem with the Organisation of American States – he had put forward a number of initiatives. He visited Caracas in January 2003 and again in May, and he eventually supported the idea that the opposition should organise the gathering of signatures – for what became known as the 'recall referendum'.

In December 2003, after several months' campaigning, the collection of signatures took place up and down the country over a period of four days. Booths and tables were placed in streets and markets, and the event took place in an atmosphere of civic pride. At its conclusion, the opposition claimed to have collected 3,477,000 signatures, sufficient to provoke a referendum.

The government, for its part, insisted that there had been widespread fraud. The National Electoral Council (CNE) took note of their claim, and began an intense scrutiny of the signature lists. After much argument, the CNE pronounced that only 1,911,000 signatures were legitimate. Of the rest, 375,000 were judged to be invalid, and 1,200,000 were considered to be of doubtful legitimacy. To achieve the 20 per cent figure required for the recall referendum, some 525,000 of the 'doubtful' signatures would need to be legitimised through a fresh scrutiny of the votes cast.

After several months of wrangling between government and opposition in the early part of 2004, both parties agreed that the CNE could permit signatories to confirm their signatures, and this formal procedure took place over a period of three days at the end of May 2004. On June 3, the CNE announced the result: there were sufficient signatures to permit the holding of a recall referendum.

To general surprise, Chávez accepted the challenge with relish. He said that he welcomed it, pointing out that he himself had been instrumental in including the referendum clause in the constitution. In practice, he knew that he was in a strong position, and his campaign struck the country like a whirlwind. It played to all his strengths as a military strategist and a political organiser. Soon he had put together a voter registration drive, reminiscent of the attempt to put black people on the election roll in the United States in the 1960s, and this produced hundreds of thousands of new voters. As already mentioned, he also embarked on a campaign to give citizenship to long-term immigrants. Thousands of these migrants had never become naturalised. Now they were not just permitted, but actually encouraged, to take up their right to citizenship, and most of them, of course, favoured Chávez. The CNE calculated that between 2 and 3 million new voters were registered in the months leading up to the referendum. As the campaign got under way, Chávez supporters were organised to patrol the shanty towns and the most remote areas of the country to get the vote out with maximum efficiency.

An unexpected bonus for Chávez in the course of the year was the dramatic and perhaps semi-permanent increase in the world oil price, to nearly US$50 a barrel. This was a five-fold increase in as many years, the result of the US war in Iraq, the general decrease in world oil supplies, and increased demand from China and India. The firm stand of OPEC, orchestrated by Venezuela, had also played its part. Much of this extra oil revenue went into the various health and education missions in the shanty towns, which undoubtedly became a powerful inducement for the population to vote in favour of Chávez.

The image of Chávez at home was also helped by the changing political attitude towards him abroad, particularly in Latin America. After nearly six years in power, armed with little more than revolutionary rhetoric and what was, after all, little more than a moderate social-democratic programme, Chávez had become the leader of the emerging opposition in Latin America to the neo-liberal hegemony of the United States. Other presidents were climbing over themselves to be photographed with him, to share in his reflected glory. He patched up relations with Colombia and Chile, hitherto cool, and in July 2004 he reinforced his friendly relations with Brazil and Argentina, signing an association agreement with their Mercosur trading union.

Once perceived by his neighbours as a bit of an oddball, Chávez now appeared as a Latin American statesman. Up and down the continent he had become the man to watch. Closely allied to Castro, he had begun to rival the Cuban leader in his fierce denunciations of George W. Bush, voicing an anti-imperialist strategy that went down well with most Latin Americans. His message was heard not just in Venezuela but in the rest of the continent, where the elites were virtually alone in their endorsement of the economic and political recipes devised in Washington. Chávez had retained his popularity as a result, while support for overtly pro-US leaders in Latin America – Vicente Fox in Mexico and Alejandro Toledo in Peru – had dwindled to nothing. Even the politically cautious President Lula in Brazil was seen to be struggling in the polls, with the loss of control over São Paulo and Porto Alegre in state elections at the end of 2004.

The Venezuelan opposition, united in the *Coordinadora Democrática* but divided politically and with no charismatic rival to Chávez to front their campaign, continued to behave as though their referendum victory was certain. They imagined fondly that they would achieve a victory comparable to that of the opposition to the Sandinistas in Nicaragua in 1990. They discussed plans for a post-Chávez government and watched closely the ever-dubious and endlessly conflicting opinion polls, placing their evaporating hopes on the 'don't knows'. Yet their referendum campaign was dull and lacklustre. They simply did not have sufficient supporters on the ground to match the panache and fervour of those in the Chávez camp. Their third attempt to derail the government was clearly doomed long before the polls opened.

On August 15, 2004, to the dismay of the opposition and to the surprise of international observers gathered in Caracas, Chávez secured a stunning victory. The referendum designed to lead to his overthrow provided him with an overwhelming majority. Some 5,800,600 people (59.25 per cent of the electorate) voted for Chávez to remain as president, while 3,989,000 (40.74 per cent) wished him to go. The Chávez victory was the opposition's third defeat in as many years. They cried 'fraud' immediately, but no one paid much attention, especially after the result was endorsed by Jimmy Carter and the observers from the OAS.

Chávez now had to be recognised as the undisputed president, and as if to show that the referendum result was no mere fluke it was followed by further victories in the election for mayors and state governors two months later. When the results came in on October 31, 20 out of 22 states were shown to have voted for Chávez candidates. Juan Barreto, the government candidate, won Greater Caracas, formerly controlled by Alfredo Peña, while Diosdado Cabello won the nearby state of Miranda, formerly held by Eugenio Mendoza. Of the important states, only Zulia remained in the hands of the opposition.

After nearly six years in power, Chávez was now in an unprecedented and unassailable position. He was a president backed by the popular vote, he had a majority in the National Assembly, and he had the support of almost all the regional governors. This was the moment he had been waiting for after the long years of fighting off the coup attempts of the opposition. Now at last he had an opportunity to put his programme into practice, and to plan for a more ordered and less hectic, less improvisational form of government. He moved swiftly to re-establish his authority, and his revolutionary credentials.

First he put the final touches to the government's control over *Petróleos de Venezuela*, a process that had begun the previous year after the failure of the oil stoppage. He appointed Rafael Ramírez, the minister of energy and mines, to take over the corporation, replacing Ali Rodríguez. The significant of the appointment lay in the fact that Ramírez retained his position as minister of energy. For the first time, the representative of the elected government had direct control over both *Petróleos de Venezuela* and the government ministry. Ali Rodríguez, meanwhile, the architect of so many reforms of the oil corporation and the protagonist of so many battles, was appointed minister of foreign affairs. He was charged with spearheading a new oil-based foreign policy, involving fresh initiatives in many lands, and beginning the task of bureaucratic reform in a ministry still harbouring innumerable placemen and women from the previous era.

Next Chávez turned his attention to the newly elected regional governors. They were expected to prepare development plans for their states that would be considered by a new policy-making body, the *Ente Coordinador de la Presidencia*, that would produce a programme for the next stage of the Bolivarian Revolution. In the meantime, they were urged to move ahead with the agrarian reform that had lain dormant since 2002.

The third important change was the further reform of the judiciary. The Supreme Court and its composition had been a bone of contention between government and opposition ever since the court had failed to bring the coup plotters of April 2002 to justice. The National Assembly now agreed to enlarge the Supreme Court, appointing 17 new judges and bringing the total from 20 to 32. With the increase in numbers, the government hoped to speed up and clean up an inefficient and corrupt system of justice. Inevitably, opposition spokesmen claimed that this would lead to government control of the Supreme Court, and those involved in the April coup began consulting their lawyers.

A fourth change on the domestic front was the start of a more robust attitude by the government towards the delinquency of the privately owned media. A new media law was passed by the National Assembly to regulate the behaviour of radio, television, and the newspapers. The opposition and its international allies expressed concerns about the freedom of the press, although the new laws merely brought Venezuela into line with similar legislation in the countries of Western Europe. Samuel Moncada, the Oxford-educated minister of higher education, noted that the laws were designed to create 'democratic control over the media'.

While the opposition and the media were debating these changes, Chávez cleverly withdrew from the domestic scene in November and December 2004 in order to repair his alliances with distant friends in the oil business. He travelled first to Libya and Iran, and also to Russia, Spain, and Qatar. He needed to shore up OPEC's commitment to a stable oil price, and to ensure that Vladimir Putin's recovery of the old Soviet state-owned oil industry – privatised in the Yeltsin era and handed over to gangsters – would mean tacit support for OPEC's objectives. He was not disappointed. Russia would put money into the modernisation of the oil industry of Venezuela and would also sell helicopters and assault rifles to the armed forces. Iran promised further cooperation, while Spain, under its new socialist government, was also keen to cooperate. The Spanish were anxious to erase the memory of the Aznar government's support for the April coup. In Qatar, Chávez visited the studios of Al-Jazeera, the radical Arab television station, with a view to securing advice for the Latin American channel that he hoped to inaugurate.

Chávez, with his professed interest in a multipolar world, wanted Venezuela to diversify its diplomatic and commercial contacts so that it might eventually escape from its eternal position of dependence on the United States. China was high on his list of potential friends, and he secured a warm welcome in Beijing in December, repeating his enthusiasm for Mao Tse-tung which he had voiced on his previous visit in October 1999. 'I think if Mao Tse-tung and Bolívar had known each other they would have been good friends because their thinking was similar,' Chávez told his Chinese hosts. 'Their inspiration came from the same place. It came from humanitarianism ... I think if Bolívar had come to China he would have become a socialist.'

The Chinese listened politely, and signed up for a series of economic exchanges, including the purchase of Venezuelan oil and the sale of a satellite, for possible use by Chávez's Latin American station.

Chávez had one further important call to make at the end of 2004 – to Havana. Fidel Castro had invited the unknown Venezuelan colonel to Cuba ten years earlier, in December 1994, to give a lecture on Simón Bolívar at the University of Havana. His bet on Chávez had proved to be one of Castro's better investments in foreign politicians. Chávez had just come out of prison at the time of his first visit, and his future was far from clear, but Castro was guilty of insider trading. He knew perfectly well that Chávez was a left-wing officer, in contact with pro-Cuban leftist groups in Venezuela, and possessed of considerable popular appeal. In the perennial Cuban search for allies on the Latin American mainland, Chávez was clearly worth a small punt.

Yet even the well-informed and farsighted Castro must have been surprised by the return on his investment. The two leaders now gathered again in Havana in December 2004 to celebrate the tenth anniversary of their first meeting. They addressed a meeting in the Karl Marx Theatre in which Castro reminded the audience of Chávez's optimistic and outspoken speech at the University of Havana ten years earlier, and praised him for his 'qualities as a great revolutionary':

> You promised to come back one day, with your hopes and dreams come true. You have returned, and you have returned a giant, now not only as the leader of your people's victorious revolutionary process but also as an important international figure, loved, admired and respected by many millions of people all over the world – and especially by our people.

Chávez and Castro then criticised the US scheme for a free trade area of the Americas, and proposed their own plan instead: the Bolivarian Alternative for the Americas. This would eliminate trade barriers and tax obstacles, as well as providing incentives for investment and increasing cooperation between banks.

The two leaders also signed an agreement that would codify their close relationship. Venezuela would never be able to replace the old Soviet Union as the milch cow of the Cuban Revolution, but Chávez's promise to fund a number of industrial and infrastructure projects in Cuba was very welcome to a country whose economy was still seriously distorted by the US embargo first imposed in November 1960 and ratcheted up in the years since. Yet more significant was the provision to Cuba of Venezuelan oil, at a minimum price of US$27 a barrel (almost half the world price at that moment), flowing across the Caribbean at the rate of 53,000 barrels a day.

Cuba, for its part, as Chávez pointed out, had been providing Venezuela with thousands of doctors, spread out in newly built health clinics across the country. This extraordinary Cuban initiative had played an important role in securing the Chávez victory in the referendum.

It was just five years since Chávez and Castro had joined together in the friendly game of baseball that was described at the start of this book. Many dramas had occurred in both countries during the following years, and the close personal friendship between the two leaders – one a revolutionary autocrat with vast intelligence and experience, the other a revolutionary soldier on a fast learning curve, with a pacifistic outlook and a profoundly democratic sentiment – had played an important role in their development.

Opposition leaders in Caracas often attacked Chávez for seeking to 'Cubanise' Venezuela, and it is certainly true that Chávez has drawn much comfort and inspiration from the example of the Cuban Revolution. Yet the trajectory of the Bolivarian Revolution has proved to be very different from the experience of Cuba. Venezuela, unlike Cuba, had a strong democratic tradition in the twentieth century which has been upheld and respected by Chávez. Unlike Cuba, Venezuela also does not have a lasting quarrel with the United States that dates back for nearly two centuries.

Yet revolutions in the former Latin American colonies of Spain are bound to have certain familiarities and complementarities. There is a shared historical experience of conquest and settlement, of slavery and extermination, and of struggle against racism and colonialism. The twin legacies of Simón Bolívar and José Martí are recognised and acknowledged in both countries. With wisdom and good fortune, Cuba may one day be 'Venezuelanised', opening up to the kind of democratic practice that has proved so successful in Venezuela. If the 'Cubanisation' of Venezuela were to lead to the permanent establishment of the social programmes that have made Cuba a legendary example throughout the world, then all Venezuelans, and not just the great poor majority, might well come to appreciate its advantages.

EPILOGUE:
THE MILITARY AND CIVIL SOCIETY

President Chávez is interested in education and in economic development, yet he is first and foremost a soldier. Two of the historical figures
that he has placed on a pedestal, Bolívar himself and Ezequiel Zamora,
are unambiguously military. 'I understand the soul of the army,' Chávez
once told me, 'and I am part of that soul.' One of his ambitions has
been to integrate the armed forces into the life of civil society.

For many people outside Latin America, particularly in the quarter
of a century since General Pinochet overthrew Salvador Allende in
September 1973, it has been almost impossible to think of a military
leader without conjuring up the grotesque image of the *gorila*, the
general and his military junta in dark glasses presiding over an authoritarian and repressive regime. Few recall the handful of leftist military
rulers who have taken the side of the poor and the peasants, and pushed
through radical reforms in the teeth of fierce opposition from local oligarchs and the United States. Few remember that Allende recruited
progressive officers to serve in his government.

Chávez knows well that many people, in Latin America and beyond,
are reticent about supporting a government with influential military
participation, even when democratically elected. He recalls that his generation of Venezuelan soldiers were genuinely shocked at the Chilean
coup, yet they were also impressed by the progressive military governments of Peru and Panama. Chávez is proud of his military antecedents,
and he believes firmly that soldiers have a right to be brought out into

society, and that they should not permanently be banished to their barracks. He wants to see a revolution in the relationship between the military and the civilian sectors of society. He is pleased that soldiers now have a right to vote, and he wants them to engage in social work and to participate in government.

'Chávez is part of an atypical generation of officers,' José Vicente Rangel once explained to me. 'They emerged in the period when the Venezuelan army was coming out of the guerrilla struggle of the 1960s. During that time the army – and all the armies of the region – had been Pentagonised. The US School of the Americas in Panama, and the US military "advisers", and the "national security doctrine" all played an important role.'

In the 1970s, once the guerrilla phenomenon had faded away, these officers 'began to search for new motivations. They started to study in the universities, and made connections with civil society.' As the economic and social situation in the country got worse, they 'began to experience the social crisis at first hand'. Since they were no longer 'cooped up in the ghetto of the barracks', the more senior officers were affected by the extent of government corruption, an additional and decisive factor. According to Rangel:

> Corruption had a rather special impact on the armed forces. A large part of the officer corps was involved in it. I think they may have been encouraged in this by the civilian political leadership, which may have thought that corrupting the senior officers would guarantee their support and neutralise their discontent. This may have neutralised the top echelons, but it created great discontent further down, among officers who were studying and had contact with students. They began to notice that the senior officers were taking part in a bonanza, and that some of them were enriching themselves very rapidly.

When I discussed this development with Chávez, he emphasised the humiliation suffered by the junior officers of his generation: 'The lack of balance in the country affected the military. At one extreme of the pendulum were the *gorilas*, at the other the eunuchs. Over many years the Venezuelan military were eunuchs: we were not allowed to speak; we had to look on in silence while we watched the disaster caused by corrupt and incompetent governments. Our senior officers were stealing, our troops were eating almost nothing, and we had to remain under tight discipline. But what kind of discipline was that? We were made complicit with the disaster.'

Chávez had sought to bring the military into civil society, 'but not as *gorilas*, not as Hitler or Mussolini, no, none of that. The idea is to return the military to their basic social function, so that both as citizens and as an institution they can be incorporated into the democratic development projects of the country.'

During the early years of the Chávez government, the military worked on their own social project, the Plan Bolívar 2000 that began in the first month of the Chávez presidency. The idea was to mobilise the spare capacity of the armed forces and to link up with local community groups so that together they might restore the country's increasingly derelict social infrastructure. Soldiers were encouraged to make their facilities available to local communities – their barracks, their sports grounds, and their canteens. They were to use their spare manpower to help in the repair of schools and roads. Mobile field hospitals were sent out into remote villages and slums 'as if to a war zone'.

After the mudslide tragedy of December 1999 in the state of Vargas, the metaphor proved uncomfortably apt. 'Thank goodness we had had the experience of the Plan Bolívar,' Chávez told me.

'We had been working on it for ten months in the coastal area, and it was just as well, for the military had become sensitised to these issues. They had already been working in what was to be the disaster zone on humanitarian tasks; it didn't cost us anything to use this huge human potential to help in the task of rescuing people and saving lives.'

Chávez recognises that the military have been going further than mere social work. They have been 'incorporating themselves, little by little, into the political leadership of the country, though not into *party* politics'.

Chávez remains bitterly hostile to the two political parties that dominated the country for so many years, and he does not really like political parties at all. His hostility derives partly from the political theorists once active in *La Causa Radical*. A large section of this leftist grouping from the 1970s, who had developed an ideology similar of that of the German Greens and were early critics of the established parties of the Fourth Republic, formed *Patria Para Todos* (PPT), which formed part of the coalition supporting Chávez in the 1990s. The president's own party, the Fifth Republic Movement, has remained a fairly moribund affair, and the two principal parties that support him, the Movement for Socialism and the PPT, are forever squabbling among themselves. Even the old Communist Party, also in the government coalition, is but a shadow of its former self. In practice, the Bolivarian Revolution has been supported by a broad coalition of grassroots organisations rather than by any organised political party with disciplined activists and an agreed ideology.

Chávez has also used the military to promote a modest internationalism. He points out that officers still 'go to the United States, but they also go to Cuba, to Bolivia, and to Brazil, to talk about the Plan Bolívar. They explain to people that the Venezuelan armed forces now have a social function.'

Reporters have always been susceptible to the charms of Latin America's radical strongmen, and I have been no exception. Graham Greene fell in love with the late General Omar Torríjos, the left-wing ruler of Panama who persuaded Jimmy Carter to hand over the Panama Canal, and is one of Chávez's models. Gabriel García Márquez never disguised his affection for Fidel Castro, another of Chávez's heroes; while many Peruvian intellectuals were hypnotised by the late General Juan Velasco, who pioneered the 'military road to socialism' in the 1960s – an example that Chávez also cherishes. Chávez has the same magnetic charisma as his predecessors, but he is an attractive and audacious colonel with a difference: his unsuccessful attempt to seize power by force in 1992 was subsequently ratified by a grateful people at elections – over and over again. By the end of 2004, Chávez had passed the electoral test eight times in six years, a record unparalleled in Latin America. He expects to win again in the presidential elections of 2006.

Much of his programme still remains to be spelt out. Yet he has issued a new prospectus for development in South America, and one with implications for Washington as well. For his hostility to neo-liberalism and globalisation, his support for the rights of indigenous peoples, his determination to use the oil rent to create a less hungry and more educated population, and his search for an agricultural strategy that would allow his people to feed themselves put Chávez in tacit alliance with the anti-globalisation protesters springing up all over the world since the conference of the World Trade Organisation in Seattle in 1999. Globalisation may be the disease of the new millennium, but antibodies to combat it are slowly being created. Speaking to the Social forum in the Porto Alegre in January 2005, Chávez put the word socialism onto the Venezuelan agenda for the first time.

Hugo Chávez has proved to be an interesting and significant figure, an honest man with the interests of his people at heart, who hopes to change the history of his nation for the better. After six years in government we know him for what he has proved himself to be. He is not a Mussolini, nor is he the dangerous Bonapartist once so brilliantly evoked by Marx. He is not a dictator in the making, nor is he an anachronistic throwback, advocating the failed economic and political recipes of yesteryear.

Chávez is a man of the left, a radical searching for new forms of politics, and new structures of economic organisation. He is also seeking different ways of perceiving the future of international relations within Latin America, and between the two Americas. His Bolivarian Revolution represents a possible future for Latin America, a genuine alternative to globalisation and neo-liberalism.

Clearly he has a utopian vision, not uncommon in a continent from which utopias are believed to spring, and in the nature of things it would be foolish not to imagine that his dreams may eventually be betrayed. Yet he has summoned some of the best people in the country to his side, and he has laid down the framework for a recovery of the history of Venezuela that may eventually lead to a cultural revival capable of resisting the US colossus.

With an intelligent and discriminating attitude towards the politics of oil, and with a powerful rhetoric directed towards the excesses of neo-liberalism, he has already got the economy of Venezuela moving again, in a manner beneficial to the bulk of its impoverished population, most of whom have missed out on the advances of the twentieth century.

Radical leaders in Latin America tend to come to a sticky end. Free elections have often turned up winners who are too far to the left to be easily countenanced by governments in Washington. Successive US governments have had innumerable arrows in their quiver for the destruction of regimes they disapprove of. Their weapons include the threat of destabilisation through economic and political means, the financing of opposition groups, and the manipulation of hostile press campaigns. In some circumstances they may involve a *coup d'état*, an assassination or an outright military invasion. These have all been tried in Latin America in the past half century, and some of them have already been experienced by the Bolivarian Revolution. It remains permanently at risk and under threat.

Maybe this great revolutionary experience will be prematurely cut short. Maybe it will all end in tears. Many radical projects in Latin America have been left, like corpses on a gibbet, to turn and twist in the wind. The proposals of Comandante Chávez and his Bolivarian Revolution deserve a better fate.

A SONG FOR BOLÍVAR

Our father who art in the earth, in the water, in the air
of all our great and silent breadth,
all bears thy name, father, in our land:
thy name the sugar cane raises to the sweetness,
Bolívar tin has a Bolívar brilliance,
the Bolívar bird over the Bolívar volcano,
the potato, the saltpetre, the special shadows,
the currents, the veins of phosphoric stone,
all that is ours comes from thy extinguished life,
thy heritage was rivers, plains, bell towers,
thy heritage is this day our daily bread, father.

I came upon Bolívar, one long morning,
in Madrid, at the entrance to the Fifth Regiment.
Father, I said to him, are you, or are you not, or who are you?
And, looking at the Mountain Barrack, he said:
'I awake every hundred years when the people awake.'

Pablo Neruda, translated by Donald D. Walsh

APPENDIX A
CHÁVEZ AND CASTRO IN HAVANA

Remarks by Fidel Castro at a ceremony to present the Order of Carlos Manuel de Céspedes to Hugo Chávez, President of the Bolivarian Republic of Venezuela, on the 10th anniversary of his first visit to Cuba, given at the Karl Marx Theatre, Havana, on December 14, 2004:

In order to know who Hugo Chávez is, you need to remember what he said in the speech he gave at the Great Hall in the University of Havana exactly ten years ago today, on December 14, 1994. I have selected some of the things he said, and although they might seem rather extensive, you will find them full of revolutionary content and spirit. When Chávez mentioned the fact that I had met him at the airport, he said the following words:

'When I had the enormous but pleasant surprise of being met at the José Martí International Airport by Fidel himself, I said to him, "I don't deserve this honour, I hope that I shall deserve it one day in the months and years to come." I say the same thing to you, dear fellow Cubano-Latino-Americanos: One day we hope to come to Cuba to offer our help, to offer each other mutual support in a Latin American revolutionary project, steeped as we have been for centuries in the idea of an Hispanic-American, Latin-American, Caribbean continent integrated into the single nation that we are.

'We are on our way to this goal, and as Aquiles Nazoa said of José Martí, we feel we belong to all eras and to all places, and we move like the wind after that seed which fell here one day and here, in fertile ground, sprouted and grew tall like we always said it would – and I am not just saying this now here in Cuba, because I am in Cuba and because, as we say in my land, on the Venezuelan plains, I feel safe and supported. We used to say the same thing in the Venezuelan army before we were insurrectionary soldiers; we said it in Venezuelan drawing rooms and military schools: "Cuba is a beacon of Latin American dignity and we have to look on her as such."

'There is no doubt that interesting things are happening in Latin America and the Caribbean; there is no doubt that our famous poet and writer, who belongs to this America of ours, Pablo Neruda, was utterly right when he wrote that Bolívar awakens every hundred years when the people awake.

'There is no doubt that we are in an era of peoples' awakening, of resurrection, of strength and hopes; there is no doubt, Mr President, that the wave whose arrival you are announcing or announced and continue to announce in that interview which I have referred to earlier, "A Grain of Corn", can be felt, its presence felt throughout Latin America.

'Weary of the existing level of corruption, we were sufficiently daring to found a movement in the ranks of the Venezuelan national army, and we swore to dedicate our lives to building a revolutionary movement and to the revolutionary struggle in Venezuela, and now in the Latin American context.

'We began to do this in the year marking the bicentennial of Bolívar's birth. But we can see that next year is the centenary of the death of José Martí, we can see that the coming year is the bicentennial of the birth of Marshal Antonio José de Sucre, we can see that the coming year is the bicentennial of the rebellion and death of the Afro-Venezuelan José Leonardo Chirinos on the coast of Coro, in Venezuela, the land, by the way, of the forebears of Antonio Maceo.

'Time calls to us and drives us; this, there is no doubt, is the time to walk down new paths of hope and struggle. We are engaged in doing that, dedicating ourselves now to our revolutionary labour in three basic areas which I am going to take the liberty of summarising for you, to invite you to exchange ideas with us, to invite you to forge ties of unity and of labour, of building something concrete.

'In the first place, we are determined to raise an ideological flag that is relevant and beneficial to our land of Venezuela, to our lands of Latin America: the Bolivarian flag.

'As we undertake this ideological work of reassessing history, and the ideas that were born in Venezuela and on this continent 200 ago, and as we plunge into history in search of our roots, so we have designed and put before the Venezuelan and international public the ideas of that Simón Bolívar who called for Latin American union in order to oppose a developed nation, as a kind of counterbalance to the ambitions of the North, a North that was already beginning to loom over our Latin American lands with its claws unsheathed; the ideas of that Bolívar who, almost from his grave, already in Santa Marta said: "Soldiers take up the sword to defend social guarantees"; the ideas of that Bolívar who said that the best system of government is that which bestows the greatest amount of happiness on its people, the greatest amount of political stability and social security.

'This deeply embedded root, this Bolivarian root which has been joined by time and by history itself to the Robinsonian root, taking as its inspiration the name of Samuel Robinson or that of Simón Rodríguez, whom very few Latin Americans know because we were told when we were very little: "Bolívar's teacher". And that's where he remained, as if stigmatised by history, the eccentric madman, wandering like the breeze through the countries of Latin America, and dying at a ripe old age.

'Simón Rodríguez called on Americans from the southern lands to make two revolutions: the political and the economic revolution. He called on people to build a model of a social economy, a model of a people's economy. He bequeathed to us, as a kind of challenge, and appropriate for any moment that Latin America might face, the idea that Latin America could not continue in its servile imitation of others, but that it had to be original, and he called on us to invent or fall by the wayside. That old man, mad according to the bourgeoisie of his time, who wandered about when already old and forgotten, gathering abandoned children, and who said, "Children are the building blocks of the future republican building, come hither and polish the building blocks so that this building may be solid and luminous!"

'We, as soldiers, are engaged in that search, and today we are ever more convinced of the need for the Venezuelan army to return to what it once was: a people's army, an army to defend what Bolívar called the social guarantees.

'That would be the first element in a really relevant effort, Comandante: to consolidate this ideological work, incorporating these two names, Bolívar and Martí, as a tool for lifting the spirits and the pride of Latin Americans.

'Another element in our effort, and for this we have to strengthen our ties with the peoples of Latin America, is our organisational work.

'When we were in jail we got our hands on many documents about how the Cuban people went about organising themselves after the triumph of the Revolution, and we are determined to organise an immense social movement in Venezuela: the Revolutionary Bolivarian Movement 200. And, what is more, we are calling for the creation of the National Bolivarian Front this coming year. We are calling on students, peasants, native peoples, on those of us soldiers who are no longer in the army, on intellectuals, workers, fishermen, dreamers, on everybody to build this front, a huge social front which can take on the challenge of transforming Venezuela.

'In Venezuela, no one knows what might happen at any moment. We are coming up to an election year, 1995 – in one year's time, in December, there will be more elections in Venezuela, illegal, illegitimate elections, that will be marked by abstentions – you won't believe this – of on average 90 per cent; in other words, 90 per cent of Venezuelans won't cast a vote, they don't believe in what politicians say, they believe in almost no political party.

'This year our hope is that, with the Bolivarian Revolutionary Movement, with the National Bolivarian Front, we can polarise Venezuela. The people who take part in the electoral process – there are some honest people who do, people whom we respect, it's the electoral process we don't believe in – that's one pole; and the other pole, the one we are going to nourish, to push and to strengthen, is the demand coming from the streets, from the people, calling for elections to a National Constitutional Assembly to redefine the republic's deepest foundations, which are falling apart; Venezuela's legal foundations, its political foundations, its economic foundations, its moral foundations even, are at rock bottom, and that's something you can't fix with Band-aids.

'Bolívar said: "Political gangrene cannot be cured with palliatives" and Venezuela is totally and utterly riddled with gangrene.

'A green mango will ripen, but a rotten mango never ripens; the seed of a rotten mango must be saved and planted so that a new plant may grow. That is happening in Venezuela today. There is no way the system can cure itself.

'In Venezuela we do not reject armed struggle. There are still – and the polls taken by the government itself say so – more than 80 per cent of the Venezuelan military who have a favourable opinion of us – in the army, the navy and the air force, and the National Guard.

'In spite of all this, in our country we have strength and, in addition to all of that, we have an extremely high percentage of Venezuelans on our side, especially, my dear friends, that 60 per cent of Venezuelans – this is something else you are not going to believe – who live in a critical state of poverty.

'It's unbelievable, but it's true: in twenty years in Venezuela more than $200 thousand million just evaporated. So, where is the money? President Castro asked me. In the foreign bank accounts of almost everyone who has been in power in Venezuela, civilians and soldiers, who filled their pockets, protected by the power they held.

'We have had an amazingly positive impact on the overwhelming majority of Venezuelans, and you can understand that, with these two forces behind us, we are prepared to give all we have for a much-needed change in Venezuela. This is why we have not ruled out using the weapons of the people-in-the-barracks to find the right way if this political system decides, as it appears to have decided, to batten down the hatches again and to find the ways and means to manipulate and cheat the people.

'We are asking for a Constitutional Assembly and next year – as I already said – we are going to be pushing this as a short-term strategic solution.

'A sovereign economic model is a long-term project; it is a project that will need twenty to forty years. We do not wish to continue to have a colonial economy, a complementary economic model.

'This is a project we have already presented in Venezuela under the name of the Simón Bolívar National Project, but with our arms stretched out to the Latin American continent and to the Caribbean. This is a project in the context of which it is not adventurist to think, politically speaking, of an association of Latin American states. Why not think of that, it was the original dream of our Liberators? Why should we continue to be fragmented? In the political arena, that is the scope of this project, which is neither ours nor is it original, it is at least two hundred years old.

'Think of how many positive experiences Cuba has had in the cultural arena, in the economic arena – in the context of this almost war economy that Cuba is enduring – in the sports arena, in the health arena, in the arena of caring for people, for human beings, which is the homeland's first objective, its subject.

'It is in this arena, or in this third element, that of the long-term project of political transformation, that we stretch out our hands to experience, to the men and women of Cuba who have spent years thinking about and working towards this continental project.

'The coming century, in our opinion, is a century of hope; it is our century, it is the century when the Bolivarian dream, Martí's dream, the Latin American dream will be reborn.

'Dear friends, you have honoured me by sitting here tonight to listen to the ideas of a soldier, of a Latin American who is fully and for ever committed to the cause of revolution in this America of ours.'

Chávez had a perfectly structured revolutionary political and economic thinking, a coherent thinking in both strategic and tactical terms. Much earlier than anyone might have thought at that time, the Bolivarian process was to overthrow the oligarchy in a transparent contest, and virtually without resources the Constitutional Assembly of which Chávez spoke to us was established. A far-reaching revolution was set in motion in Bolívar's glorious country.

As you can see, he said very candidly in that speech: 'We have not ruled out armed struggle in Venezuela.' This important subject was something we discussed in the many hours of conversation and exchange of ideas we had during that visit.

The Bolivarian leader preferred to conquer power without spilling blood. He was, however, extremely concerned that the oligarchy would resort to a *coup d'état*, backed by the military top brass, to halt the movement set in motion by the rebel officers on February 4, 1992.

I remember that he said to me: 'Our idea is to avoid difficult situations and bloodshed; our plan is to build alliances with social and political forces, because, in 1998, we could launch a vigorous political campaign with considerable electoral strength, with the support of the people and of broad sectors in the armed forces, and take power in this traditional way. I think that would be our best strategy.'

I have not forgotten my laconic but sincere comment: 'That is a good way.'

And things happened just as he said they would. In 1998 the Bolivarian Revolutionary Movement, an alliance of patriotic forces and of the left, built and led by him, won a landslide victory in that year's elections – with the support of the people and the sympathy and solidarity of a majority in the military, especially the young officers. It was a good lesson for revolutionaries: there are no dogmas nor only one way of doing things. The Cuban Revolution itself was also proof of that.

I have, for a very long time, had the very deeply held conviction that, when a crisis comes, leaders arise. So Bolívar arose when Napoleon occupied Spain, and the imposition of a foreign king created the conditions that facilitated the independence of the Spanish colonies in this hemisphere. So Martí arose when the right moment came for the independence revolution in Cuba. So arose Chávez when the dreadful social and human situation in Venezuela and Latin America determined that the time to fight for the second, real independence had come.

The battle is now harder and more difficult. A hegemonic empire in a globalised world – the only superpower which remains after the Cold War (that period of prolonged conflict between two radically different political, economic and social ideas) – raises an enormous obstacle to the only thing that today can save humankind's most basic human rights, and even its very survival.

The crisis the world is going through today does not, and cannot, affect only one country, or subcontinent or continent; it affects everyone. Therefore, that imperial system and the economic order it has imposed on the world cannot be sustained. Peoples which have decided to fight, not only for their independence but also for their very survival, can never be defeated, even when we are talking of only one people.

It is impossible to ignore what has happened in Cuba over almost half a century, or to ignore the enormous social, cultural, and human advances made by our country in spite of the longest economic blockade known to history. It is impossible to ignore what happened in Vietnam, impossible to ignore what is happening in Iraq today.

What is happening in Venezuela today is another powerful example. Neither the *coup d'état*, nor the oil coup, nor the recall referendum backed by almost all of the media could prevent the Bolivarian Revolutionary Movement's landslide victory; it received almost 60 per cent more votes for NO on August 15 and had another colossal victory in the regional governorships, something unprecedented that the world observed with amazement and sympathy.

At the same time, a battle is being waged about the standards and rules that the empire has imposed in order to weaken and divide our peoples and impose its rotten, discredited representative democracy …

To put the finishing touches on this historic ceremony, both governments will this night sign a Joint Declaration on the ALBA, the Bolivarian Alternative for the Americas, the Bolivarian conception of economic integration, and we will sign a bilateral agreement to begin putting this concept into practice, both of which documents will make history.

Hugo, you said ten years ago that you didn't deserve the honours you were being given by those who, when the news began to reach us of your history, your behaviour, and your ideas while you were in prison in Yare jail, had perceived your qualities as a great revolutionary.

Your organisational ability, your teaching skills with young officers, your noble thoughts and steadfastness in adversity have made you worthy of these and of many more honours.

You promised to come back one day, with your hopes and dreams come true. You have returned, and you have returned a giant, now not only as the leader of your people's victorious revolutionary process but also as an important international figure, loved, admired and respected by many millions of people all over the world – and especially by our people.

Today the well-deserved honours of which you spoke, and the two decorations we have bestowed on you, seem rather small. What moves us most is that you have returned, as you promised, to share your Bolivarian and Martíst struggles with us.

Long live Bolívar and Martí!

Long live the Bolivarian Republic of Venezuela!

Long live Cuba!

May our ties of brotherhood and solidarity last for ever!

APPENDIX B
THE RIGHTS OF INDIGENOUS PEOPLES

The articles of the Venezuelan constitution of December 1999 regarding the rights of indigenous peoples:

Chapter VIII

Article 119

The State recognises the existence of the indigenous peoples and communities, their social, political and economic organisation, their cultures, their customs and practices, languages and religions, as well as their habitat and native rights to the lands which they ancestrally and traditionally occupy and which are necessary to develop and guarantee their way of life. It is the role of the State, with the participation of the indigenous peoples, to demarcate and guarantee the right to the collective ownership of the same, which shall be inalienable, imprescriptible, non-sequestrable and non-transferable under the terms of the Constitution and the law.

Article 120

The exploitation by the State of natural resources in indigenous areas shall be carried out without harm to the cultural, social and economic integrity of the same, and is subject to prior warning and consultation of the respective indigenous communities. The benefits accruing to the indigenous peoples from this exploitation shall be in accordance with the Constitution and the law.

Article 121

The indigenous peoples have the right to maintain and develop their ethnic and cultural identity, as well as their cosmology, values and spirituality and their sacred sites and forms of worship. The State will promote respect for and dissemination of the cultural products of the indigenous peoples, who have the right to their own form of education and to a multicultural and bilingual educational regime which reflects their own socio-cultural characteristics, values and traditions.

Article 122

The indigenous peoples have the right to an integral health [service] which takes into account their practices and cultures. The State recognises their traditional medicine and complementary therapies, in accordance with bio-ethical principles.

Article 123

The indigenous peoples have the right to maintain and promote their own economic practices, based on reciprocity, solidarity and exchange, their traditional productive activities and their participation in the national economy, and to define their priorities. The indigenous peoples have the right to professional training services and to participate in the drafting and execution of specific programmes of training, technical and financial assistance services which strengthen their economic activities within the framework of local sustainable development.

Article 124

The collective intellectual property of the indigenous peoples in regard to their technological knowledge and innovations is guaranteed. Every activity relating to genetic resources and the knowledge associated with the same will be for [their] collective benefit. The patenting of ancestral resources and knowledge is forbidden.

Article 125

The indigenous peoples have the right to political participation. The State shall guarantee indigenous representation in the National Assembly and in the deliberative bodies of federal and local entities with an indigenous population, in accordance with the law.

Article 126

The indigenous peoples as cultures with ancestral roots form part of the Venezuelan nation, State and people, unique, sovereign and indivisible, and under the terms of this Constitution have a duty to safeguard the integrity and sovereignty of the nation.

The term 'people' should not be interpreted as having any implications in regard to the rights that this term may confer under International Law.

APPENDIX C
SAUCE OF WONDER

**Richard Gott relishes a strange connection between
Worcestershire and Venezuela**

Reprinted from the *Guardian* (London), December 11, 1976

At the turn of the century in Caracas, after an outside concert by the band, the European-oriented Venezuelan gentry would repair for a social cup of chocolate, then one of the country's chief products, to 'La India', the Caracas equivalent of Sacher's or Demmel's in Vienna. Nowadays 'La India' is a company, not a coffee house, the Venezuelan subsidiary of the General Foods Corporation, a powerful United States transnational company. Its manager, Bill MacClarence, is a graduate of the Harvard Business School and has been with General Foods for 25 years.

Among the foods he produces for the discriminating palate of the Venezuelan middle class is *Salsa Inglesa* – English sauce. On the strangely familiar label it proclaims defiantly and unpronounceably in Spanish, 'Worcestershire Sauce'. The label itself is familiar because it says 'Lea and Perrins, the original and genuine'. The sauce in fact is made under licence in Venezuela by an American company that pays royalties to the British firm in Worcestershire, contributing doubtless to the 'invisibles' that keep Britain afloat.

Now if there is one thing that the countries of Latin America do not lack it is the wherewithal and the traditional skill to make an immense variety of sauces, chutneys and condiments. Hot and salty, sweet and savoury, the material is there – red peppers, green peppers, chili peppers, mangoes, plantain and ají. A cuisine cultivated, protected and enriched through the centuries by an oppressed but resourceful peasantry. So it comes as some surprise that there should be such a large demand in Venezuela for Lea and Perrins.

But look along the shelves of a suburban supermarket in Caracas and there is another bottle of *Salsa Inglesa*, 'French's Worcestershire Sauce', made this time by a British company, Reckitt and Colman of Hull. It has a Venezuelan subsidiary, Atlantic Venezolana, which makes Worcestershire Sauce under licence from the H.T. French Company of Rochester in the United States – a British company manufacturing Worcestershire Sauce in Venezuela and paying royalties to an American company for the privilege of doing so. Atlantic Venezolana, perhaps to the delight of the Venezuelan housewife, also makes Brasso, Robinson's Barley Water, and Cherry Blossom shoe polish.

Two companies making Worcestershire Sauce in Venezuela might seem one too many, but not of course to those who dislike monopolies and extol the virtues of competition. And competition there certainly is. Further along the supermarket shelf stands yet another brand, 'McCormick's Worcestershire Sauce', made by McCormick de Venezuela, a subsidiary of the McCormick Company of Baltimore, manufactured under licence from nobody. The boss of McCormick de Venezuela, Manuel Mosteiro Pérez, is a Cuban exile who used to sell the company's sauce and mayonnaise in Havana. The revolution put paid to that. The Cuban subsidiary was confiscated. Now he flogs the stuff all over Latin America.

Nor does the story end here. Also on sale is 'Royal Worcestershire Sauce' (perhaps to be eaten off Royal Worcester dishes), produced by a subsidiary of Standard Brands. The president of the Venezuelan company is Eduardo Pinilla Pocaterra. As the name implies, he has little land – but his family owns plenty of banks. He did a spell at the University of New York's Graduate School of Business, where clearly he learned to put the Venezuelan taste for Worcestershire Sauce to profitable ends.

Heinz, 'the one you love', has also launched a Worcestershire Sauce onto the Venezuelan market. The boss of Alimentos Heinz de Venezuela, Louis Pacini, hails from Massachusetts, and used to be an operations officer in the US Army's Counter-Intelligence Corps in France and Austria in the 1950s. Now he just sells food.

So, five brands of Worcestershire Sauce are sold in Venezuela, mostly by American companies. A basic component of most of them, the soya bean, has to be imported. Venezuela can no longer feed itself and has a massive annual import bill for food. The companies that benefit are American: Kraft, Kellogg, Del Monte, Great Plains Wheat de Venezuela (cables: USWHEAT), National Biscuit and Quaker. They, and many more, are well established in Venezuela, though they don't make Worcestershire Sauce.

What about Nelson Rockefeller, the American who seems to control much of Latin America? Well, he owns the supermarket. Or at least he did until Carlos Andrés Pérez, the Venezuelan president, decided to nationalise it. How about nationalising Lea and Perrins? It wouldn't be difficult to give it a new name: Lea and Pérez.

BIBLIOGRAPHY

Arvelo Ramos, Alberto, *El dilema del Chavismo: una incógnita en el poder*, José Agustín Catalá, Caracas, 1998

Bilbao, Luís, *Chávez, después del golpe y el sabotaje petrolero*, Editorial Fuego Vivo, Puerto La Cruz, 2003

Blanco Muñoz, Agustín, *Habla el Comandante: testimonios violentos*, UCV, Caracas, 1998

Boustany, Nora, 'Venezuela's Aspiring Innovator', *Washington Post*, Friday September 24, 1999

Bravo, Douglas, and Argelia Melet, *La otra crisis, otra história, otro camino*, Oríjinal Editores, Caracas, 1991

Briceño Porras, Guillermo, *El extraordinário Simón Rodríguez*, Caracas, 1991

Brito Figueroa, Federíco, *Tiempo de Ezequiel Zamora*, José Agustín Catalá, Caracas, 1995

Britto García, Luís, *El poder sin la máscara: de la concertación populista a la explosión social*, 2nd edition, Alfadil Ediciones, Caracas, 1989

Burgos, Elizabeth, 'Base-ball: imposition impériale ou affirmation du sentiment national?' L'ordinaire latino-américain, No. 187, Université de Toulouse-le-Mirail, January–March 2002

Buxton, Julia, *The Failure of Political Reform in Venezuela*, Ashgate, Aldershot, 2001

Buxton, Julia and Nicola Phillips, *Case Studies in Latin American Political Economy*, Manchester University Press, Manchester, 1999

Castañeda, Jorge, *Utopia Unarmed: the Latin American Left after the Cold War*, Random House, New York, 1994

Castro, Orlando, *Orlando Castro*, Editora Anexo, Caracas, 1998

Chávez, Hugo, *The Fascist Coup against Venezuela: speeches and addresses, December 2002–January 2003*, Ediciones Plaza, Havana, 2003

Chávez, Hugo, *Discursos fundamentales: ideología y acción política*, Vol. 1, 1999, Foro Bolivariano de Nuestra América, Caracas, 2003

Coppedge, Michael, *Strong Parties and Lame Ducks: presidential partyarchy and factionalism in Venezuela*, Stanford University Press, Stanford, 1994

Coronil, Fernando, *The Magical State: nature, money and modernity in Venezuela*, University of Chicago Press, Chicago, 1997

Díaz Rangel, Eleazar, *Todo Chávez: de Sabaneta al golpe de abril*, Caracas, 2002

Dieterich, Heinz, *Hugo Chávez: con Bolívar y el Pueblo, nace un nuevo proyecto latinoamericano*, Editorial 21, Buenos Aires, 1999

Elizalde, Rosa Miriam and Luis Báez, *Chávez nuestro*, Casa Editora, Havana, 2004

Ellner, Steve, and Daniel Hellinger (eds), *Venezuelan Politics in the Chávez Era: class, polarization and conflict*, Lynne Rienner, Boulder, 2003

Ewell, Judith, *Venezuela: a century of change*, Hurst and Co., London, 1984

Garrido, Alberto, *Guerrilla y conspiración militar en Venezuela*, José Agustín Catalá, Caracas, 1999

Garrido, Alberto, *La historia secreta de la revolución bolivariano*, Mérida, 2000

Garrido, Alberto, *Mi amigo Chávez: conversaciones con Norberto Ceresole*, Caracas, 2001

Giordani, Jorge A., *La propuesta del MAS*, UCV, Caracas, 1992

Gott, Richard, *Guerrilla Movements in Latin America*, Thomas Nelson, London, 1971

Gott, Richard, *In the Shadow of the Liberator: Hugo Chávez and the transformation of Venezuela*, Verso, London, 2000

Grüber Odreman, Hernán, *Antecedentes históricos de la insurrección militar del 27-N-1992*, Caracas, 1993

Grüber Odreman, Hernán, *Soldados alerta!* Caracas, 2004

Harnecker, Marta, *Hugo Chávez Frías: un hombre, un pueblo*, Bogotá, 2003

Henry, James, *Banqueros y lavadolares: el papel de la banca internacional en la deuda del Tercer Mundo, la fuga de capitales, la corrupción y el antidesarrollo*, Tercer Mundo Editores, Bogotá, 1996

Iglesias, María Cristina, *Salto al futuro: conversaciones con Pablo Medina (y otros)*, Ediciones Piedra, Papel o Tijera, Caracas, 1998

Kornblith, Míriam, *Venezuela en los 90: las crisis de la democracia*, Ediciones IESA, Caracas, 1998

Krehm, William, *Democracies and Tyrannies of the Caribbean*, Lawrence Hill & Co., Westport, 1984

Langue, Frédérique, *Hugo Chávez et le Venezuela: une action politique au pays de Bolívar*, L'Harmattan, Paris, 2002

Ledezma, Eurídice, 'Crísis política y nacionalismo, en Venezuela, Mexico, y Peru: un estudio comparado', unpublished thesis, Universidad Complutense de Madrid, 1998

López Maya, Margarita, 'El ascenso en Venezuela de La Causa R', *Revista Venezolano de Economía y Ciencias Sociales*, UCV, Caracas, 2–3, 1995

López Maya, Margarita (ed.), *Lucha popular, democracia, neoliberalismo: protesta popular en America Latina en los años de ajuste*, Editorial Nueva Sociedad, Caracas, 1999

McCaughan, Michael, *The Battle of Venezuela*, Latin America Bureau, London, 2004

McCoy, J. (ed.), *Venezuelan Democracy under Pressure*, North-South Centre, New Brunswick, 1995

Maringoni, Gilberto, *A Venezuela que se inventa: poder, petróleo e intriga nos tempos de Chávez*, Editora Fundacao Perseu Abramo, São Paulo, 2004

Martín, Américo *et al.*, *Chávez y el movimiento sindical en Venezuela*, Alfadil Editores, Caracas, 2002

Martínez Galindo, Román, *Ezequiel Zamora y la batalla de Santa Inés* (prologo Hugo Chávez), Vadell Hermanos, Caracas, 1992

Medina, Pablo, *Rebeliones*, Caracas, 1999

Mieres, Francisco *et al.*, *PDVSA y el golpe*, Editorial Fuentes, Caracas, 2002

Moleiro, Moisés, *El poder y el sueño*, Editorial Planeta Venezolano, Caracas, 1998

Müller Rojas, Alberto, *Relaciones peligrosas: militares, política y estado*, Fondo Editorial Tropykos, Caracas, 1992

Naím, Moisés, *Paper Tigers and Minotaurs: the politics of Venezuela's economic reforms*, Carnegie Endowment, Washington, 1993

Olavarría, Jorge, *El efecto Venezuela*, 3rd edition, Editorial Panapo, Caracas, 1996

Olavarría, Jorge, *Historia viva: articulos publicados en El Nacional, marzo 1998–marzo 1999*, Caracas, 1999

Olavarría, Jorge, *Historia viva, 2002–2003*, Alfadil Ediciones, Caracas, 2003

Peña, Alfredo, *Conversaciones con José Vicente Rangel*, Editorial Ateneo de Caracas, Caracas, 1978

Petkoff, Teodoro, *Hugo Chávez, tal cual*, Los Libros de la Catarata, Madrid, 2002

Ramírez Rojas, Kléber, *Historia documental del 4 de febrero*, UCV, Caracas, 1998

Robinson, Max, *La raíz robinsoniana de la revolución bolivariano en Venezuela*, Caracas, 2004

Rodríguez, Simón, *Sociedades americanas*, Biblioteca Ayacucho, Caracas, 1990

Rodríguez-Valdés, Angel, *Los rostros del golpe*, Alfadil Ediciones, Caracas, 1992

Romero, Celino, 'Pacific Revolution', *World Today* (London), Vol. 25, No. 10, October 1999

Sánchez Otero, Germán, *Cuba desde Venezuela*, CONAC, Caracas, 2004

Santodomingo, Roger, *La conspiración 98: un pacto secreto para llevar a Hugo Chávez al poder*, Alfadil Ediciones, Caracas, 1999

Sanz, Rodolfo, *Diccionario para uso de: Chavistas, Chavologos y Antichavistas*, Caracas, 2004

Stepan, Alfred, *The State and Society: Peru in comparative perspective*, Princeton University Press, Princeton, 1978

Tarre Briceño, Gustavo, *El espejo roto: 4F 1992*, Editorial Panapo, Caracas, 1994

Vivas, Leonardo, *Chávez: la última revolución del siglo*, Editorial Planeta Venezolano, Caracas, 1999

Williamson, John (ed.), *The Political Economy of Reform*, Institute for International Economics, Washington, 1994

Zago, Angela, *La rebelión de los Angeles*, Fuentes Editores, Caracas, 1992

Zapata, Juan Carlos, *Los ricos bobos*, Alfadil Ediciones, Caracas, 1995

INDEX